Interpreting Company Reports and Accounts

INTERPRETING COMPANY REPORTS AND ACCOUNTS

Geoffrey Holmes and Alan Sugden

THIRD EDITION

WOODHEAD-FAULKNER · CAMBRIDGE

Published by Woodhead-Faulkner Limited,
Fitzwilliam House, 32 Trumpington Street,
Cambridge CB2 1QY, England
and 27 South Main Street,
Wolfeboro, New Hampshire 03894-2069, USA

First published 1979
Second impression 1980
Third impression 1981
Second edition 1982
Second impression 1983
Third impression 1983
Fourth impression 1984
Third edition 1986
Second impression 1986
Third impression 1986

© Geoffrey Holmes and Alan Sugden 1979, 1982, 1986

British Library Cataloguing in Publication Data

Holmes, Geoffrey, *1926–*
    Interpreting company reports and accounts.—3rd ed.
    1. Financial statements
    I. Title   II. Sugden, Alan
    657'.33   HF5681.B2

    ISBN 0-85941-325-X
    ISBN 0-85941-326-8 Pbk

Library of Congress Cataloging in Publication Data

Holmes, Geoffrey Andrew
    Interpreting company reports and accounts.

    Includes index
    1. Financial statements.   2. Corporation reports.
    I. Sugden, Alan.   II. Title.
    HF5681.B2H63   1986   657'.33   85-26642
    ISBN 0-85941-325-X
    ISBN 0-85941-326-8 (pbk.)

Typeset by Rowland Phototypesetting Ltd, Bury St Edmunds, Suffolk
Printed in Great Britain by St Edmundsbury Press Ltd, Bury St Edmunds, Suffolk

PREFACE

'Published accounts are utterly and absolutely useless.'
Clive Jenkins

Many non-trade-unionists might agree with Clive Jenkins on this point, but we believe they are wrong. Given a sound knowledge of the basic components of a balance sheet and profit and loss account, *anybody with a reasonably enquiring mind* can learn a great deal about a company by studying its report and accounts and by comparing it with other companies, and we have written this book to provide the basic knowledge required and to give the reader (be he student, investor, company director or trade-unionist) a line-by-line guide on how to take a set of reports and accounts to pieces.

A careful, systematic examination of accounts can also provide warning of when a company is taking undue risks, when it is 'window dressing' to cover up a poor performance, or when it is 'netting off' figures to hide embarrassing items.

In addition, an examination of accounts over several years can give a very good picture of the long-term trends of a company's fortunes, distinguishing between a company that is growing at an incredible speed (in which case don't believe it), is growing at a prudent speed (in which case consider investing), or is static or on the decline (in which case avoid or sell).

Analysing accounts, sorting out the good, well-run companies from the less reliable ones, all the time asking further questions and keeping an eye out for warning signals is, in our view, fun. We hope that once you have mastered the nuts and bolts of the process you will find it fun, too.

Note to the third edition

This edition reflects various events that have taken place since the second edition was published in September 1982, including the publication of the Companies Act 1985, which consolidates the greater part of the 1948, 1967, 1976, 1980 and 1981 Acts and other company legislation; the revision of the regulations for the admission of securities to Listing to comply with EEC directives; important changes to company taxation introduced in the 1984 Budget; and the continuing development of accounting standards, including those on the capitalisation of financial leases and merger accounting.

Many of the examples have been updated to illustrate the use of the new formats for profit and loss accounts and balance sheets introduced by the Companies Act 1981, and a number of new examples have been added.

This edition also describes the impasse that has been reached on the development of an accounting standard for inflation accounting, and makes some constructive suggestions on how this impasse might be overcome.

Acknowledgements

We would like to thank Geoffrey Fryer, head of The Stock Exchange quotations department, John Jeffrey-Cook of chartered accountants Moores & Rowland, Rory Tapner of stockbrokers Rowe & Pitman, and Robin Corner, Simon Hichens and Stephen Lynam of merchant bankers J. Henry Schroder Wagg, for their help and advice on various aspects of the third edition.

G.H.
A.S.

CONTENTS

Chapter 1

INTRODUCTION TO ACCOUNTING PRACTICE

This book is intended as a practical guide to the interpretation of reports and accounts. In it frequent reference is made to the legal, accounting and Stock Exchange requirements that accounts have to meet, but this is done in the context of what interesting information to look out for, rather than to show how a set of accounts should be prepared.

Useful guides to *compiling* accounts include:

The Companies Act 1985 – A guide to the accounting and reporting requirements, published by the Institute of Chartered Accountants in England and Wales.

Companies Act 1985 – Model reports and accounts, published for the Institute of Chartered Accountants in Scotland by Gee & Co.

Financial Reporting – A Survey of UK Published Accounts, published annually by the Institute of Chartered Accountants in England and Wales.

Information which reports and accounts must contain

The annual report and accounts is usually the principal way in which shareholders and others can keep themselves informed on the activities, progress and future plans of a company.

Although the style and content vary with the directors' views on the use of the report and accounts as a public relations vehicle – an increasing number of companies distribute a summary of their report and accounts to all employees or include one in their house newspaper, and some even produce a separate 'company profile', while others argue the risks of disclosing anything in case it may be of use to competitors – there is a minimum amount of information that *must* be disclosed to comply with the law. Amongst these requirements, the annual report and accounts has to contain four basic components: a directors' report, a profit and loss account, a balance sheet and an auditors' report.

In addition, when the company's shares are listed on The Stock Exchange, London, the report and accounts have to contain more information (see Section 5 of The Stock Exchange's *Admission of Securities to Listing*, known as 'The Yellow Book'). Companies listed on The Stock Exchange also have to produce a half-yearly or interim report.

Accounting standards

The Accounting Standards Committee, a committee representing the Institute of Chartered Accountants in England and Wales, the Scottish and Irish Institutes, the Chartered Association of Certified Accountants, the Institute of Cost and Management Accountants and the Chartered Institute of Public Finance and Accountancy, produces papers giving guidance on the treatment and presentation of various aspects of a company's accounts. These papers are published in two series:

1. *Exposure Drafts* (EDs), which propose methods to be used, and form the basis for discussion and comment in the development of official standards. Once these standards are agreed they are published as:

2. *Statements of Standard Accounting Practice* (SSAPs). These place, on members who are directors or officers of companies, the onus of ensuring that the standards are fully understood by other directors and within the company, and that significant departures are

disclosed and explained in the accounts, while members acting as auditors are also required to justify any significant departures if they concur with them.

A number of the accounting requirements contained in SSAPs have subsequently been incorporated in Companies Acts.

The production of EDs and SSAPs is a continuing process: a list of those currently extant is contained in Appendix 1. One of them, SSAP 10, requires the annual report and accounts to contain a fifth basic component, a Source and Application of Funds Statement.

Fundamental accounting concepts

Four fundamental concepts are laid down in SSAP 2 *(Disclosure of Accounting Policies)*:

1. *The going concern* concept: the accounts are compiled on the assumption that there is no intention or need to go into liquidation or to curtail the current level of operations significantly.
2. The *accruals* (or matching) concept: revenue and costs are accrued (accounted for) as they are earned or incurred, not as the money is received or paid, and revenue and profits are matched with associated costs and expenses by including them in the same accounting period.
3. The *consistency* concept: accounting treatment of like items is consistent from one period to the next.
4. The concept of *prudence*, which is the overriding concept, demands that:

(a) Revenue and profits are not anticipated;
(b) Provision is made for all known liabilities (expenses and losses), whether the amount is known with certainty or has to be estimated.

Accounting policies

SSAP 2 requires the accounting policies (the various bases on which the accounts have been prepared) to be disclosed as a note to the accounts. The note is usually No. 1 and, typically, includes the basis for accounting for:

(a) sales (treatment of VAT and duties);
(b) deferred taxation;
(c) depreciation of fixed assets;
(d) investment grants;
(e) research and development;
(f) stocks and work in progress;
(g) extraordinary items;
(h) translation of currencies;

plus any items specially related to the company's business, such as the treatment of long-term contracts, hire-purchase transactions or growing timber.

The balance sheet and profit and loss account

(The remainder of this chapter provides an introduction to the balance sheet and profit and loss account for those who are not already familiar with them. Experienced readers may like to turn straight to Chapter 2.)

The *balance sheet* is a statement of the assets and liabilities of a company on a given day, i.e. on the

---

Example 1.1   The new company's balance sheet

Liabilities		Assets	
Ordinary share capital	£100,000	Cash	£100,000

Example 1.2   The balance sheet after acquisition of fixed and current assets

Liabilities		Assets	
	£		£
Ordinary share capital	100,000	*Fixed assets*	
		Freehold land and buildings	60,000[1]
		Fixtures and fittings	15,000[2]
		Motor vehicles	2,500[4]
Current liabilities		*Current assets*	
Creditors: due within 1 year	20,000[5]	Stock (of goods)	40,000[3]
		Cash	2,500[6]
	120,000		120,000

balance sheet date. The *profit and loss account* is a record of the activities of a company for a given period of time; this period, which is called the accounting period, is normally a year, and the balance sheet always has to be drawn up on the last day of the company's accounting period.

When a company is formed the *members* (shareholders) subscribe for shares. For example, let us suppose that a company is formed with a share capital of 100,000 ordinary shares with a nominal value of £1 each, and that all the shares are issued at *par* (are issued to members at their nominal value of £1 each). The balance sheet will then look like Example 1.1.

Supposing the company then:

1. buys a freehold shop for £60,000,
2. fits it out for £15,000, and
3. stocks it with £40,000 worth of goods.

It also:

4. buys a van for £2,500.

The shop, the fittings and the van are all paid for with cash, and so are half the goods, but:

5. the other half of the goods are supplied on credit; i.e. the suppliers do not require immediate payment, so they become creditors of the company (*creditors* are people to whom the company owes money);
6. by this time most of the original £100,000 has been spent: £100,000 − 60,000 − 15,000 − 20,000 − 2,500 = £2,500 cash remaining.

The balance sheet would then look like Example 1.2 (superior figures refer to items in the above list).

Fixed assets are assets not held for resale but for use by the business. *Current assets* are cash and other assets that the company expects to turn into cash (e.g. stock), and *current liabilities*, usually described as *Creditors: due within 1 year*, are all the liabilities that the company expects to have to meet within twelve months. In modern accounting practice the current liabilities are normally shown below the current assets on the assets side of the balance sheet, and the total of the current liabilities is deducted from the total of the current assets to give what is called *net current assets*.

Let us suppose that the company then trades for a year, during which time it:

7. sells goods for £290,000, their cost plus a profit margin, and
8. buys goods for £220,000 in addition to the initial purchase of £40,000, which is called the *opening stock* (except for the first year this is the stock on hand at the end of the previous year).

9. At the end of the year, on the last day of the company's accounting year, there is £85,000 of stock, valued at cost price, on hand. This is called the *closing stock*.
10. Wages and other expenses for the year amount to £72,000.
11. In addition, a provision is made for the wear and tear on fixed assets during the year. This is calculated so that the cost of each fixed asset is written off over its expected life. The provision is called *depreciation* and, using the most common method of depreciation, the 'straight line' method:

$$\text{Depreciation for the year} = \frac{\text{Cost of asset}}{\text{Expected useful life}}$$

For our company the depreciation charge for the year would be worked out as follows:

Fixed asset	Cost	Life	Annual depreciation £
Building	£50,000	50 years	1,000
Fittings	£15,000	10 years	1,500
Motor van	£2,500	5 years	500
Depreciation charge for the year[11]			3,000

Notice that depreciation is charged only on the cost of the building (here assumed to be £50,000), not on the value of the land (assumed to be £10,000), because depreciation is provided only on assets with a finite useful life.

Example 1.3 overleaf shows how the profit and loss account for the first year's trading would be calculated.

During the year the company borrowed money to finance increased stock and to allow its customers to run accounts, normally payable monthly. The borrowings were of two types:

12. a 20-year loan of £25,000 secured on the freehold land and buildings – this is called a mortgage debenture because the lender of the money (the debenture holder) has first claim on the property if the company goes into liquidation;
13. an overdraft facility with the company's bank, with a limit of £10,000 (i.e. the bank allows the company to borrow on its current account any amount it likes up to a maximum of £10,000).

In Example 1.3 the interest on these borrowings has, for simplicity, been included in 'Wages and other expenses'. It would normally be shown separately.

At the end of the year:

14. debtors (customers owing money to the company) owed a total of £24,000;

Example 1.3   The first year's profit and loss account

	£	£	£
Sales (or Turnover)			290,000[7]
less Cost of goods sold:			
Opening stock	40,000[8]		
Purchases	+220,000[8]		
	260,000		
Closing stock	−85,000[9]		
Cost of goods sold		175,000	
Wages and other expenses		72,000[10]	
Depreciation		3,000[11]	
			250,000
Profit before tax			40,000
Corporation Tax (assuming the company pays tax at a rate of 40%)			16,000
Profit after tax			24,000
Dividends (the directors recommend a further 10% on the nominal value of the issued share capital having paid an interim dividend of 5%, making 15% in all)			15,000
Retained profits (to be ploughed back into the company)			9,000

15.   trade creditors were £38,000 – so a little less than half the stock was being financed by suppliers.

Our final illustration (Example 1.4) shows the balance sheet at the end of the year drawn up in the modern way, with the assets less creditors above the capital and reserves, rather than assets on one side and liabilities on the other. Notice that:

16.   fixed assets are shown at cost *less* depreciation to date;
17.   companies normally have a small amount of cash in hand, even if they have an overdraft;
18.   the final dividend, 10% out of a total of 15% for the year, has not yet been paid;
19.   net current assets = current assets − current liabilities, i.e. £109,500 − 50,000 = £59,500;
20.   *ordinary shareholders' funds* = ordinary share capital issued plus reserves.

Example 1.4   The balance sheet after the first year's trading

	£	£
Fixed assets[16]		
Freehold land and buildings		59,000[11]
Fixtures and fittings		13,500[11]
Motor vehicles		2,000[11]
		74,500
Current assets		
Stock	85,000[9]	
Debtors	24,000[14]	
Cash[17]	500	
	109,500	
Current liabilities		
(or Creditors: due		
within 1 year)		
Trade creditors	38,000[15]	
Dividends payable[18]	10,000	
Overdraft[17]	2,000[13]	
	50,000	
Net current assets[19]		59,500
Total assets less current liabilities		134,000
Creditors: due after more than 1 year		
Mortgage debenture		25,000[12]
		109,000
Capital and reserves		
Ordinary share capital		100,000
Reserves (retained profits)		9,000
Ordinary shareholders' funds[20]		109,000

Chapter 2

FORMING A COMPANY

Incorporation of a company

(References: Companies Act 1948, Sch. 1, Tables A and B, which were *not* reproduced in the Companies Act 1985, but are in statutory instruments under S.3 and S.8 of that Act.)

When a company is formed by incorporation under the Companies Acts a Certificate of Incorporation is issued and the company assumes a legal identity separate from its shareholders.

Before incorporation can take place, a Memorandum of Association and Articles of Association have to be drawn up and filed with the Registrar of Companies in England and Wales or with the Registrar of Companies in Scotland.

Memorandum of Association

The Memorandum lays down the rules which govern the company in its relations with the outside world. It states the name of the company; the country in which the Registered Office will be situated; the objects of the company (i.e. activities the company may pursue); the authorised share capital, the nominal value of the shares; a list of initial subscribers and whether the liability of members (shareholders) is limited. An example is given in Table B of the First Schedule to the Companies Act 1948.

Articles of Association

The Articles lay down the internal rules within which the directors run the company. The main items covered are:

(a) the issue of shares, the rights attaching to each class of share, the consent required for the alteration of the rights of any class of shareholders, and any restrictions on the transfer of shares;

(b) the procedure for general meetings and for altering the authorised share capital;

(c) the election and retirement of directors, their duties and their powers, including borrowing powers;

(d) the declaration of dividends;

(e) the procedure for winding up the company.

A model set of Articles is given in Table A of the First Schedule to the Companies Act 1948.

Members' (shareholders') liability

The liability of members (shareholders) of a company can either be limited by shares or by guarantee, or the liability can be unlimited.

Limited by shares
This is the method normally used for a company engaged in business activities. If the shares are *fully paid*, the members' liability is limited to the money they have put up: the maximum risk a shareholder runs is to lose all the money he has paid for his shares, and no further claim can be made on him for liabilities incurred by the company. If the shares are only *partly paid*, shareholders (and to a limited extent former shareholders) can be called upon to subscribe some or all of the unpaid part, but no more than that.

Limited by guarantee
This method is used for charitable and similar organisations, where funds are raised by donations and no shares are issued. The liability is limited to the amount each member personally guarantees, which is the maximum each member may be called upon to pay in the event of liquidation. This form of incorporation is not normally used for a business.

Unlimited

This method is used by professional firms that want the tax advantages of being a company; the members have joint and several liability in the same way as a partnership (each member can individually be held entirely responsible).

Chartered company

Companies may also be established by Royal Charter, the method used before any Companies Acts existed; for example, the PENINSULAR & ORIENTAL STEAM NAVIGATION COMPANY was incorporated by Royal Charter in 1840. The legal position of a chartered company is similar to an incorporated company, except that any change to the Articles involves a petition to the Privy Council.

Public company

(Reference: Companies Act 1985, Sections 1(3), 11 and 25.)

A public company is defined as one:

(*a*) which is limited by shares or guarantee, with a minimum issued share capital of £50,000 (the shares must be at least 25% paid up, with any share premium fully paid up); and
(*b*) whose Memorandum states that it is a public company; and
(*c*) which has been correctly registered as a public company.

All other companies are private companies.

The name of a public company must in all cases end either with the words 'Public Limited Company' or with the abbreviation 'PLC', neither of which may be preceded by the word 'Limited'.

A public company does not automatically have its shares listed on The Stock Exchange, but the process of obtaining a listing (see Chapter 3) is often referred to as 'going public', as a private company cannot obtain a listing on The Stock Exchange, and the processes of obtaining a listing and of becoming a public company are often carried out together.

Private company

A 'private company' is a company that is not a public company (CA 1985, S.1(3)).

A company limited by shares or by guarantee (not being a public company) must have 'limited' as the last word in its name (CA 1985, S.25). Thus all companies whose names end with 'limited' are private companies.

Close company

(Reference: Income and Corporation Taxes Act 1970, Section 282.)

Broadly speaking, a close company is one which is under the control of five or fewer persons or their associates *or* is under the control of its directors.

A close company is required to distribute at least 50% of trading income less Corporation Tax and all its investment income less tax, unless larger retentions can be shown to be needed for the continuing requirements of the business. If insufficient is distributed, the company is assessed as having distributed the required total: the difference is apportioned to the shareholders, treated as paid to them, and they are taxed accordingly. This process, called 'apportionment', is sometimes still referred to as 'shortfall', its correct name prior to 1973.

A listed company is not a close company if shares carrying not less than 35% of the voting power are unconditionally and beneficially held by the public.

The Stock Exchange requires a listed company to include, with its annual report, a statement showing whether or not, as far as the directors are aware, the company is a close company.

Small and medium-sized companies

Small and medium-sized companies are defined by Section 248 of the Companies Act 1985 as companies meeting at least two of the following criteria:

	Small company	*Medium-sized company*
Turnover not exceeding	£1.4m	£5.75m
Balance sheet total not exceeding	£0.7m	£2.8m
Average number of persons employed not exceeding	50	250

Small and medium-sized private companies are exempted from some of the requirements of the Companies Acts (CA 1985, Sch.8).

Chapter 3

ADMISSION TO LISTING

Stock Exchange listing – 'quoted companies'

(References: *The Stock Exchange (Listing) Regulations 1984*; The Stock Exchange, London's book *Admission of Securities to Listing* – known as 'The Yellow Book'.)

Provided that it meets certain criteria, a public company may have its shares and/or debentures, unsecured loan stocks and warrants 'listed', i.e. included in The Stock Exchange Official List, so that a market is 'made' in the securities. Although it is usual for all the securities of a company to be listed, it is possible for this not to be the case. For example, SAINSBURY's preference shares were listed for many years before its ordinary shares were offered to the public.

Companies which have securities that are listed are often referred to as 'quoted companies', 'having a quotation' or 'being listed', although it is the company's securities that are listed, not the company itself. 'Having a quotation' is simply the old term for being 'listed', and The Stock Exchange department which deals with applications for listing is still called the Quotations Department.

Requirements for listing

The minimum legal requirements that a company has to meet before any of its securities can be listed are laid down in *The Stock Exchange (Listing) Regulations 1984*, a statutory instrument which implements in the United Kingdom three EEC directives, known as the Admission directive, the Listing Particulars directive and the Interim Reports directive.

These requirements are incorporated in The Stock Exchange's *Admission of Securities to Listing* (The Yellow Book), together with The Stock Exchange Council's own requirements.

Listing Particulars (prospectus)
Section 3 of The Yellow Book contains details of the contents of Listing Particulars, which have to be supplied to The Stock Exchange's Quotations Department for approval prior to listing, and which have to be included in any prospectus inviting initial public subscription for the company's shares.

The Listing Particulars are designed to ensure that the company makes available sufficient information on its history, current position and future prospects to enable the general public to assess the value of the company's shares as an investment, and they are very comprehensive. The prospectus issued by a company when it goes public is therefore a most valuable source of information for the analyst.

Minimum size of issue
The Stock Exchange has to satisfy itself that sufficient dealings are likely to take place in the class of security for which application is being made to make a realistic market, and thus justify a listing. The Yellow Book lays down two minimum criteria for listing – the expected market value of the securities for which listing is sought (the expected market price multiplied by the number of shares issued and to be issued: currently a minimum of £700,000 for shares and £200,000 for debt securities), and the proportion of shares to be held by the public (currently 25% of any class of share).

Keeping the public informed
The Stock Exchange also has to ensure that the general public will be kept satisfactorily informed of the company's activities and progress in the future, and that the shareholders' interests will be

adequately protected: this is done by requiring an applicant for listing to accept 'Continuing Obligations' as a condition of admission to and subsequent maintenance of listing.

Continuing Obligations

Chapter 2 of Section 5 of The Yellow Book contains details of the *Continuing Obligations* of listed companies, designed to protect shareholders and to keep them properly informed. It requires the company to submit to The Stock Exchange through the company's brokers proofs *for approval* of all circulars to holders of securities, notices of meetings, forms of proxy and notices by advertisement to holders of bearer securities. It also requires the company to notify The Stock Exchange of profit announcements, dividend declarations, material acquisitions, changes of directors, proposed changes in the nature of the business and any other 'information necessary to enable holders of the company's listed securities and the public to appraise the position of the company and to avoid the establishment of a false market in its securities'.

In addition, amongst various requirements on interim reports, proxy voting, registration of securities and several other topics, the *Continuing Obligations* require companies to circulate with the annual report:

(a) the directors' reasons for any significant departure from standard accounting practices;
(b) a geographical analysis of the turnover of operations outside the United Kingdom and Ireland, and of contribution to trading results if 'abnormal';
(c) the name of the principal country in which each subsidiary operates;
(d) certain particulars of each company in which the group holds 20% or more of the equity capital;
(e) the amount of interest capitalised by the company (or group) during the year;
(f) details of each director's beneficial and non-beneficial interests in the company's shares and options;
(g) information on holdings, other than by directors, of 5% or more of any class of voting capital;
(h) a statement of whether the company is or is not a close company;
(i) particulars of significant contracts during the year in which any director is or was materially interested;
(j) particulars of the waiving of emoluments by any director, and of the waiving of dividends by any shareholder.

Companies are also expected to issue their report and accounts within six months of their year end, but the six-month period may be extended if they have significant overseas interests.

Methods of obtaining a listing

Chapter 3 of Section 1 of The Yellow Book describes the five ways in which a company can obtain a listing. Briefly, they are as follows:

1. *Offer for sale*, the most common method; both new and/or existing shares can be offered to the public. The issuing house or the sponsoring broker purchases the shares from existing shareholders and/or from the company, and offers them on to the general public at a slightly higher price.
2. *Offer for sale by tender*, a variation on method 1 which allows applicants to bid for securities at or above a minimum issue price. The shares are then all sold at one price, the 'striking price', which may be the highest price at which all the shares can be sold, or a little lower if this is necessary to ensure a good spread of shareholders.
3. *Public issue by prospectus*, a rare method; shares are offered direct to the public by the company. Only new shares can be offered.
4. *Placing*, used for small issues (under £3 million); the shares are sold to institutional investors, and the general public is not invited to subscribe. A proportion of the shares have to be offered to the jobbers to ensure that a reasonable market can be started in the shares, i.e. so that other investors have an opportunity to buy the shares through any stockbroker.
5. *Introduction*, used where the company's shares are already widely held and/or are already listed outside the United Kingdom; there is no formal offer of shares, but a listing is obtained for existing shares.

Methods 1 to 4 are referred to broadly as 'new issues', because the company's shares are new to the stock market, although methods 1, 2 and 4 do not necessarily involve the issue of any new shares.

The Unlisted Securities Market

(Reference: The Stock Exchange, London's booklet *Unlisted Securities Market* – known as 'The Green Book'.)

The Unlisted Securities Market (USM) was launched by The Stock Exchange in November 1980 to provide a recognised market for the securities of smaller, less mature companies. Although the shares of USM companies are in law 'unlisted', they are dealt in on The Stock Exchange just like any listed shares; however, entry to the USM was made much easier than obtaining a full listing:

1. Only 10% of the equity need be made available to the general public rather than the 25% normally required for the full listing.

2. The company is required to have been trading for only three years (full listing five years).

3. Both the cost of entry and the annual charge are considerably less than for a full listing.

4. Being in law 'unlisted', there is no requirement to comply with EEC directives on listed companies.

Chapter 4

SHARE CAPITAL AND RESERVES

SHARE CAPITAL

Authorised and issued share capital

When a company is formed the authorised share capital and the nominal value of the shares are established and written into the company's Memorandum of Association. At the same time the procedure for increasing the authorised share capital is included in the company's Articles of Association; this procedure usually requires the passing by simple majority of an ordinary resolution at a general meeting of shareholders. Thereafter the directors of the company cannot issue new shares in excess of the authorised limits, nor can they issue any form of securities which have rights to subscribe for shares (e.g. convertibles and warrants: see below) if the full exercising of these rights would involve the issue of shares in excess of the authorised share capital.

Both the authorised share capital and the issued share capital are shown in the company's balance sheet.

Types of share capital

Although all shares are referred to generally as 'risk capital', as the shareholders are the first investors to lose if the company fails, the degree of risk can vary within the same company from hardly any more than that of an unsecured lender to highly speculative, with prospects of reward usually varying accordingly. The main types of shares, in increasing order of risk, the order in which they would rank for distribution in the event of liquidation, are:

(*a*) preference shares;
(*b*) ordinary shares;
(*c*) deferred shares;
(*d*) warrants to subscribe for shares.

Unlike interest paid on loan capital, distributions of profits to shareholders are not an 'allowable expense' for company taxation purposes; i.e. dividends have to be paid out of profits *after* Corporation Tax has been deducted, although the present imputation tax system does concede to shareholders an associated tax credit on dividends, as explained in Chapter 13.

Preference shares

Preference shares carry a fixed rate of dividend, normally payable half-yearly, but unlike the holders of loan capital, who can take action against a company in default of interest payments, preference shareholders have no legal redress if the board of directors decides to recommend that no preference dividends should be paid. However, if no preference dividend is declared for an accounting period, no dividend can be declared on any other type of share for the period concerned, and the preference shareholders usually become entitled to vote at shareholders' general meetings. (Provided their dividends are paid, preference shares do not normally carry a vote.)

Varieties of preference shares (see Example 4.1) can include one or a combination of the following features:

1. *Cumulative.* If the dividend on a cumulative preference share is not paid on time, payment is postponed rather than omitted. When this happens, the preference dividend is said to be 'in arrears', and these arrears have to be paid by the company before any other dividend can be declared. Arrears of cumulative preference dividends must be shown in a note to the accounts.

2. *Redeemable*. The shares are repayable, normally at their nominal (par) value, in a given year, e.g. 1990, or when the company chooses within a given period, e.g. 1988/92.
3. *Participating*. In addition to receiving a fixed dividend, shareholders participate in an additional dividend, usually a proportion of any ordinary dividend declared.
4. *Convertible*. Shareholders have the option of converting their preference shares into ordinary shares, usually on an unchanged nominal value basis within a given period of time, the conversion period.

Example 4.1 Varieties of preference share

A company has four types of share, listed below. In 1981 it pays no dividends; in 1982 it pays preference dividends only, including arrears of cumulative preference dividends, and in 1983 and 1984 it also pays ordinary dividends of 4p and 12p respectively. The participating preference shareholders are entitled to half the ordinary dividend in addition to their fixed 3.5% per annum.

The net dividend payable on each type of share, all of £1 nominal value, would be

	1981	1982	1983	1984
5.6% Cumulative preference	Nil	11.2p	5.6p	5.6p
7% Redeemable preference 1982	Nil	7p	Nil	Nil (redeemed)
3.5% Participating preference	Nil	3½p	5½p	9½p
Ordinary £1 share	Nil	Nil	4p	12p

(The rate of dividend on a preference share is normally quoted net of associated tax credit (see page 85).)

Ordinary shares

Ordinary shares usually form the bulk of the share capital of a company. Ordinary shareholders are normally entitled to all the profits remaining after tax and preference dividends have been deducted although, as explained later, not all these attributable profits are likely to be distributed. Ordinary shareholders are entitled to vote at general meetings, giving them control over the election of directors.

Until recently companies were not allowed to issue redeemable ordinary shares. Under Section 159 of the Companies Act 1985 they are now allowed to do so, provided they also have shares in issue which are not redeemable; i.e. the share capital of a company cannot consist solely of redeemable shares. A company may now also purchase its own shares, subject to a large number of conditions, including the prior approval of its shareholders (see page 16).

Ordinary stock

Ordinary stock is a historical legacy from the days when every share in issue had to be numbered; some companies used to convert their shares into stock when they became fully paid (as this avoided the bother of numbers), and a few companies have carried on doing so.

Ordinary stock is equity capital. It can, in theory, be transferred in any monetary amount, while shares can only be bought and sold individually; in practice ordinary stock is normally traded in multiples of £1, so the terms 'ordinary share' and 'ordinary stock' are effectively synonymous.

Non-voting shares

A number of companies have more than one class of share (other than preference shares), with differing rights on voting and/or dividends and/or on liquidation. The most common variation is in voting rights, where a second class of share, identical in all other respects to the ordinary class, carries either no voting rights (usually called N/V or 'A' shares), or carries restricted voting rights (R/V shares).

The trend over the last few years has, however, been towards the abolition of non-voting shares, and it is becoming increasingly difficult (if not actually impossible) to raise new money by the issue of non-voting shares. Several companies, led by MARKS & SPENCER in 1966, and including SEARS and RANK, have enfranchised their non-voting shares, giving modest scrip (free) issues to voting shareholders by way of compensation.

Investing in shares that do not have full voting power is very much a case of *caveat emptor* (buyer beware). You may find yourself invested in a company like C. H. BAILEY, where the B shares, largely family-held, carry 100 times the voting rights of the more widely held A shares and where, for the inconvenience of outside shareholders, the AGM was held in 1985 at 10.30 a.m. on 2 January, in Cardiff. Or you may find yourself invested in a company like ACROW, where the founder, Bill de Vigier, and his son-in-law between them held over 50% of the voting shares; de Vigier ran ACROW extremely successfully for many years, but built up a mountain of debt because he steadfastly refused to enfranchise the N/V shareholders and have a rights issue to broaden his equity base. When, in the early 1980s, the bottom fell out of the crane market and the strength of sterling hit exports (a very large part of ACROW's turnover), the bankers finally withdrew their support. When we asked de Vigier, two years earlier, why he

11

didn't enfranchise and have a rights issue, he replied 'Not while I'm alive. The banks have never refused to lend me money in the past, why should they do so in the future?'

The same warning applies to companies where all shares (other than preference shares) carry equal voting rights, and one person effectively controls more than 50% of the votes; other shareholders are relying very heavily on that one person, but at least the controlling shareholder doesn't enjoy power that is disproportionate to his stake in the company.

Deferred shares

Another, but less common, class is the deferred share, where no dividend is payable either:

(*a*) until ordinary shareholders' dividends have reached a certain level,
 or
(*b*) until several years after issue: e.g. CRODA in 1978 made a scrip issue of deferred ordinary shares which do not rank for dividend until 1988.

Partly paid shares

When a company does not need all the proceeds of an equity issue immediately (e.g. an oil exploration company with a lengthy drilling programme) or wishes to have guaranteed recourse to further

equity finance in certain circumstances (e.g. a merchant bank wanting ample cover for liabilities), it may issue partly paid shares, i.e. shares for which subscribers pay for only part of the nominal price at the time of issue. Partly paid shares, once issued, place an obligation on the holder to subscribe the unpaid-up portion at the company's call, and there are legal safeguards to prevent the device of holders transferring their shares to a non-creditworthy person in order to avoid paying the call.

Details of partly paid shares issued by a company are shown in the balance sheet (e.g. HAMBROS, as shown below).

Where a company holds partly paid shares, details should be shown under 'contingent liabilities' (CA 1985, Sch. 4, para. 50 (2)), e.g. BURMAH OIL, illustrated below.

Shares can be issued with part of the issue price payable on application and the remainder payable shortly afterwards, before registration (i.e. before the company registers the shares in the holder's name). However, if shares are to remain partly paid after registration, The Stock Exchange will not normally allow them to be admitted to listing.

Warrants

Warrants are transferable options granted by the company to purchase new shares from the com-

HAMBROS PLC *Note 12 to the balance sheet at 31 March 1984*

Share capital

	Authorised £000	1984 £000	1983 £000
2,000,000 £2 shares, allotted, 50p called up and paid	4,000	1,000	1,000
100,000,000 5p limited voting shares,	5,000		
86,653,235 called up and fully paid		4,333	4,328
1,126,500 ½p called up and paid		5	6
1,000,000 £1 non-voting shares, called up and fully paid	1,000	1,000	1,000
	10,000	6,338	6,334

BURMAH OIL *Balance sheet*

Note 24   Other commitments and contingent liabilities

	1983 £ million Group	1982 £ million Group	1983 £ million Company	1982 £ million Company
(a) Amounts uncalled on partly paid shares:				
Subsidiaries			2.0	2.1
Trade investments	0.2	5.1	0.2	5.1
	0.2	5.1	2.2	7.2

pany at a given price, called the 'exercise price'. The warrant is normally exercisable only during a given time period, the exercise period, although one or two perpetual warrants have been issued.

Warrants can be issued on their own, but are usually issued attached to new issues of unsecured loan stock to give the stockholder an opportunity of subsequently participating in the equity of the company; the warrant element makes the issue more attractive and is sometimes referred to as the 'sweetener' (see Chapter 5).

Once the loan stock plus warrants 'package' is issued the warrants can be detached ('stripped') and sold separately, providing a high risk/high reward form of equity investment. For example, if the ordinary shares of a company stood at 100p, warrants with an exercise price of 75p would then be worth a minimum of 25p. If the ordinary shares doubled to 200p then the warrants would be worth a minimum of 125p, a fivefold increase. In practice warrants command a premium over the ordinary price minus exercise price, although this premium tends to fall over the life of the warrant, reaching zero at the end of the exercise period. Warrants are comparatively rare in the United Kingdom, where the majority have been issued in bid situations.

A very clear explanation of the behaviour of warrant prices in practice is given in R. A. Brealey's book *Security Prices in a Competitive Market*.

Share schemes for directors and employees

A number of companies have encouraged share ownership amongst their staff for many years (ICI, for example, introduced a profit-sharing scheme as long ago as 1954, under which employees received a salary-related allocation of shares each year, according to the profitability of the company), but it is only in the last few years that governments have actively encouraged wider share participation by the introduction of substantial tax concessions. These concessions now apply to three types of scheme: savings related share option schemes (SAYE schemes), profit-sharing schemes and, most recently, share option schemes. The first two have proved very popular; by the end of 1984 380 SAYE and 450 profit-sharing schemes had been approved by the Inland Revenue.

Savings related share option schemes (SAYE schemes)
In this type of scheme, if 'approved' under the Finance Act 1980, an employee enters into a 'save as you earn' contract for a minimum of five years and at the same time is given an option to subscribe for shares with the sum saved at a given price, which must not be more than 10%

below the market price at the start of the SAYE contract.

At the end of the SAYE contract period the employee can either use the lump sum from the SAYE contract to exercise the option, if the shares have done well in the mean time, or he can keep the cash. In either case he will not be charged income tax, but any profit on disposal is subject to assessment for capital gains tax. The total number of options outstanding under the scheme will be shown in the annual report and accounts (e.g. GREENALL WHITLEY, illustrated here).

GREENALL WHITLEY *Report of the Directors 1983*
Employment Report
In further development of the company's employment policy, savings-related share option schemes have operated since 1975. To date 963,982 Ordinary shares have been issued to employees and there were a further 1,113,640 Ordinary shares reserved against the exercise of options granted pursuant to the savings-related share option schemes at 30th September 1983.

Profit-sharing schemes
In this type of scheme, introduced by Labour under pressure from the Liberals, companies have, since 1978, been allowed to allocate up to a maximum sum per employee (currently £1,250 p.a. or 10% of earnings if less) to be used to purchase shares at full market value through specially created trusts.

The shares have to be held in trust for at least two years; income tax has to be paid only if the shares are sold within seven years, and then only on a reducing scale according to how long they have been held, but normal capital gains tax rules apply.

Share options
These are like warrants, except that they are not normally transferable, and may lapse on termination of the holder's directorship of or employment by the company. For options granted before the concessions of the Finance Act 1984, income tax is payable when the options are exercised on the amount by which the market price of the shares at the time exceeds the exercise price, whether or not the shares are sold at that time. If the shares are subsequently sold at a higher price, an assessment for capital gains tax will arise.

Under the Finance Act 1984 there is no tax liability when the options are exercised, but when the shares are sold there is an assessment for capital gains tax on the amount by which the selling price exceeds the exercise price.

Details of the number of options granted, the period during which they may be exercised and the subscription price payable should be shown in the accounts. For example:

BOC *Note on capital and reserves*

Senior Executives' Share Option Scheme
Of the unissued shares, 8,300,000 Ordinary shares were, at 30th September 1983, reserved for the Senior Executives' Share Option Scheme approved by shareholders on 30th July 1982. At 30th September 1983 options under that Scheme were outstanding in respect of a total of 2,197,790 Ordinary shares and are exercisable at dates between 8th September 1986 and 8th September 1989 at 200p per share.

Partly paid shares
As the amount paid up is usually very small, and the call is normally payable at the holder's request, partly paid shares issued under executive incentive schemes are very similar to options from the company's point of view. From the holder's point of view the tax advantages of share options under the Finance Act 1984 are so great that partly paid shares are unlikely to be used as executive incentives in the future.

Details of all types of partly paid shares are shown in the balance sheet under 'Share capital' (e.g. BRITISH LAND, shown here).

BRITISH LAND *Balance sheet*

Note 8   Shareholders' Funds

	1984
	£000
Shares of 25p each:	
Fully paid	26,008
Share incentive scheme – 2½p paid	6
	26,014

Strictly speaking, options granted and partly paid shares issued to directors and employees under incentive schemes produce potential dilution of equity earnings in the same way as warrants, but in practice they are usually sufficiently small in relation to a company's issued equity to be ignored.

Shares purchased with loans
Section 153 (4) (c) of the Companies Act 1985 allows loans to employees, but not to directors, for the purpose of purchasing fully paid shares in the company; the aggregate amount of any outstanding loans must be shown in the company's balance sheet. Because of the tax advantages of other schemes, loans for the purchase of shares are likely to become increasingly rare.

The investors' viewpoint
Companies that encourage employee share participation on favourable terms are generally regarded as more likely to prosper than those which do not. In particular, companies that grant options to executive directors and key senior staff, on whose efforts the success of a company largely depends, can expect better than average performance. In short, giving the directors and employees a 'slice of the action' should be regarded as a plus point for investing in a company.

Limitations on the issue of further equity

There are three limitations to the issue of further equity.

First, as already mentioned, there must be sufficient share capital authorised.

Secondly, The Stock Exchange's *Continuing Obligations* for listed companies forbids the issue of equity, convertibles, warrants or options for cash, other than to the equity shareholders of the company, except with the prior approval of ordinary shareholders in general meeting, and the approval of The Stock Exchange. The Stock Exchange normally restricts issues of equity capital by way of placings to protect the interests of existing shareholders (see The Yellow Book, Section 1, Chapter 2, para. 2.3), but these restrictions can be relaxed when market conditions or the individual circumstances of a company justify doing so.

Thirdly, Section 100 of the Companies Act 1985 prohibits the issue of shares at a discount, i.e. for less than their nominal value.

Rights issues

A rights issue is an issue of new shares offered to shareholders in proportion to their existing holdings at a discount to the current market price. The discount varies according to the 'weight' of the rights issue; 1 new share offered for every 8 or 10 shares already held would be regarded as a 'light' issue, probably requiring a discount of around 15%, while more than 1-for-4 would be 'heavy' and likely to need about 20% discount, or more if the company is in poor health. At these discounts underwriting would be arranged to ensure buyers for any shares not taken up by shareholders, but companies occasionally choose to make a rights issue at very much below the market price, the lowest price normally permitted being the par value of the shares.

The effect on the balance sheet of an issue at par is to add the total nominal value of the shares being issued to the issued share capital, and to show the cash received on the assets side. The expenses of the issue would normally be written off either to profit and loss account or against share premium account.

If the new shares are issued above par, the nominal value of the shares issued is added to the issued share capital and the difference between the issue price and the nominal price of each new share, i.e. the premium at which the shares were issued, is added to the share premium account. For example, in July 1983 RIO TINTO-ZINC made a 1-for-6 rights issue of 44,106,395 ordinary 25p shares at 450p per share. The issue added £11.1m to the ordinary share capital (44.1m × 25p) and £187.5m (44.1m × 425p premium), less expenses, to the share premium account, as illustrated here.

RIO TINTO-ZINC *Note 22 to 1983 balance sheet*

	1983 £m	1982 £m
Issued share capital		
Ordinary shares of 25p each	77.3	66.2
Share premium		
At 1 January	115.8	68.6
Premium on shares issued	187.5	47.2
Expenses of rights issue	(6.5)	
At 31 December	296.8	115.8

There are two methods of dealing with convertible stock in a rights issue. Either the holders are offered new shares on the basis of the number of ordinary shares they would hold on full conversion, or the stock has its conversion terms adjusted to allow for the rights issue, whichever method is laid down in the convertible's trust deed (see Chapter 5). Similarly, either warrant holders are offered new shares or the warrant's exercise price is adjusted.

Scrip issues

A scrip issue, also known as a bonus or capitalisation issue, is a free issue of additional new shares to existing shareholders, made by capitalising reserves. For example, WATTS BLAKE BEARNE made a 1-for-4 scrip issue in 1980, with the following effect on the balance sheet:

	At 31 Dec 1979 £000	Post scrip £000
Share capital:		
preference	146	146
ordinary	3,278	4,098
Reserves	15,708	14,888
Shareholders' funds	19,132	19,132

As a scrip issue is basically a bookkeeping transaction, the share price would normally be expected to adjust accordingly (e.g. would fall from 125p to 100p with a 1-for-4), and it is open to debate as to whether scrip issues serve any useful purpose. The main arguments in favour are the following:

(a) Scrip issues are popular with the investing public, and therefore enhance share prices. Research shows that shares tend to outperform the market after the announcement of a scrip issue, but that companies make scrip issues only when they are doing well, i.e. when their share price would be expected to outperform just as much without the scrip issue.

(b) A 'heavy' share price in the market, say over £2, tends to make the shares harder to trade and artificially depresses the price. Scrip issues can be used to scale the price down.

(c) A scrip issue, being 'paid for' out of reserves, enables retained profits and/or the increased value of assets to be reflected by an increased share capital.

(d) The rate of dividends, expressed as a percentage of an unrealistically small share capital, can look excessive.

(e) An issued share capital of at least £1 million is needed for Trustee status.

The last argument appears to be the only factual one in favour of scrip issues; the remainder are psychological, although only a sound and flourishing company is likely to be able to make substantial scrip issues every few years. WATTS BLAKE BEARNE's record illustrates this well: the company also made a 1-for-2 scrip issue in 1970, a 1-for-3 in 1972, a 1-for-4 in 1976 and a 1-for-2 in 1978.

The arguments against scrip issues are firstly the administrative costs incurred and secondly the increased risk of the share price subsequently falling very close to or below par, thus precluding a rights issue. The cost is relatively small, but reducing the market price can cause serious embarrassment if the company wants, at a later date, to make a rights issue only to find that its share price is too low to do so.

Share splits

Where a company feels its share price is 'heavy' but does not want to capitalise reserves – i.e. it does not want to make a scrip issue – it can split its shares into shares with a smaller par value. For example, in 1982 GEC split its 25p shares, which were standing at around £12 at the time, into 5p shares, and the share price moved to around 240p.

Stock (scrip) dividends

There are two types of stock or scrip dividends:

(a) where the company issues shares instead of paying cash dividends – shareholders have no choice (as ULTRAMAR did in the 1970s);

(*b*) where each shareholder can choose whether he or she wishes to receive a cash dividend or a stock dividend.

Between 1973 and 1975 tax legislation enabled shares issued by companies in lieu of cash dividends at the choice of individual shareholders, i.e. type (*b*) above, to be assessed for Capital Gains Tax on subsequent disposal rather than being treated as income received in the year of distribution. The number of shares was calculated to give the same value as the *net* dividend payable, and each shareholder could elect to receive a stock dividend in lieu of a cash dividend if he preferred the former.

An alternative method, adopted by one or two companies (for example, RIO TINTO-ZINC), was to create a separate class of *accumulating ordinary shares*, which ordinary shareholders could switch into so as to receive stock dividends automatically.

The tax concession was of considerable advantage to shareholders paying more than the standard rate of Income Tax, and was abolished when a Labour government returned to power. Thus stock dividends became fairly rare; they may still be paid in lieu of cash, but they can only avoid Income Tax assessment provided the stock dividend is not an alternative to cash, i.e. type (*a*) above.

Vendor consideration

This is the use of new shares to pay for an acquisition. In the balance sheet the value of the shares issued is shown as an increase in liabilities under share capital and share premium account, balanced on the other side by the assets acquired. If the value of the tangible assets falls short of the market value of the shares issued, the difference (i.e. the premium the acquirer has paid) can either be written off straight away against reserves, or taken into the balance sheet as 'goodwill' – an intangible asset.

For example, in 1983 GREENALL WHITLEY made several acquisitions and gave details of assets acquired and how their purchase was funded at the bottom of its source and application of funds statement (see illustration below). The sum of £2,724,000 was provided by the issue of shares, and the overall cost exceeded the value of the tangible assets acquired by £7,000.

Supplementary information on shares

Details of shares and debentures issued during the year should be given in a note to the balance sheet (CA 1985, Sch. 4, paras 39 and 41). The terms for redemption of all redeemable shares and the details of all outstanding rights to acquire shares either by subscription or conversion should also be given (CA 1985, Sch. 4, paras 38 (2) and 40).

Company purchasing its own shares

Under Sections 162 to 169 of the Companies Act 1985, a company may purchase its own shares, providing it doesn't buy in all its non-redeemable shares. Each contract for purchases outside the normal market must be authorised in advance by a special resolution. General authority may be given for market purchases up to a maximum number of shares, within a given price range and within a maximum of 18 months from the date the resolution is passed.

Several property companies were quick to take advantage of this concession to purchase their ordinary shares at a price below asset value, thus increasing the asset value of the remaining shares. For example, SAMUEL PROPERTIES passed the following resolution at an EGM held on 17 June 1983:

'That the Company be generally and unconditionally authorised to make market purchases of not more than 2,893,900 shares of 25p each at not more than 150 pence nor less than 82 pence per share providing that this authority shall expire on 17th December, 1984.'

GREENALL WHITLEY *Source and application of group funds statement 1983*

Summary of the effects of acquisitions made during the year

	£000		£000
Net assets acquired:		Discharged by:	
Tangible fixed assets	15,521	Cash	1,964
Depreciation	(242)	Bank loans	4,275
Net current assets	799	Mortgage loans	6,624
	16,078	Proceeds from issue of shares	2,724
Net premium on acquisition	7	Minority interests	498
	16,085		16,085

The annual report subsequently recorded the purchase of 500,000 of the Company's 25p ordinary shares in the year ending 30 June 1983 at a price of 120p each; this helped to increase the net assets per share during the year from 189p to 209p.

Other companies have followed suit, most notably GEC, which spent over £150 million on buying its own shares in the year to 31 March 1985.

Reduction of share capital

Under Section 135 of the Companies Act 1985 a company may, with court approval, reduce its share capital in any way and, in particular, may:

(a) reduce or extinguish liability on share capital not fully paid up;
(b) cancel any paid-up share capital which is lost or unrepresented by available assets; and
(c) repay any paid-up share capital in excess of its requirements.

Where the net assets no longer exceed the paid-up value of the issued share capital, the reserves will appear negative in the balance sheet. Take, for example, the balance sheet of a company which has 1 million £1 ordinary shares in issue and reduces this to 1½ million 25p shares to remove a substantial accumulation of losses (Example 4.2):

The amount of £625,000 nominal of capital and

Example 4.2 Effect of share capital reduction on the balance sheet

	Before reduction £000	After reduction £000
Issued share capital	1,000	375
Share premium account	206	—
Other reserves	(831)	—
Shareholders' funds	375	375

the share premium account of £206,000 have been cancelled.

Arrangements and reconstructions

If a company wishes to make an arrangement with its creditors or shareholders, including a re-organisation of the company's share capital by consolidation of different classes and/or division into different classes, it can do so under Section 425 of the Companies Act 1985. A meeting has to be called for each class of creditor or shareholder concerned, at which a resolution to make the arrangement requires at least three-fourths by value of those present to vote in favour; after subsequent sanction by the court, the arrangement is then registered with the Registrar of Companies and becomes binding on all creditors and shareholders concerned.

RESERVES

Reserves can arise in several ways:

(a) by the accumulation of profits, either by retained profits from the profit and loss account or from the sale of assets;
(b) by the issue of shares or loan capital at a premium, i.e. at more than their nominal value: the issue can be either for cash or as consideration (payment) in an acquisition;
(c) by the purchase or repayment of loan capital below its nominal value;
(d) by upward revaluation of assets (see page 35);
(e) by the acquisition of assets at below their balance sheet value.

They can be reduced by losses, issue and redemption expenses, revaluation deficits and the writing-off of goodwill. In addition, some companies take foreign currency adjustments direct to reserves.

The balance sheet formats in Schedule 4 of the Companies Act 1985 require reserves to be shown

in three main subdivisions: Share premium account, Revaluation reserve, and Other reserves. Reserves should not include provision for deferred taxation, or any other provision.

Capital and revenue reserves

By law certain reserves are non-distributable (cannot be paid out as dividends) and the Articles of a company may further restrict distribution.

Prior to the Companies Act 1967 a company was required to distinguish between reserves available for dividend (revenue reserves) and those not available (capital reserves), and although in law this distinction is no longer compulsory some companies still make the division between capital reserves and revenue reserves in their accounts.

Share premium account

(Reference: Companies Act 1985, Section 130.)

When shares are issued at a premium over their nominal value, the premium element must, by law, be credited to the share premium account, unless the rules of merger accounting apply (see page 108).

The share premium account has to be shown separately on the balance sheet and no part may be paid out to shareholders except on liquidation or under a capital reduction scheme authorised by the court. It is permissible, however:

(a)   to capitalise the share premium account to pay up unissued shares for distribution to shareholders as a *bonus* issue (otherwise known as a scrip or capitalisation issue), for instance:

Ordinary share capital	£100,000
Share premium account	£85,000

Company makes 1-for-2 scrip issue:

Ordinary share capital	£150,000
Share premium account	£35,000

(b)   to charge to the share premium account:

(i)   the preliminary expenses of forming a company;

(ii)   the expenses and commissions incurred in any issue of shares or debentures;

(iii)   any discount on the issue of loan capital;

(iv)   any premium paid on the redemption of debentures.

Revaluation reserve

The surplus (or shortfall) on the revaluation of assets should be credited (or debited) to a separate reserve, the revaluation reserve. The amount of the revaluation reserve shall be shown 'under a separate sub-heading in the position given for the item "revaluation reserve" in the balance sheet formats, *but need not be shown under that name*'. (*Our italics!* CA 1985, Sch. 4 para. 34.)

Foreign currency equalisation

Some companies with overseas borrowings and overseas assets keep a running total of the effect of currency exchange rates in a separate reserve.

Reserve funds

Where a reserve is represented by earmarked assets (e.g. quoted securities, an endowment policy and/or cash specifically set aside), it is called a reserve *fund*.

For example, if a company issues a £250,000 debenture repayable in 20 years and decides to set aside £8,000 each year towards the cost of eventual redemption (the old-fashioned type of sinking fund as described in Chapter 5), it will treat it as a separate fund, investing the money in earmarked

assets, usually risk-free gilt-edged securities, to earn interest between now and the redemption date.

Debenture redemption reserve funds are comparatively rare these days as almost all debenture issues now either have no sinking fund at all or provide for a small proportion of the debenture to be redeemed by drawings or repurchase each year, rather than setting the money aside in a fund.

Capital redemption reserve

Shares may only be redeemed or purchased by the company out of distributable profits or out of the proceeds of a new issue of shares. Where redemption or purchase is out of distributable profits, an amount equal to the amount by which the company's issued share capital is diminished must, by law, be transferred to a reserve, called the *capital redemption reserve* (CA 1985, S. 170). This reserve is shown separately under Other reserves.

The idea behind the law is to prevent a company's overall share capital plus non-

---

Example 4.3   Capital redemption reserve

1. Initial position:

Issued share capital	£
30,000 £1 Redeemable preference shares	30,000
100,000 £1 Ordinary shares	100,000
	130,000
Reserves	
Revenue reserve (retained profits)	75,000

2. Company then uses retained profits to redeem all the preference shares:

Issued share capital	£
100,000 £1 Ordinary shares	100,000
	100,000
Reserves	
Capital redemption reserve	30,000
Revenue reserve (retained profits)	45,000

3. Company then decides to make a 3-for-10 scrip issue, which brings the issued share capital back to £130,000.

Issued share capital	£
130,000 £1 Ordinary shares	130,000
	130,000
Reserves	
Revenue reserve (retained profits)	45,000

distributable reserves from being reduced when share capital is repaid: the reserve can never be distributed except upon liquidation or in a capital reduction scheme, but it can be capitalised by a bonus issue, as in Example 4.3.

Movements to and from reserves

The Companies Act 1985 requires the source of any increase and the application of any decrease in reserves to be disclosed (Sch. 4, para. 46 – see example on page 97).

Chapter 5

LOAN CAPITAL

The advantages of borrowing

If a company confidently expects that its return on capital (i.e. the trading profit expressed as a percentage of the capital the company employs) will exceed the cost of borrowing, then borrowing will increase the profit attributable to the ordinary shareholders.

There are, however, various limitations on the amount a company can borrow, which we will discuss later in this chapter, and borrowing also increases risk.

The risk of borrowing

The risk of borrowing is twofold: firstly the interest on most borrowings has to be paid promptly when due (unlike dividends on shares, which can be deferred or omitted altogether) and secondly most borrowings have to be repaid by a certain date (unlike most share capital, which is only repayable on liquidation).

In a poor year, interest charges can drastically reduce the pre-tax profits of a heavily borrowed company. Take, for example, two companies that are identical except that one, Company A, is financed entirely by shareholders while the other, Company B, is financed half by shareholders and half by borrowing, which bears a fixed rate of interest of 10% per annum.

The table in Example 5.1 shows the profitability of the two companies with varying rates of return on capital employed: in an average year Company B earns 15% on money borrowed at 10%, and so gains 5% on £500,000, adding £25,000 to pre-tax profits. This extra profit, after tax, adds 2½p to the earnings attributable to each of the 500,000 shares that Company B has issued, making the earnings per share 10p compared with 7½p for Company A.

In a good year the advantage of borrowing will enhance Company B's earnings per share even more (20p compared with 12½p for Company A) but in a poor year, as our table shows, all the trading profit is used servicing the borrowings of Company B, while Company A still manages to earn £25,000 after tax for its shareholders.

The point at which the two companies do equally well as far as their shareholders are concerned is shown on the graph in Example 5.1. Their earnings per share are both 5p when the return on capital employed is 10% per annum; as one would expect, borrowing at 10% to earn 10% neither adds to nor detracts from Company B's profits. As the graph also shows, borrowing makes a company's profits more volatile, and the risk of borrowing is further increased when money is borrowed at a variable rate of interest (e.g. on overdraft). If interest rates had risen above 10% in our example's 'poor year', Company B would have actually made a loss.

We will come back to the effects of borrowing in Chapter 23, but let us now look in detail at various types of borrowing.

Types of borrowing

There are many ways in which a company can borrow money, the main characteristics of different types of debt being:

(a) the length of time for which the money is borrowed;
(b) the rate of interest paid;
(c) the security offered to the lender by way of charges on the assets of the company;
(d) the negotiability of the debt instrument (i.e. does the lender receive a piece of paper which he can sell if he wishes to disinvest before the date of repayment?);

Example 5.1   Financing by share capital and by borrowing

	Company A			**Company B**		
Issued equity (£1 shares)	£1,000,000			£500,000		
Borrowings (10% interest)	Nil			£500,000		
	Good year	*Average year*	*Poor year*	*Good year*	*Average year*	*Poor year*
Rate of return	25%	15%	5%	25%	15%	5%
	£000	£000	£000	£000	£000	£000
Trading profit	250	150	50	250	150	50
Interest	—	—	—	50	50	50
Pre-tax profit	250	150	50	200	100	0
Taxation (50%)	125	75	25	100	50	0
Profit after tax	125	75	25	100	50	0
Earnings per share	12.5p	7.5p	2.5p	20p	10p	0p

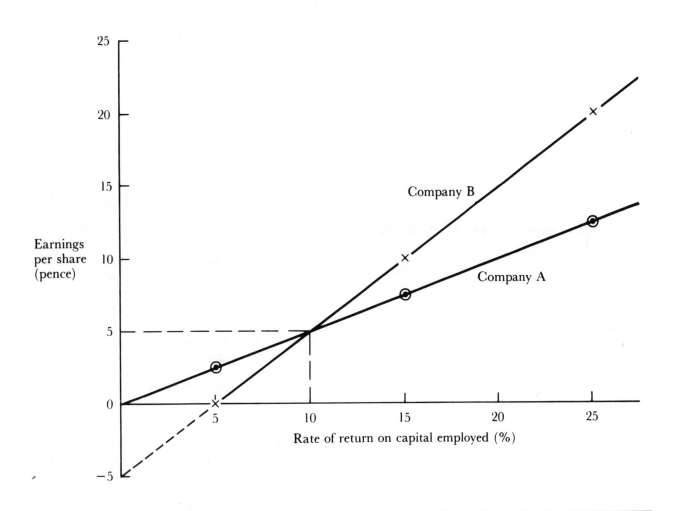

(e) the flexibility to the company and to the lender in the timing of borrowing and repayment;

(f) any deferred equity option given to the lender.

A company's borrowings fall broadly into three categories:

1. Issues of debentures and unsecured loan stock, which can be held by the general public, and can be bought and sold in the same way as shares.
2. Loans from banks and other financial institutions.
3. Bank overdrafts (described in Chapter 10).

Categories 1 and 2 are shown separately in the balance sheet, with a note describing the terms on which each loan is repayable and the rate of interest, dividing them into secured and unsecured loans, and giving the aggregate amount of:

(a) bank loans;
(b) other loans wholly repayable within five years;
(c) other loans, wholly or partly repayable more than five years after the balance sheet date.

Loans that are wholly repayable within one year should appear under 'Creditors: amounts falling due within one year' where Format 1 in the Companies Act 1985 is used, but in Format 2 all creditors come under a single heading. This is an important point to watch, because a loan coming up for repayment may significantly weaken the company's liquidity position, and can be a very serious threat to a company that is already short of funds if it is likely to have any difficulty refinancing the loan.

Security given to the lender – debentures and unsecured loan stock

When a company wishes to issue loan capital it can offer the lender some specific security on the loan. If it does so, the loan is called a debenture (£100 units) or debenture stock (usually units of £1); if not it is an unsecured loan stock (ULS), and these are the two main types of loan capital raised from the general public.

Debentures

Debentures can be secured by fixed and/or floating charges described below, the most common type of debenture being one that is secured on specific land or buildings, sometimes called a mortgage debenture. Other examples are:

1. *Tonnage debenture*, secured on the revenues of specific long-term contracts between the company and their customers, e.g. BRITISH OXYGEN COMPANY's series of Tonnage Debenture Stocks, 9% 1988 and 1990 and 11½% 1992.

2. *Wagon debenture*, secured on railway rolling stock. Although common in the United States there has only been one recent issue in the United Kingdom, the PROCOR (UK) 11¼% Wagon Debenture Stock 1993/98.

Fixed charge

A fixed charge is similar to a mortgage on a house. The company enters into a debenture deed which places a charge on specific identifiable assets. This gives the debenture holder a legal interest in the assets concerned as security for the loan, and the company cannot then dispose of them unless the debenture holder releases the charge (which he is unlikely to do unless he is offered some equally good alternative security). If the company defaults or falls into arrears on interest payments or capital repayments, the debenture holder can either:

(a) appoint a Receiver to receive any income from the assets (e.g. rents) *or*
(b) foreclose, i.e. take possession and sell the assets, using the proceeds of the sale to repay the debenture holders in full; any surplus remaining is then paid to the company, but if the proceeds of selling the assets charged are insufficient to repay the debenture holders in full, the debenture holders then rank equally with unsecured creditors for the shortfall.

Floating charge

This is a general charge on the assets of a company. But the debenture holder has no legal interest in the assets unless and until an event specified in the debenture deed occurs; for example, if the company goes into liquidation or ceases trading, or falls behind with interest payments or capital repayments, or exceeds specified borrowing limits. In the event of default the debenture holder can then appoint a Receiver, who takes physical possession of the assets of the company. The Receiver can also be appointed as the Manager or a separate Manager can be appointed to continue running the company, or the Receiver can sell off the assets; the former course is adopted if possible, because a company can normally be sold as a going concern for more than the breakup value.

The ranking of ULS

In a liquidation the holders of unsecured loan stock rank equally with other unsecured creditors, that is after debenture holders and preferential creditors (tax, rates and certain obligations to employees). In practice trade creditors often restrict a company to 'cash with order' terms if they see it running into difficulties, and to that extent a ULS tends to rank behind suppliers.

Typical characteristics of debentures and ULS

Interest
Most debentures and ULS carry a fixed annual rate of interest (known loosely as the 'coupon') which is payable (normally half-yearly) regardless of the company's profitability. Interest is deductible before the company is assessed for tax, i.e. it is an allowable expense for tax purposes, and therefore costs the company less than the same amount paid out in dividends on shares.

Redemption
Each issue is normally for a given term, and is repayable at the end of the term (at the redemption date) or, where there is a redemption period (e.g. 1993/97), it is repayable when the company chooses within that period. A few irredeemable stocks do exist, e.g. BRITISH ELECTRIC TRACTION 5% Perpetual Debenture, redeemable (at 130%) only in the event of voluntary liquidation, but they are rare.

Liquidation
In the event of liquidation, debenture holders are entitled to repayment in full from the proceeds of disposal of the charged assets. Then the ULS holders and other unsecured creditors, and the fixed charge debenture holders if not already fully satisfied, rank equally after preferential creditors, and have to be repaid before the shareholders are entitled to anything.

Specific characteristics – the trust deed

Where a debenture or loan stock is to be issued to more than a very small number of holders, and particularly when it is going to be listed on The Stock Exchange, a trustee or trustees are appointed to represent the holders collectively, and the company enters into a trust deed rather than a debenture deed.

For listing, The Stock Exchange also requires that at least one trustee must be a trust corporation which has no interest in or relation to the company which might conflict with the position of the trustee. A large insurance company or the specialist LAW DEBENTURE CORPORATION is often appointed as trustee.

The deed contains all the details of the issue, except the issue price, including:

(a) details of fixed and floating charges, together with provision for *substitution* (securing further assets to replace secured assets which the company may subsequently wish to dis-

pose of during the term of the loan). Provision may also be made for *topping up* (securing further assets if the value of secured assets falls below a given limit);

(b) redemption price and redemption date or period, together with any sinking fund arrangements;

(c) conditions under which the company may repurchase in the market, by tender and from individual holders;

(d) redemption price in the event of liquidation;

(e) conditions for further *pari passu* (equal ranking) issues, restrictions on prior borrowings and, for ULS, overall borrowing limits;

(f) minimum transferable unit;

(g) powers to approve modifications to the terms and conditions.

The trust deed may also include restrictive clauses, for example:

(h) to prevent the nature of the company's business being changed; this is known as a 'Tickler' clause, after the celebrated case of the jam manufacturer who was taken to court by the holders of an unsecured loan stock;

(i) to prevent major disposals of the company's assets – a 'disposals' clause;

(j) to restrict the transfer of assets between charging subsidiaries (those within the charging group, i.e. included in the charge on assets) and other subsidiaries – sometimes known as a 'ring fence' clause.

Treatment of expenses on issue and of profit or loss on redemption

The expenses of issuing debentures and ULS, and any profit or loss on issues not made at par, are normally shown as an extraordinary item. For example, TRANSPORT DEVELOPMENT GROUP made an unsecured loan stock issue of £10 million nominal in 1983 at £97.941% and the accounts showed 'Discount and costs on issue of loan stock' as an extraordinary item of £292,000. However, in the same year WESTLAND wrote off the expenses of a £30 million debenture issue directly against reserves, showing 'Debenture issue expenses written off – (Net of tax)' as a £148,000 deduction in a note on reserves, and the gross amount of £306,000 as an application in the Source and Application of Funds statement, so there is no hard and fast rule about the treatment of the profit/loss and expenses of an issue.

With redemptions, the normal practice is also to show any profit/loss as an extraordinary item; for example, the note on extraordinary items in TRAFALGAR HOUSE's 1983 accounts showed:

	1983	1982
	£000	£000
Surplus on redemption of loan stocks	5,308	1,101

But some companies treat profit on redemption as a *normal* item in their profit and loss account; for example, BICC GROUP's 1983 accounts showed operating profit as including:

Profit on redemption of debentures and bonds	£0.5m

In our view, profits and losses on the issue and redemption of loan capital should be treated as extraordinary items. They should not be included in the calculation of a company's normal earnings.

Sinking funds

Some debenture and loan stock issues make provision for part or all of the stock to be redeemed gradually over a period of time by means of a sinking fund.

The normal method for a sinking fund to redeem stock is by annual or six-monthly drawings (lotteries of stock certificate numbers), with the company in some cases having the option of purchasing stock in the market if it can do so at or below the drawing price. The company may also be allowed to invite holders to tender stock for redemption.

There are three types of sinking fund, described below.

Original concept – no early redemptions

The sinking fund or redemption reserve fund, as originally conceived, was a fund into which a company put a given sum each year, the money being invested in government or other safe fixed-interest securities rather than being used to make early redemptions. The sums, together with interest earned, went on accumulating in the balance sheet year by year until the redemption date. This method is now rarely used.

Non-cumulative

Each year in which the sinking fund is in operation the company normally sets aside enough cash to redeem a fixed amount of stock, expressed as a given percentage of the total issue, and uses it to redeem stock on or by the date of the second interest payment (Example 5.2).

Example 5.2   Non-cumulative sinking fund

A 25-year stock with a 2% sinking fund starting at the end of the 5th year would be redeemed at the rate of 2% per annum at the end of years 5 to 24, leaving 60% of the stock to be redeemed at redemption date.

Provided redemptions each year are by drawings at par, the *average life* of a stock can be calculated by working out the average life of the stock redeemed by the sinking fund, in this case 14½ years, and then weighting it by the percentage redeemed by the sinking fund, in this case 40%:

$$\text{Average life} = \frac{(14\frac{1}{2} \times 40\%) + (25 \times 60\%)}{100\%}$$

$$= 20.8 \text{ years}$$

Cumulative

In a cumulative sinking fund the cash used for redemption each year is variable and normally consists of a fixed amount of cash plus the amount of interest saved by prior redemption (Example 5.3).

Example 5.3   Cumulative sinking fund

If our previous example had been a £10m issue of a 25-year stock with a 10% coupon and a cumulative sinking fund starting at the end of year 5, and if all redemptions were made by drawings at par, then the annual redemptions would be:

End of year	Fixed amount of cash £	Variable amount (interest saved) £	Stock redeemed in year £	Total stock redeemed £	Stock remaining £
4	Nil	Nil	Nil	Nil	10,000,000
5	200,000	Nil	200,000	200,000	9,800,000
6	200,000	20,000	220,000	420,000	9,580,000
7	200,000	42,000	242,000	662,000	9,338,000
8	200,000	66,200	266,200	928,200	9,071,800

and so on. The average life can be calculated by time-weighting each year's redemption, e.g. 200,000 × 5 years plus 220,000 × 6 years, etc. ÷ 10,000,000. However, if redemptions are made by purchases in the market or by tender at below the redemption price, the amount redeemed will be greater, the amount of interest subsequently saved will be larger and the whole process of redemption will accelerate.

Yields

The yield on an irredeemable security is the gross amount of income received per annum divided by the market price of the security. Redeemable securities have two yields, their running yield and their gross redemption yield.

Running yield

The running yield is the same as the yield on an irredeemable security: it measures *income* and is concerned purely with the annual gross interest and the price of the stock; for instance, an 8% unsecured loan stock issued at £98% will yield 8% ÷ 0.98 = 8.16% at the issue price, or a 4½% debenture purchased at £50% will give the purchaser a yield of 9%, ignoring purchase expenses.

Redemption yield

The *gross* redemption yield is rather more complicated, as it measures 'total return'; i.e. it takes into account both the stream of income and any capital gain (or loss) on redemption. It is *not* just the sum of the running yield and the capital gain per annum, but is obtained by discounting the future interest payments and the redemption value at a rate that makes their combined *present value* equal to the current price of the stock. (The concept of discounting to obtain *present value* is explained in Appendix 2.) The rate required to do this is the gross redemption yield (Example 5.4).

Typical gross redemption yields for a well secured debenture are ¾% to 1½% above the yield on the equivalent gilt-edged security (i.e. a UK government stock of similar life and coupon), and 1% up to 5% or more for ULS, depending very much on the quality of the company and the amount of prior borrowings (borrowings that would rank ahead in a liquidation). *Net* redemption yields (i.e. the yields after tax) vary with the individual holder's rate of income tax payable on the stream of interest payments and the rate of tax payable on any capital gain on redemption.

Redemption date

When a stock has a final redemption period, e.g. 1999/2004, it is assumed in computing redemption yields that the company will choose the earliest date for redemption, 1999, if the stock is currently standing above par, otherwise the latest date, 2004.

When there is a sinking fund which allows redemptions only by drawings, the average life can be calculated accurately and should therefore be used as the number of years to redemption in calculating redemption yields. However, if the company is allowed to redeem by purchase in the market or by inviting tenders, the stockholder can no longer be sure that early drawings at par will take place, and the average life is therefore ignored.

Example 5.4   Gross redemption yield

A 6% debenture due for redemption at £105% in four years' time is standing in the market at £90. Interest is payable in the normal manner, half-yearly in arrears (at the end of each six months). The present value of the stock is the sum of the present values of the eight future six-monthly interest payments discounted at $\sqrt{(1 + i)}$ per half-year (where i expressed as a decimal = gross redemption yield).

$$\frac{3}{(\sqrt{1 + i})} + \frac{3}{(\sqrt{1 + i})^2} + \ldots + \frac{3}{(\sqrt{1 + i})^8}$$

plus the present value of the sum received on redemption in eight half-years' time:

$$\frac{105}{(\sqrt{1 + i})^8}$$

Solving for i by trial and error:

Value of i		Present value of income		Present value of redemption	Total
10%	=	19.48	+	71.72	= £91.20
11%	=	19.09	+	69.15	= £88.24

Inspection suggests that the gross redemption yield on a market price of £90 is about 10½%, and a more accurate figure can be obtained by further manual calculation or by computer. Alternatively, the yield can be obtained from Bond Tables.

The amount a company can borrow

The amount a company can borrow may be limited by the following:

(a)   Its borrowing powers. The directors' borrowing powers are normally limited by a company's Articles of Association, and cannot be altered except with the approval of shareholders at a general meeting. Borrowing powers are usually expressed as a multiple of shareholders' funds (issued share capital plus reserves, less goodwill).

(b)   Restrictions imposed by existing borrowings. The terms of the trust deeds of existing loan capital may restrict or preclude the company from further borrowing. In particular the terms of an unsecured loan stock may include a clause preventing the company from issuing any loans that rank ahead of the stock concerned, and unduly restrictive clauses are often the reason for companies redeeming loan capital in advance of the normal redemption date.

(c)   The lender's requirement for capital and income cover.

(*d*) The lender's general opinion of the company and its overall borrowing position.

Capital and income covers

These are two standard measures the intending purchaser of a debenture or loan stock may use to assess the security of his investment.

The *capital* or asset cover can be calculated in two ways, on a simple basis or on a 'rolled-up' basis.

Using the simple basis, the cover is the total capital less all prior-ranking stocks, divided by the issued amount of the stock in question.

Using the 'rolled-up' basis, the cover is the total capital divided by the stock in question plus all prior-ranking stocks.

As Example 5.5 shows, the two equal-ranking ULS issues are three times covered on a simple basis (£60 million total capital less £15 million prior-ranking debenture, divided by the total of £15 million ULS), but only twice covered on a rolled-up basis. The more conservative rolled-up basis is normally used for assessing capital covers.

For a floating charge debenture a rolled-up capital cover of at least 3 or 4 is expected by the lender, and 2½ times is the normal minimum for an unsecured loan stock, but both depend on the quality of the assets, i.e. the likely realisable value of the assets on the open market in the event of a liquidation.

The *income* cover is normally worked out on a rolled-up rather than a simple basis: i.e. it is the number of times the interest on a stock plus the interest on any prior-ranking stocks could be paid out of profits before interest and tax. This cover can also be expressed as a *priority percentage*, showing the percentile ranking of a stock's interest, with earnings before interest and tax representing 100% (Example 5.6).

Interest should normally be several times covered, although a lower income cover may be acceptable in some highly geared situations, e.g. in some property companies, where assured rental income provides safe cover.

A company's overall borrowing position

There are a variety of methods of measuring a company's overall borrowing position: the two main ones are *gearing* and *debt/equity ratio* (which is known as 'leverage' in the United States).

Gearing is most commonly defined as loan capital plus bank and other borrowings expressed as a percentage of capital employed (Example 5.7).

Example 5.7 Gearing and debt/equity ratio

Loan capital	£24,000	
Bank overdrafts	£10,000	£34,000
Ordinary shares	£14,500	
Reserves (*less* goodwill)	£21,500	£36,000
Capital employed		£70,000

Gearing $= \dfrac{34,000}{70,000} = 49.1\%$

Debt/equity ratio $= 34,000:36,000 = 0.94$ or 94%

Example 5.5 Capital cover

Capital	Amount	Cumulative total	Simple cover	Rolled-up cover
	£000	£000		
6% Debenture	15,000	15,000	4.0	4.0
8% ULS	10,000			
10% ULS	5,000	30,000	3.0	2.0
Ordinary shares	12,000			
Reserves (less goodwill)	18,000	60,000		
Total capital	60,000			

Example 5.6 Income cover

A company has £5.76 million of earnings before interest and tax, and the following loan capital, with the ULS and the CULS ranking equally:

Nominal value of issue	Annual interest	Cumulative interest	Times covered	Priority percentage
£12m of 6% Debenture	£0.72m	£0.72m	8.0	0–12½%
£10m of 8% ULS	£0.80m			
£8m of 5% CULS	£0.40m	£1.92m	3.0	12½–33⅓%

Gearing of 33.3% (debt/equity ratio of 50%) would be a reasonable level for an average company, although companies with steady profits can borrow more highly, while those in cyclical industries would be wise to have little or no gearing.

Convertible loan capital

Convertible loan capital, which is usually convertible unsecured loan stock (CULS) rather than convertible debentures, entitles the holder to convert into ordinary shares of the company if he so wishes (see also convertible preference shares, Chapter 4).

The coupon on a convertible is usually much lower than the coupon needed for the issue of a straight unsecured loan stock with no conversion rights. This is because a convertible is normally regarded by the market as deferred equity, valued on the basis of the market value of the shares received on conversion plus the additional income enjoyed before conversion (the coupon on issue being higher than the yield on the ordinary shares).

Because convertibles are a form of deferred equity, listed companies can issue them without shareholders' prior approval only as a rights issue or as part or all of the consideration in an acquisition. In a takeover situation the bidder can use a suitably pitched convertible to provide the shareholders of the company being acquired with a higher initial income than they would receive from an equivalent offer of the bidder's ordinary shares. This is particularly useful when a bidder with low-yielding shares wants to avoid the shareholders of the company he wishes to acquire suffering a fall in income if they accept his offer.

In recent years CULS have become increasingly popular with investors, particularly with gross funds (e.g. pension funds), which are attracted by their higher income and by the greater security a convertible provides for both income and capital compared with the equity. From a company's point of view, CULS is cheaper to service than convertible preference shares, as the interest on the former is deducted before Corporation Tax is assessed.

Terms of a convertible loan

The holder has the option of converting into ordinary shares during a given period in the life of the debenture or ULS (the conversion period), at a given conversion price per share, expressed as so many shares per £100 of stock, or as so much nominal stock per ordinary share (Example 5.8).

Example 5.8   Convertible loan: TATE & LYLE

TATE & LYLE issued a 13% convertible unsecured loan stock 1994/99 in October 1976 in connection with the acquisition of MANBRÉ & GARTON. The stock is convertible into 34.32 ordinary £1 shares per £100 of stock on 15 April in any year up to and including 1989, and these conversion terms will be adjusted for any *scrip issues* to the ordinary shareholders in the meantime. Any *rights issues* to ordinary shareholders will also be made to the holders of the convertible as if they had already exercised their outstanding conversion rights (rather than making an adjustment to the conversion terms, as is done in some convertible issues).

If more than 75% of the stock is converted, TATE & LYLE has the right to force remaining stockholders to convert or redeem straight away; this is a fairly standard condition in a convertible stock, enabling the company to clear a convertible off its balance sheet once most of it has been converted. Stock that remains unconverted at the end of the conversion period can be redeemed by TATE & LYLE at any time from 30 April 1994 and all outstanding stock will be redeemed on 30 April 1999, the final redemption date.

The period between issue and the first date for conversion is sometimes called the 'rest period', and the period from the last date for conversion and the final redemption date the 'stub'. Diagrammatically the TATE & LYLE convertible can be shown as:

Rest period	Conversion period	Stub
1976 1978		1989 1999

A rest period of two or three years is normal, and most conversion periods run for at least four or five years. Some of the earlier convertible issues had little or no stub, but several years is now fairly standard because if convertible holders decide not to exercise their conversion rights the company concerned is probably not doing very well and would not want to be faced with having to redeem the stock immediately the conversion rights lapsed.

Another piece of convertible jargon is the *conversion premium*. This is the premium one pays by buying the ordinary shares via the convertible rather than buying them direct. For example, if the TATE & LYLE convertible in Example 5.8 was standing at £140% (per £100 nominal) and the ordinary shares were standing at 383p, the cost of getting into the ordinary shares through the convertible would be £140 ÷ 34.32 = 408p, a conversion premium of about 6½%.

A good indication of the likely market price of a convertible can be obtained by discounting the future income advantage to present value and adding it to the market value of the underlying equity. Where conversion terms vary during the conversion period, sometimes called *stepped conversion* (e.g. DRAYTON CONSOLIDATED TRUST's 7½% CULS 1993), the calculation has to be done for each set of terms and the highest result taken. One caveat to this method is that if the price of the ordinary shares is very depressed, the price of the CULS in the market can become mainly dependent on its value as a fixed-interest security, particularly if the conversion period has not long to run.

Warrants

Where a company is reluctant to raise loan capital when very high long-term interest rates prevail, or investors are reluctant to commit themselves to purely fixed-interest securities, loan capital can be raised with a lower coupon by attaching warrants to issues of stock. For example, REDLAND attached one warrant to each US$1,000 bond in its finance company's issue of 9½% Guaranteed Bonds 1991 to help raise US$25m in the Eurobond market in 1979.

Warrants, already described in Chapter 4, are long-term options granted by the company, entitling holders to subscribe for ordinary shares during some specified period in the future at some specified price, called the exercise price. They are normally detachable and exercisable as soon as the stock to which they are attached is fully paid, and in some issues stock can be surrendered at its nominal value as an alternative to cash payment when the warrants are exercised.

In a takeover situation, warrants can provide a more flexible way for the bidder to give loan stock an equity interest than convertibles, because the number of warrants, sometimes called the 'equity kicker', can be varied as the company wishes, while the quantity of ordinary shares to which convertible holders are entitled is defined within a narrow range by the limit the market will accept on the conversion premium.

On the other hand, a drawback to warrants is that they will seldom be exercised until close to the final exercise date, because they are bought by investors who want the gearing they provide, so the future flow of money into the company's equity is more chancy than a convertible.

Details of a warrant's exercise rights are normally shown in the company's annual report and accounts; for example, REDLAND reported an adjustment to warrant holders' rights in a paragraph in the directors' report in 1980, illustrated below. This information is now repeated each year at the bottom of the Financial Calendar, also illustrated below.

REDLAND *1980 Directors' report*

Redland Finance NV Warrants
In view of the capitalisation issue an appropriate adjustment has been made to the rights of the holders of the warrants which were originally attached to the 9½% Guaranteed Bonds. Warrant holders now have the right to require the Depository to procure the subscription of £176 for 125.71 Ordinary Shares in REDLAND Limited at a price of 140p per share.

REDLAND *1984 report and accounts*

Financial calendar
Holders of warrants of Redland Finance NV, which were originally attached to the 9½% Guaranteed Bonds 1985/91, can subscribe for ordinary shares of Redland PLC at 140p per share until 15 March 1991. Each warrant entitles the holder to subscribe for 125.71 shares. Only whole shares will be allotted but fractional entitlements can be aggregated. The fractions arose from the adjustment following the capitalisation issue in 1980. Before that time each warrant carried the right to subscribe for 100 shares at 176p per share.

Chapter 6

FIXED ASSETS

(References: SSAP 12 *Accounting for Depreciation*; SSAP 19 *Accounting for Investment Properties*; SSAP 22 *Accounting for goodwill*.)

Schedule 4 to the Companies Act 1985 requires fixed assets to be presented in the balance sheet under three headings: *Intangible assets*, *Tangible assets* and *Investments*; we deal with the first two in this chapter, and with Investments in Chapter 7.

Definitions

Intangible (fixed) assets
These include capitalised development costs (see page 67); concessions, patents and trademarks; and goodwill. Goodwill is the amount by which the value of a business as a whole exceeds the value of its individual assets less liabilities; it is normally only recognised in the accounts of a company when it acquires another business as a going concern, i.e. when purchased.

Most companies write purchased goodwill off against reserves as soon as it arises, but it may be carried in the balance sheet, in which case it should be amortised through the profit and loss account over its estimated useful life. (See Chapter 15 for goodwill on consolidation.)

Tangible (fixed) assets
Those long-lived assets not held for resale in the ordinary course of business but for the purpose, directly or indirectly, of earning revenue. Thus they include not only things like plant and machinery which are actually used to provide the product, but assets used to house or support its operations, such as land, buildings, furniture, vehicles, ships and aircraft. They may also contain leased assets (see pages 64–65).

Depreciation
A measure of the loss of value of an asset due to use, the passage of time and obsolescence, including the amortisation of fixed assets whose useful life is predetermined (e.g. leases) and the depletion of wasting assets (e.g. mines).

Book value
Traditionally fixed assets are shown in the balance sheet at cost less aggregate depreciation to date (i.e. at net book value). This book value is not, and does not purport to be in any sense, a valuation, though fixed assets, particularly land and buildings, are quite frequently revalued. Sometimes, but by no means always, the valuation is taken into the books.

Companies Act requirements on fixed assets

The requirements of the Companies Act 1985 with regard to fixed assets are complex. In summary they are as follows:

(a) Fixed assets may be shown on a historical cost basis, or at valuation, or at current cost (see Chapter 22), and should be classified under headings appropriate to the business.

(b) Land must be analysed into freehold, long leaseholds (over 50 years unexpired) and short leaseholds.

(c) Where fixed assets are included on a historical cost basis, the aggregate figure for the following amounts must be shown under each heading:
(i) cost;
(ii) provision for depreciation since acquisition;
(iii) the book value (i minus ii).

(d) Where fixed assets are included at a valuation, the amount so included must be shown, together with the years and amounts of the valuations and, for assets valued during the year, the names of the valuers and the basis of valuation (see page 35, Example 6.9).

(e) Where fixed assets are included at valuation or at current cost, historical cost details must also be disclosed.

(f) Particulars must be given of additions and disposals during the period.

Disclosure requirements on depreciation

Schedule 9 of the Companies Act 1985 requires companies to disclose:

(a) the amount of depreciation charged to revenue;

(b) if depreciation has been calculated on other than book value;

(c) any amounts, additional to depreciation, charged by way of provision for renewal of fixed assets;

(d) if no provision has been made for depreciation or replacement; or the method used if other than by depreciation charge or provision for renewals.

SSAP 12 requires companies to disclose the method of depreciation used for each category of asset, together with the effective useful lives assumed.

Rates of depreciation

The following are typical rates (using the straight line method of depreciation, described below):

Freehold land	Nil
Freehold buildings	2% = 50-year life
Leasehold property:	
Long leases (over	
50 years)	2% = 50 years
Short leases	Over life of the lease
Plant and machinery	10% = 10 years
Vehicles	20% = 5 years
Ships, according to type	4–10% = 10–25 years
Furniture and equipment	10% = 10 years

Subnormal depreciation charges

Where a company is charging a subnormal rate of depreciation, or is omitting to charge depreciation on assets (other than freehold land), it will report higher than normal pre-tax profits, and the figures should be adjusted accordingly in any analysis.

Where depreciation is shown in the accounts

Depreciation appears in several places; EDBRO (HOLDINGS) provides an example of what a good set of accounts shows:

1. In the profit and loss account, as a note to

the item 'Operating profits' (opposite): the charge for the year.

2. In the balance sheet, as a note to the item 'Fixed assets' (opposite): the charge for the year and the cumulative amount to date.

3. In the statement of accounting policies:

EDBRO (HOLDINGS) *Note on accounting policies*

Depreciation

The charge for depreciation is calculated to write off the cost of tangible fixed assets less government grants over their expected useful lives from the dates they come into use. Depreciation rates are:

Freehold land	Nil	
Freehold buildings	4%	(reducing balance)
Long leasehold land		
and buildings	4%	(reducing balance)
Plant and equipment:		
Plant and machinery	10%	(straight line)
Office equipment	20%	(straight line)
Motor vehicles	20%	(straight line)

In addition, the auditors' report may mention depreciation. For example, J. B. EASTWOOD's 1976 accounts showed that the company had not provided for depreciation on freehold or long leasehold properties nor on poultry house equipment, but instead had charged the cost of all replacements (an unspecified amount) direct to revenue. If depreciation had been charged at, say, a modest 2% on the book value of the assets concerned, the profits would have been reduced by more than £0.4 million, material in relation to the reported pre-tax profits of £7 million, and even more material in the previous year, when the company reported a loss of £0.5 million. Their auditors, the leading firm of PEAT, MARWICK, MITCHELL & CO., qualified their auditors' report accordingly:

J. B. EASTWOOD *Auditors' report*

. . . in our opinion the fixed assets concerned (other than land) depreciate by reason of use coupled with the effluxion of time and provision should therefore be made for such depreciation in arriving at the profit of the group.

In any analysis of Eastwood's accounts, the estimated depreciation omitted (£0.4 million) should be deducted from the reported figure for pre-tax profits.

Methods of depreciation

The most common method or basis of depreciation, used by over 80% of major companies, is the

EDBRO (HOLDINGS) *Profit and loss account, note on operating profits*

	1984 £000
Operating profits are shown after charging: depreciation	756
auditors' remuneration (etc. . . .)	

EDBRO (HOLDINGS) *Balance sheet, note on tangible fixed assets*

	Land and buildings Freehold	Long leasehold	Plant and equipment	Total
	£000	£000	£000	£000
Depreciation at start of year	884	793	3,788	5,465
Exchange differences	(32)	(1)	(21)	(54)
Charge for the year	13	110	633	756
Eliminated on disposals	—	—	(177)	(177)
Depreciation at end of year	865	902	4,223	5,990

straight line (or fixed instalment) method. Other methods include:

(a) the declining balance (or reducing balance) method;
(b) the sum of the years' digits method;
(c) the production unit method;
(d) the annuity method;
(e) the sinking fund method.

The straight line or fixed instalment method

Depreciation under the fixed instalment method is computed as follows (see also Example 6.1):

$$\text{Annual depreciation} = \frac{\text{Cost} - \text{Residual value}}{\text{Expected useful life}}$$

The straight line method is ideal where the service provided by the asset continues unabated throughout its useful life, as might be the case with a 21-year lease of a building; and it is *generally used wherever the equal allocation of cost provides a reasonably fair measure of the asset's service*, for example, for buildings, plant, machinery, equipment, vehicles and patents. It is easy to calculate, and conceptually simple to understand.

The declining balance or reducing balance method

The declining balance method used to be the most popular method of depreciation; but it has largely been supplanted in recent years by the straight line method.

Example 6.1   Straight line depreciation

If a machine having an estimated useful life of five years is purchased for £10,000, and is expected to have a residual value of £1,000 at the end of that life, depreciation will be:

$$\frac{£10,000 - £1,000}{5} = \frac{£9,000}{5} = £1,800 \text{ per annum}$$

and the accounts will show:

End of year	Depreciation for the year (shown in the P & L account)	Cost	Provision for depreciation to date	Net book value
	£	£	£	£
1	1,800	10,000	1,800	8,200
2	1,800	10,000	3,600	6,400
3	1,800	10,000	5,400	4,600
4	1,800	10,000	7,200	2,800
5	1,800	10,000	9,000	1,000

Under the declining balance method, the annual depreciation charge represents a fixed percentage of the net book value brought forward (i.e. cost less aggregate depreciation). The calculation of the annual charge is simple enough once the appropriate percentage has been determined, but this requires the use of tables, a slide rule or a calculator.

$$\text{Depreciation rate (as a decimal)} = 1 - \sqrt[n]{\frac{\text{Residual value}}{\text{Cost}}}$$

where n = useful life in years.

Example 6.2 illustrates the calculation.

Among the disadvantages of the declining balance method are these:

(a) Most users do not calculate the rate appropriate to each particular item of plant, but use standard percentages, which tend to be too low rather than too high.

(b) Unless notional adjustments are made to cost and residual value, it is impossible to calculate satisfactorily a declining balance rate if the residual value is nil – the net book value can never get to nil, as it can only be reduced by a proportion each year.

(c) Even if the asset is assigned a nominal scrap value (say £1 so that it is not overlooked in the books) or if there is some residual value but it is small in relation to cost, the method is unlikely to be satisfactory without notional adjustments, because it leads to such high charges in the early years, as Example 6.3 shows.

The sum of the years' digits method

The sum of the (years') digits method is not commonly found in the United Kingdom, though

Example 6.3   Declining balance depreciation, small residual value

Taking our previous example of plant costing £10,000, but with a residual value of £200 instead of £1,000, we get:

Year	Year's depreciation £	Compared with £
1	5,425	3,690
2	2,482	2,328
3	1,135	1,470
4	520	927
5	238	585
Accumulated depreciation at the end of year 5	9,800	9,000
Residual value	200	1,000

it is used a good deal as a method of allowing accelerated depreciation in the United States (where accounting depreciation, provided it is computed by an acceptable method, is used for tax purposes too). It is occasionally found in the United Kingdom in connection with activities like leasing which involve heavy outlays in early years, when it is often referred to as 'the rule of 78'.

In this method, the cost less any residual value is divided by the sum of the years' digits to give what, for the purpose of this explanation, may be termed a unit of depreciation. In the last year of expected life, one unit of depreciation is provided; in the next to last, two; in the one before that, three; and so on.

The sum of the years' digits is simply the sum of

Example 6.2   Declining balance depreciation

The rate for the machine in Example 6.1 would be computed as follows:

$$\text{Depreciation rate} = 1 - \sqrt[5]{\left(\frac{£1,000}{£10,000}\right)} = 1 - 0.631 = 0.369 = 36.9\%$$

Thus the rate to apply is 36.9%.

End of year	Depreciation for the year (shown in the P & L account) £	Cost £	Provision for depreciation to date £	Net book value £
1	3,690	10,000	3,690	6,310
2	2,328	10,000	6,018	3,982
3	1,470	10,000	7,488	2,512
4	927	10,000	8,415	1,585
5	585	10,000	9,000	1,000

shown in the balance sheet

Example 6.4   Sum of the years' digits method of depreciation

Taking our example of a machine costing £10,000, with an estimated life of five years and a residual value estimated at £1,000: the sum of the years' digits is 15, and a unit of depreciation is thus (£10,000 − £1,000) ÷ 15 = £600, so:

End of year	Depreciation for the year (shown in the P & L account)	Cost	Provision for depreciation to date	Net book value
		◄————— shown in the balance sheet —————►		
	£	£	£	£
1	3,000	10,000	3,000	7,000
2	2,400	10,000	5,400	4,600
3	1,800	10,000	7,200	2,800
4	1,200	10,000	8,400	1,600
5	600	10,000	9,000	1,000

the series: $(1 + 2 + 3 + 4 + \ldots + n)$, where n represents the expected life of the asset.

The formula for computing the sum of the digits is $n(n + 1) \div 2$, where n is the number of years. Thus, to apply the sum of the digits to an asset having a life of 5 years, the divisor (i.e. the sum of the years' digits) is $5(5 + 1) \div 2 = 15$, and the first year's depreciation is 5/15ths of (cost minus residual value), the second year's 4/15ths, and so on (see Example 6.4).

It is interesting to compare the balance sheet value of this asset year by year with the value under the straight line and the declining balance methods, as shown in Example 6.5.

It can be seen that if the annual book value under the declining balance method is plotted, it follows a curve which in mathematical terms is asymptotic, that is, it gets nearer and nearer to the horizontal axis (i.e. to 0), but if the residual value is zero it would never quite get there (i.e. a charge for depreciation is made however long the asset lasts, be that charge ever so small), whereas the value under the sum of the digits method is reduced in decreasing steps, year by year, reaching residual value at the end of the asset's expected life, regardless of the size of the residual value, if any. Thus, although there is a similarity in the charges produced by the two methods, the sum of the digits method does not need the notional adjustments of the declining balance method to cope with small or nil residual values.

The production unit method

In this method, depreciation is charged according to the number of units produced in the period (see Example 6.6 overleaf):

$$\text{Charge per unit} = \frac{\text{Cost} - \text{Residual value}}{\substack{\text{Estimated number of units} \\ \text{to be produced during the} \\ \text{asset's effective lifetime}}}$$

This method can be used only where all the units an asset produces are identical or involve the same 'work value'. It makes costing of machine costs simple; and has the result of charging high depreciation where a machine is being used round the clock (which is not unreasonable); but it can be very misleading in that there is no charge for

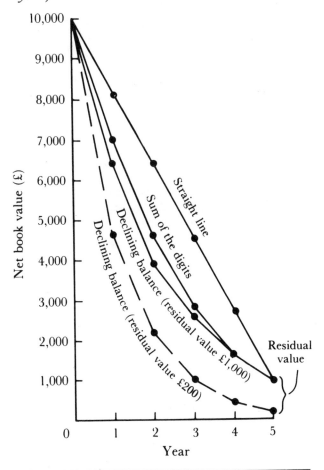

Fig. 6.5   Comparison of depreciation methods (for an asset costing £10,000, residual value £1,000, useful life 5 years)

Example 6.6   Production unit depreciation

An asset costing £10,000 is estimated to have a residual value of £1,000 at the end of its useful life, which is 300,000 units.

$$\text{Depreciation per unit} = \frac{£10,000 - £1,000}{300,000} = 3p$$

Thus, the charge in a period in which 80,000 units were produced would be £2,400.

depreciation if the machine lies idle – though clearly an unused asset still depreciates with the lapse of time, e.g. through corrosion, and the idleness of a machine may indicate an earlier than estimated end to its useful life.

The annuity method

The annuity method is sometimes used for the amortisation of leasehold properties, i.e. to write off the premium (the initial cost of the lease) over the term of the lease.

The annual depreciation charge under the annuity method is calculated by dividing the cost of the asset (less the present value of any expected residual value) by the present value of an annuity of 1 per annum for the estimated life of the asset.

An *annuity* is simply an annual payment, normally for a defined number of years (or for someone's lifetime), so the present value of an annuity of 1 for *n* years is the present value of 1 receivable in one year's time, plus that of a further 1 receivable in two years' time and so on, up to the last payment of 1 in *n* years' time.

A more detailed explanation of the concept of present value is given in Appendix 2, together with examples of a present value table and an annuity table.

Example 6.7 gives a simple illustration of the calculation:

Example 6.7   Calculating present value of an annuity

If $n = 3$ and the interest rate is 15%, then the present value of an annuity of 1 is

$$\frac{1}{(1.15)} + \frac{1}{(1.15)^2} + \frac{1}{(1.15)^3} = 2.283$$

Returning to the calculation of depreciation – as we said, the cost of the asset less the present value of any expected residual value is divided by the present value of an annuity of 1 per annum for the estimated life of the asset to produce the annual depreciation charge. At the same time notional interest on the net book value (cost less accumulated depreciation) is taken on the credit side of the profit and loss account (Example 6.8).

Alternative annuity method

An alternative way of using the method, at one time used by public utilities, and used by property companies in Canada, shows the net amount (i.e. depreciation less notional interest) as 'depreciation', and not a depreciation charge and a separate credit for interest. This has the effect of producing a rising charge: a low charge in the early years and a high one in the later years.

Example 6.8   Annuity method of depreciation

Take the case of a five-year lease costing £9,000, with no residual value; if interest is taken to be 15% the present value of an annuity of 1 for 5 years is 3.352 (see table in Appendix 2) and the depreciation charge is thus:

$$\frac{£9,000}{3.352} = £2,685$$

The computation then proceeds as follows:

Year	1 £	2 £	3 £	4 £	5 £
Cost	9,000				
Balance b/f	—	7,665	6,130	4,364	2,334
Notional interest at 15% p.a.	1,350	1,150	919	655	351
	10,350	8,815	7,049	5,019	2,685
Depreciation charge	2,685	2,685	2,685	2,685	2,685
Balance c/f	7,665	6,130	4,364	2,334	—

This method puts the company in a position similar to investing the £9,000 rather than purchasing the lease, and renting the asset for £2,685 per annum.

The sinking fund method

The sinking fund method is similar to the 'original concept' of a sinking fund to provide for the repayment of a loan, described in the previous chapter. A given sum of money is invested each year outside the business sufficient to provide, with interest, the amount of money required to replace the asset at the end of its useful life. The method is rarely used, for two main reasons:

(a) The cost of replacement is unlikely to be known with any accuracy when the asset is originally acquired.

(b) Most businesses have opportunities for investment within the business which will yield far more than is usually available from fixed-interest stocks, in which sinking funds are normally invested.

When the method is used, the amount to be set aside annually is the sum required for replacement divided by the value of an annuity of 1 in arrears for the expected life of the asset (the value an investment of 1 per annum will reach, with compound interest, by the end of the period). The value of an annuity of 1 in arrears can be obtained from annuity tables, or can be calculated as follows:

$$\text{Value} = \frac{(1 + r)^n - 1}{r}$$

where r is the interest rate (expressed as a decimal), and n is the expected life of the asset.

Further points on depreciation

Change in expected useful life
Where, through experience or changed circumstances, it is considered that the original estimate of useful life of an asset needs to be revised, the unamortised cost of the asset (net book value less residual value) should be charged over the revised remaining useful life.

Irrecoverable cost
If, at any time, the unamortised cost of an asset is seen to be irrecoverable in full (for example where production on a purpose-built machine is about to cease), it should be written down immediately to the estimated recoverable amount.

Changing method
Under SSAP 12 a change from one method of providing for depreciation to another is permissible only on the grounds that the new method will give a fairer presentation of the results and of the financial position. Where such a change is made, the unamortised cost should be written off over the remaining useful life commencing with the period in which the change is made, and the effect of the change should be disclosed in the year of change, if material.

Freehold land and buildings
Traditionally, freehold land and buildings used not to be depreciated, though the majority of companies have been depreciating freehold buildings in recent years, and SSAP 12 makes this obligatory, except for investment properties. In addition, freehold land should be written down if its value is adversely affected for any reason.

Excess depreciation

A few companies make an additional charge for depreciation to allow for the cost of replacing fixed assets, rather than just writing off the original cost of an asset over its useful life.

The amounts involved can be very large – for example, PILKINGTON charged an additional £33.7 million in 1984 – and they should be added back for the purposes of inter-company comparison.

The revaluation of assets

Traditionally, under historical cost accounting, assets appear at cost less depreciation, and they are not revalued to show their current worth to the company. But because of the effects of inflation, the practice has grown up in the United Kingdom of revaluing assets, particularly freehold land and buildings, from time to time.

Indeed, Schedule 7 para. 1 of the Companies Act 1985 requires the difference between the market value of property assets and the balance sheet amount to be disclosed in the directors' report if, in the opinion of the directors, it is significant. UK companies thus face the choice; they must either:

(a) incorporate any revaluation in the accounts,
   or
(b) disclose it in the directors' report.

Where assets are revalued and the revaluation is incorporated in the accounts, both sides of the balance sheet are affected, and depreciation from then on is based on the revalued amounts, as Example 6.9 illustrates.

Example 6.9   Effects of revaluation

A company has freehold land which cost £100,000 and buildings which cost £420,000, have a useful life of 50 years and were 10 years old on 31 December 1984. Depreciation to that date would therefore be 2% p.a. for 10 years on £420,000 = £84,000, so the balance sheet would show:

Freehold land and buildings at cost	£520,000
less depreciation to date	84,000
Book value at 31 December 1984	436,000

On 1 January 1985 the land was revalued at £380,000 and the buildings at £810,000. After the revaluation the accounts would show freehold land and buildings at the valuation figure of £1,190,000, an increase of £754,000. On the other side of the balance sheet the reserves would normally be increased by £754,000. (If, however, the company has decided in principle to dispose of the buildings, SSAP 15, para. 12 requires a provision to be made out of the revaluation surplus for the tax which would be payable on disposal, and this would be credited to deferred tax, the remainder of the surplus being credited to reserves.)

The 1985 accounts would be required to disclose:

(*a*) the basis of valuation used and the name or qualification of the valuer (CA 1985, Sch. 4, para. 43 (b);

(*b*) the effect of the revaluation on the depreciation charge, if material (SSAP 12, para. 20).

The revaluation will affect the company in several ways:

1. The annual depreciation charge on the buildings, based on the new value and the current estimate of the remaining useful life (40 years), will increase from £8,400 to £20,250 (2½% p.a. on £810,000), thus directly reducing the pre-tax profits by £11,850 in future years.

2. The overall profitability of the company, as measured by the ratio Return on Capital Employed (ROCE, described in Chapter 23), will also appear to deteriorate because the capital employed will have increased by £754,000. For instance, if the company in our example went on to make £300,000 before interest and tax in 1985, and had £2 million capital employed before the revaluation, the 1985 return on capital employed would be:

No revaluation
$$\frac{311{,}850}{2{,}000{,}000} = 15.59\%$$

Revaluation
$$\frac{300{,}000}{2{,}754{,}000} = 10.89\%$$

3. The borrowing powers of most companies are expressed as a multiple of share capital and reserves, so the increase in reserves will raise the borrowing limits, and improve the capital cover of existing lenders.

4. The higher property value may give more scope for borrowing on mortgage.

5. The increase in reserves will also increase the n.a.v., the net asset value per share, described in Chapter 23.

Revaluation deficits

Although unrealised surpluses on the revaluation of fixed assets should be credited direct to reserves, revaluation deficits should be charged to the profit and loss account to the extent that they exceed any surplus held in reserves identified as relating to previous revaluations of the same assets (SSAP 6).

Investment properties

SSAP 12 requires annual depreciation charges to be made on fixed assets, and makes it clear that an increase in the value of a fixed asset does not remove the necessity to charge depreciation. It is, however, accepted that a different treatment should be applied to fixed assets held as disposable investments.

Under SSAP 19, 'investment properties' (properties held as disposable investments rather than for use in a manufacturing or commercial process) are not depreciated, but are revalued each year at their open market value, and the valuation is reflected in the balance sheet.

Changes in the value of investment properties should be treated as a movement on an 'investment property revaluation reserve'. If, however, there is a fall in value that exceeds the balance in the investment property revaluation reserve, the excess should be charged to the profit and loss account; i.e. the reserve cannot 'go negative'.

Sales and other disposals of fixed assets

Where fixed assets are disposed of for an amount which is greater (or less) than their book value, the surplus (or deficiency) should be reflected in the results of the year, and should be disclosed separately if material (SSAP 12).

Some companies, for instance MARKS & SPENCER, habitually include an item 'profit (loss) on sales of tangible fixed assets' in a note to their profit and loss account. If the profit or loss on disposals is not disclosed it may be possible to calculate it, but companies often adjust the depreciation charge for the year to bring the net book value of the assets sold into line with the proceeds of the sale, thus hiding any profit or loss on disposal in the depreciation charge, for example in the 1982 accounts of AARONSON BROS, opposite.

It is fairly unlikely that the proceeds of sale of fixed assets happened to be exactly the same as their normally written-down book value, so it is pretty certain that the depreciation charge for 1982 was adjusted to make the figures balance.

There is nothing particularly significant in a company making small gains or losses on disposals, but it may give some indication of whether fixed assets tend to be worth more or less than their net book value.

When disposals arise because of the discontinuation of a significant part of the business, they should be dealt with as extraordinary items (see Chapter 14); in these cases the release of capital and the profit or loss previously being made by the discontinued part are probably more important than the amount by which the proceeds of the sale varied from the book value of the assets sold.

AARONSON BROS *Disposal of fixed assets in 1982 accounts*

(*a*) In the note on tangible fixed assets

	£000
Cost or valuation	
At 1st October 1981	31,914
Additions at cost	1,760
Cost of disposals	(808)
	32,866
Depreciation	
At 1st October 1981	8,869
Charge for the year	1,956
Eliminated on disposals	(274)
	10,551

The net book value of disposals is thus £808,000 − 274,000 = £534,000.

(*b*) In the Source and Application of Funds

Net additions to tangible fixed assets	1,226

The proceeds of disposal can be calculated as additions at cost − net additions = £1,760,000 − 1,226,000 = £534,000.

Government grants

(Reference: SSAP 4 *The Accounting Treatment of Government Grants*.)

Capital-based grants, such as regional development grants, introduced by the Industry Act 1972, and similar grants found in other countries, are grants which provide a refund of part of the purchase price of fixed assets. SSAP 4 requires capital-based grants to be credited to revenue (i.e. to profit) over the expected useful life of the asset concerned. There are two ways of achieving this:

1. By deducting the grant from the cost of the fixed assets (and thus reducing the subsequent annual depreciation charges). In the accounts the fixed assets simply appear net of grants, although some companies mention this in their note on accounting policies and a few, like BLUNDELL-PERMOGLAZE (illustrated below), describe 'additions at cost' in their note on fixed assets as '(less grants receivable)'.

2. By treating the grant as a deferred credit, and transferring it to revenue by annual instalments over the life of the asset concerned. Under this method government grants normally appear in several places in the accounts; for example, ENGLISH CHINA CLAYS' 1984 consolidated balance sheet included a figure of £5,842,000 for capital grants, showed movements on the capital grants account in the Source and Application of Funds statement and explained its

ENGLISH CHINA CLAYS *1983 accounts – government grants*

Source and Application of Funds

	1983 £000	1982 £000
Deduct:		
Transfers from:		
Capital grants	1,356	1,334
. . .		
Add:		
Capital grants received	1,702	1,769
. . .		

Note on Accounting Policies

Capital grants

Grants in respect of capital expenditure are credited to profit and loss account over a period of ten years. Capital grants shown in the balance sheet represent estimated total grants received or receivable to date less the amount transferred to profit and loss account.

BLUNDELL-PERMOGLAZE *Deduction of grants*

Fixed assets – tangible

	Freeholds £	Land and Buildings Leases (under 25 years) £	Plant, machinery and vehicles £	Total £
Cost or valuation				
At 31st October 1982	2,034,233	896,979	4,491,874	7,423,086
Assets acquired on purchase of subsidiary	1,355,754	—	1,653,767	3,009,521
Additions at cost (less grants receivable)	117,922	74,945	681,267	874,134
Sales and scrappings	(14,732)	—	(234,507)	(249,239)
Exchange rate adjustments	(32,612)	(228)	(38,829)	(71,669)
At 31st October 1983	3,460,565	971,696	6,553,572	10,985,833

accounting policy in a note to the accounts, as illustrated.

However, some companies using this method, like DUNLOP, deduct the balance in their government grants account from the net book value of their tangible assets in a note, rather than showing it in the balance sheet.

The arguments in favour of method 1 are, first, that commercial decisions on capital investment are (or should be) made on a 'net of grants' basis, i.e. the return on capital employed to consider is the return on the capital the company would have to put up, not the 'gross' cost, and, second, that method 1 makes accounting so much simpler.

Method 2 has the advantage of showing the extent to which government grants are contributing to and may be influencing the company's investment programme.

Less than half of UK listed companies mention government grants in their accounts, presumably because they are not material. Of those that do, about twice as many use method 1 as use method 2. From the analyst's point of view, the only disadvantage to method 1 is that companies using it seldom if ever report the amount of government grants received, although they could easily do so.

Revenue-based grants, e.g. regional employment premiums, are simply credited straight to revenue in the same period as the related expenditure and are seldom shown in the accounts.

Chapter 7

INVESTMENTS

Types of investment

Investments fall into three categories:

(*a*) Investment in subsidiaries.
(*b*) Investment in associated or related companies.
(*c*) Other investments, which may appear in the balance sheet as fixed assets, or as current assets.

Investment in subsidiaries

In simple terms, a subsidiary company is a company where the company owning the investment (the holding company) is able to control the board of directors, either by virtue of its voting power or in some other way. The holding company is required by law to produce group accounts, in which the profits, assets and liabilities of the subsidiary are merged with those of the holding company, as described in detail in Chapter 15.

Investment in associated companies

For accounting purposes, an associated company is defined by SSAP 1 as a non-subsidiary company in which the investing group or company's position in it is:

(*a*) effectively that of a partner in a joint venture or consortium; *or*
(*b*) long-term and substantial (i.e. not less than 20% of the equity voting rights).

In each case the investing group must be in a position to exercise a significant influence on the commercial and financial policy decisions of the associated company, including the distribution of profits; this is usually by representation on the board of directors.

The investing group's share of the associated company's profits before tax, taxation, extra-ordinary items and net profit retained are shown separately in the group's consolidated accounts, as described more fully in Chapter 16.

Investment in related companies

The Companies Act 1985 defines a related company as one where equity share capital is held on a long-term basis 'for the purpose of securing a contribution to that company's [the investing company's] own activities by the exercise of any control or influence' arising from that investment (Sch. 4, para. 92). Associated companies must also, by definition, be related companies, but related companies are not associated companies if the investing company holds less than 20% of the equity *and/or* is not in a position to exercise a significant influence on that company (see Chapter 16).

Other investments

While at first sight it may seem that these will consist entirely of investments of less than 20% in unrelated companies, this is not the case. Many public companies have holdings greater than 20% in other companies which are not treated as associated because the investing group is not represented on the board of directors and does not participate in commercial and financial policy decisions; there may also be special circumstances, as with GREAT UNIVERSAL STORES' holding in EMPIRE STORES:

GREAT UNIVERSAL STORES *Note on investments*

The group currently holds and held at 31st March, 1983, more than 20% of the equity share capital of the following companies . . .

Empire Stores (Bradford) plc   Ordinary share 29.9%

Empire Stores (Bradford) plc is not regarded as an associate as the Company has given an undertaking to the Secretary of State for Trade and Industry to restrict voting rights to 9.99% of the equity share capital.

Companies sometimes use surplus cash to make short-term investments in various securities, and show these under current assets.

Balance sheet presentation

Schedule 4 of the Companies Act 1985 requires other investments to be shown in the balance sheet either under fixed assets and/or under current assets. Where shown as fixed assets a further breakdown should be given, if individual amounts are material, either in the balance sheet itself or in notes:

(a) shares in group companies;
(b) loans to group companies;
(c) shares in related companies;
(d) loans to related companies;
(e) other investments other than loans;
(f) other loans;
(g) own shares.

Fixed assets – other investments

Listed investments should be shown at cost, divided into those listed on a recognised stock exchange in the United Kingdom and those listed overseas. The aggregate market value should also be shown where it differs from cost (CA 1985, Sch. 4, para. 45). *Unlisted investments*, which include securities on the USM, should be shown at cost or valuation. See example from HARRISON & CROSFIELD's accounts:

HARRISON & CROSFIELD *Note to the balance sheet*

Other investments held as fixed assets

	1983 Book value £000	Valuation £000
Shares		
Quoted in the United Kingdom	8,240	14,084
Quoted elsewhere	1,228	4,703
Unquoted	337	1,030
	9,805	19,817

Quoted valuations at market value; unquoted valuations at directors' valuation.

Holdings of more than 10%
In respect of substantial holdings, Schedule 5 of the Companies Act 1985 requires that where at the end of its financial year a company:

(a) holds in excess of one-tenth in nominal value of the issued shares of any class of *equity* share capital of another company;
or
(b) holds in excess of one-tenth in nominal value of *all* the issued share capital of another company; *or*
(c) holds shares in another company, not its subsidiary, stated in its accounts at an amount in excess of one-tenth of the amount of the investing company's total assets;

then the accounts must include:
(i) the name of the other company;
(ii) the country in which it is incorporated (if other than Great Britain); *or* (if incorporated in Great Britain) the country in which it is registered (England or Scotland) if not the same as the investing company;
(iii) the description of each class held, and the proportion held;

as illustrated here:

WHITBREAD *Note to 1984 accounts*

Other investments

. . . . . .

Particulars of significant investments comprising more than 10% of the issued capital of other companies:

	Country of Incorporation	Whitbread Equity Holding
Border Breweries (Wrexham) Ltd	UK	17%
Buckley's Brewery Ltd	UK	18%

Such holdings are occasionally referred to as 'associated companies', though they may or may not be associated companies for the purpose of SSAP 1 (see Chapter 16).

This information need not be disclosed in respect of companies incorporated or carrying on business outside the United Kingdom if the directors of the investing company consider disclosure would be harmful and the Department of Trade and Industry agrees (CA 1985, Sch. 5, para. 10).

Holdings of 20% or more
Here The Stock Exchange's requirements overlap those of Schedule 5 of the Companies Act 1985. Where the investment company or group interest in the equity capital of another company amounts to 20% or more, the following information should be given about that company:

(a) principal country of operation;
(b) its issued share and loan capital and, except where the group's interest is dealt with in the

consolidated balance sheet as an associated company, the total amount of its reserves;

(*c*) the percentage of each class of loan capital attributable to the company's interest (direct or indirect).

For example, a note to the NORCROS 1984 balance sheet on investments disclosed that 'Listed investments include a holding of 36.3% of the ordinary shares of UBM Group PLC acquired in the year at a cost of £27,095,000 . . . UBM Group PLC is registered in England and had at 28th February, 1984 Share Capital and Reserves amounting to £60,569,000 and Loan Capital of £7,128,000.'

Investments held as current assets

Other investments shown as current assets also need describing in detail (CA 1985, Sch. 4, para. 45). For example:

HARRISON & CROSFIELD *Note to the balance sheet*

Investment held as current assets

	1983 £000	1982 £000
Shares at cost less provisions		
Quoted in the United Kingdom	1,177	1,170
Quoted elsewhere	29	54
	1,206	1,224
Short term deposits	56,336	55,622
	57,542	56,846

The market value of quoted investments at 31st December 1983 was £2,074,000 (1982 – £1,712,000).

Most companies are not in business to deal in shares, nor are equities really suitable as a holding medium for liquidity (notice HARRISON & CROSFIELD's holdings of quoted investments represented only 2% of liquid resources), and the investor should be wary of any substantial amount of short-term investments (other than short-dated government stock): they may indicate a wheeler-dealer style of management.

Points to watch on substantial holdings

A holding of 5% or more may indicate:

(*a*) the possibility of an eventual bid, particularly if the holder is predatory by nature;

(*b*) a blocking position taken by the holder to protect his trade interests from the risk of the company concerned being taken over by some (larger) competitor.

There is no hard and fast rule about which is which, and a holding could indicate a blocking position pending a possible bid in the distant future. In this context it is worth checking whether directors have substantial holdings and, if so, whether any are nearing retirement age.

If the holding is of *20% or more* and the company is *not* treated as an associate, the chances are probably more in favour of a bid than a blocking position – the unwelcome holder of a substantial stake being unlikely to be given a seat on the board. If the holding is of *25% or more* the holder is in the strong position of being able to block any arrangements and reconstructions that the company might wish to make with creditors and members under Section 425 of the Companies Act 1985, which require three-fourths to vote in favour.

A substantial holding may also be the legacy of a thwarted bid, as it was with the 36.3% holding of UBM shown in the note to NORCROS's 1984 accounts.

Interlocking holdings

Where a number of companies under the same management have substantial holdings in each other or in another company, the holdings may be entirely innocent; but interlocking holdings can give scope for manipulation to the detriment of outside shareholders and should be viewed with caution.

A classic illustration of the dangers of interlocking holdings was provided by the affairs of several companies in the LOWSON GROUP, which came under investigation by the Department of Trade in 1973. The appointed inspectors found that a number of defaults in the management 'were knowingly committed by Sir Denys [Lowson] and constituted grave mismanagement of the affairs of the companies concerned' and that in some transactions 'his motive was to obtain a very substantial gain for himself and his family'.

Chapter 8

STOCKS AND WORK IN PROGRESS

(Reference: SSAP 9 *Stocks and Work in Progress*.)

Different classes of stock

Most manufacturing companies have traditionally shown stocks as a single figure under current assets, described either as 'stocks', as 'inventories' or as 'stocks and work in progress', but these terms cover three very different classes of asset:

(*a*) items in the state in which they were purchased; these include raw materials to be used in manufacture, components to be incorporated in the product and consumable stores (like paint and oil) which will be used in making it;

(*b*) items in an intermediate stage of completion ('work in progress', or in the United States 'work in process');

(*c*) finished goods.

For wholesalers and retailers, stocks are normally only goods purchased for resale.

Subclassification required by SSAP 9

SSAP 9 calls for the accounts to show the subclassification of stocks and work in progress 'in a manner which is appropriate to the business and so as to indicate the amounts held in each of the main categories'; for example, BASS's accounts give a subclassification of stocks in a note which is illustrated at the top of the next column.

Subclassification required by CA 1985

The Companies Act 1985 is more stringent than SSAP 9, requiring stocks to be analysed under the

BASS *Note to the 1983 accounts*

	£m
Raw materials	43.6
Consumable stores	14.5
Work in progress	28.4
Finished stocks	93.1
Bottles, cases and pallets	13.0
	192.6

following subheadings:

(*a*) raw materials and consumables;

(*b*) work in progress;

(*c*) finished goods and goods for resale;

(*d*) payments on account (for items of stock not yet received).

The matching principle

Where a business incurs in one accounting period expenditure on stocks which remain unsold or unconsumed at the balance sheet date, or upon work in progress which is incomplete at that date, these costs are carried forward into the following period so that they may be set against the revenue when it arises. This is an application of what accountants term the matching principle: that of matching cost and revenue in the year in which the revenue arises rather than charging the cost in the year in which the cost is incurred.

If, however, there is no reasonable expectation of sufficient future revenue to cover costs already incurred (for instance because of deterioration, obsolescence or a change in demand pattern), any irrecoverable cost should be charged to revenue in the year under review, and not carried forward. For this reason the value of stock and work in progress in the balance sheet at the end of the year (i.e. the book value) should be the lower of cost and net realisable value.

Consistency

The method of valuing stock should be consistent, and most sets of accounts include a brief statement in the notes on how stocks have been valued, e.g.:

AARONSON BROS. 'Stocks are valued at the lower of purchase price or production cost and net realisable value. In the case of finished goods, production cost comprises the purchase price of raw materials and attributable costs of production.'

RTZ. 'Stocks are valued at the lower of cost and net realisable value. Cost for raw materials and stores is purchase price and for partly processed and saleable products is generally the cost of production calculated on average or standard costing principles, including the appropriate proportion of depreciation and overheads.'

A particular point to look for is any statement of a change in the basis between year ends and, when one is made, whether any indication is given of how much difference the change has made to the year-end stock figure and to profits.

The importance of stock valuation

The accurate valuation of stock on a consistent basis is important, because quite small percentage variations can very significantly affect the profits reported in any period (Example 8.1):

Example 8.1 Stock valuation

	£	£
Sales		2,000
less Cost of goods sold:		
Opening stock	600	
add Purchases in period	1,500	
	2,100	
less Closing stock	400	
		1,700
		300
less Wages, overheads, etc.		200
Trading profit		£100

If the closing stock had been valued 10% lower at £360 and the opening stock 10% higher at £660, the cost of goods sold would have increased by £100 and the trading profit would have been wiped out.

Problems in valuing stock

Three main problems arise in valuing stock:

(a) the price to be used if an item has been supplied at varying prices;
(b) the value added in manufacture both to incomplete items (work in progress) and to completed items (finished goods);
(c) the assessment of net realisable value.

Stocks in a large retail business

Having defined the main principles and problems, let us now look at stocks in practice, beginning with the control of stocks in a large retail business, where all stocks are goods purchased for resale and the complications of WIP (work in progress) and finished goods do not arise.

The central management of most supermarkets controls the efficiency and honesty of local stores by charging goods out to those stores at *selling* price, and by maintaining overall stock control accounts in terms of selling price by broad product groups. By suitably analysing takings it will then be possible, for each of these product groups, to compare theoretical stock with actual stock:

Opening stock at selling price	Deliveries at + selling price	− Takings	Theoretical closing = stock at selling price

With this sort of operation, it is usual for the purpose of monthly, quarterly, half-yearly and annual accounts to deduct from the value of stock at selling price the normal gross profit margin, as MARKS & SPENCER's accounting policy on stocks illustrates:

MARKS & SPENCER *Accounting policies*

Stocks

Stocks which consist of goods for resale are valued at the lower of cost and net realisable value. Cost is computed by deducting the gross profit margin from the selling value of stock. When computing net realisable value an allowance is made for future markdowns.

But SSAP 9 (about which we shall have much to say later) requires that before such a figure is used for the purposes of the annual accounts, it be tested to ensure that it gives a 'reasonable approximation of the actual cost'.

Stocks in the manufacturing business

Most manufacturing businesses employ a system of cost accounting. They do so:

(*a*) as an aid to price fixing (so that they can charge the customer with the materials used and the time actually taken to complete his job – as is the case with a motor repair garage, or jobbing builder); *or*

(*b*) in order to provide the estimating department with information on which to base future estimates or tenders; *and/or*

(*c*) as a means of controlling operating efficiency.

The type of record employed varies widely, from a few scribblings on the back of an envelope, to a cost system parallel to the normal financial system, reconciled with it but not part of it, right up to a completely integral cost and financial accounting system. In all but the first of these there would normally be some form of stock record.

A problem often arises in the case of the manufacturing business over the pricing of issues from stock. When there are relatively few items, and where they are easily identifiable and can each be kept separate, each stock issue can be priced at its *specific price*, and no problem arises. But in many cases it is not possible, or not convenient, to keep identical items from different purchase consignments separate.

Several different methods of pricing issues from stock are commonly employed, and the value of the stock remaining depends on the pricing method used, as we will illustrate with Example 8.2.

Example 8.2 'STOCKOUT LTD'

'STOCKOUT LTD' purchased the following quantities of a raw material called 'Expel' during 1984:

1 February	4,800lb	at 10p per lb	£480
14 March	10,000	11p	£1,100
16 June	7,200	12p	£864
10 December	8,000	14p	£1,120
	30,000		£3,564

There was no stock on 1 January 1984. Issues during 1984 totalled 24,600 lb, leaving a closing stock on 31 December 1984 of 5,400 lb. The value of the closing stock under different pricing methods is dealt with below.

First-in first-out (FIFO)

Good storekeeping demands that goods should, so far as is possible, be used in the order in which they are received; that is to say, that those which came in first should be the first to go out, otherwise the danger of being left with stock which has deteriorated through lapse of time is greatly in-creased. The first-in first-out method of stock pricing merely assumes for accounting purposes that the normal rules of good storekeeping have been followed.

On a FIFO basis, all the stock at 31 December 1984 in Example 8.2 would be deemed to be out of the delivery on 10 December 1984, which cost 14p per lb:

Stock at 31 December 1984 =
5,400 lb at 14p = £756.

Average or weighted average price

When an organisation receives a number of deliveries during an accounting period at a series of different prices, it is reasonable to take the average price or, for more accuracy, the weighted average price.

Taking the *average price* for the year, STOCKOUT LTD's issues will be priced at:

$(10p + 11p + 12p + 14p) \div 4 = 11.75p$ per lb

Stock at 31 December 1984 =
5,400 lb at 11.75p = £634.50.

On a *weighted average price* basis, Stockout Ltd's issues would be priced at:

£3,564 ÷ 30,000 = 11.88p per lb

Stock at 31 December 1984 =
5,400 lb at 11.88p = £641.52.

Standard price

Many businesses employ a standard cost system; that is to say, they predetermine for each type of unit manufactured the price which ought to be paid for material, the material usage, the wage rate of the personnel employed to produce it, the time they should take, and so on. In such a system materials issued from store are priced at standard cost, as are work in progress at all stages and any finished goods in stock. Any variances from standard are written off as operating losses (or profits) at the time they occur.

If 'STOCKOUT LTD' adopted a standard costing system and employed a standard price of 11.5p per lb for 'Expel', a material price variance of £114 (adverse) would be written off, computed as follows:

Cost of material acquired (30,000 lb)	£3,564
Standard cost of 30,000 lb at 11.5p per lb	£3,450
Material price variance (adverse)	£114

Provided the standard price represents fairly the average cost of the material in stock, it may be employed for financial accounting purposes. Where it does not, it may be adjusted by adding back the proportion of the material price variance appropriate to the stock on hand:

Stock at 31 December 1984 at standard cost:

5,400 lb at 11.5p	£621.00
add $\frac{5,400}{30,000} \times £114$	£20.52
Stock adjusted to a weighted average cost basis	£641.52

These different methods of pricing issues each give rise to a slightly different closing stock value and thus to a slightly different profit for the year. But this is not important *provided* that a company adopts the same method consistently in each accounting period. It is not permissible to chop and change.

Replacement cost and NIFO

In the past, items in stock were occasionally stated in the accounts at replacement cost when this was lower than both cost and net realisable value. The effect of this was to increase the cost of goods sold for the period, and thus reduce reported profits. The statement of stocks at the lowest of cost, net realisable value and replacement cost is no longer (under SSAP 9) an acceptable basis of stock valuation. However, for pricing purposes (but not for either stock valuation or costing purposes) some companies employ a next-in first-out basis (NIFO) when estimating and pricing, taking account of the price they expect to pay to replace items to be taken from stock, rather than the price they themselves paid for them.

LIFO

Another method of valuation, unacceptable under SSAP 9, but commonplace in the United States, is the last-in first-out (LIFO) basis in which issues are charged at the latest price at which they could conceivably have come. This has the advantage of charging the customer with the most recent price; but in the balance sheet stocks appear at the price of the earliest delivery from which they could have arisen, on the basis that the rule of good storekeeping is (in theory only) reversed, and goods received latest are used first, and those in stock remain in stock.

In Example 8.2, the closing stock of 'Expel' would have been deemed on a LIFO basis to be from the earliest purchases:

Stock at 31 December 1984 = (4,800 lb at 10p) + (600 lb at 11p) = £546

compared with £756 on a FIFO basis, reducing profits by £210.

Thus, in a time of rising prices LIFO has the effect of:

(*a*) showing stocks in the balance sheet at a cost appropriate not to recent purchases but to

those many months or even years earlier; and, consequently,

(*b*) reducing profit made on holding stock.

Taxation of stock profits

Supposing that, in Example 8.2, Stockout Ltd had, in fact, had a closing stock of 5,400 lb of 'Expel' at the end of 1983, valued on a FIFO basis at 9p per lb = £486, then:

Stock at 31 December 1984: 5,400 lb at 14p	£756
Stock at 31 December 1983: 5,400 lb at 9p	£486
	£270

The stock profit of £270 would be subject to tax, even if the company's normal stock level of 'Expel' needed for the business was around 5,000–6,000 lb, i.e. even if the company was in no position to realise any of the profit by running stocks down. In the early 1970s, when almost all prices were rising rapidly with inflation, companies that needed to carry large stocks were very hard hit: they were taxed on their stock profits and had to find more working capital each year just to maintain the same *volume* of stock. Their plight was eventually recognised by the government, which introduced stock relief in the Finance Act 1975, but discontinued it in 1984 after inflation had eased (see Chapter 13).

The problems of stocks in an inflationary situation will be discussed further in Chapter 22.

Requirements of the Companies Act 1985 and of SSAP 9 on stocks and WIP

SSAP 9 requires that the amount at which stock and work in progress, other than long-term contracts, are stated in periodic financial statements should be 'the total of the *lower of cost and net realisable value* of the separate items of stock and work in progress or groups of similar items', i.e. each item or each group of similar items should be assessed separately.

The Companies Act 1985 allows the use of FIFO, LIFO, weighted average price or any other similar method to be used for *fungible assets* (assets substantially indistinguishable from one another) but, where the amount shown differs materially from the replacement cost (or the most recent purchase price or production cost), the amount of that difference must be disclosed (Sch. 4, para. 27).

The inclusion of overheads in cost

It was at one time accepted that companies should be free to choose whether to value work in progress and finished goods:

(*a*) at prime cost: that is to say, to exclude all overheads, *or*

(b) at variable (or marginal) cost: that is to say to exclude all *fixed* overheads, but include prime cost plus variable overheads, *or*

(c) at the full cost of purchase plus the cost of conversion (including fixed overheads too).

The Companies Act 1985 and SSAP 9 both regard (c) as the only proper method. The classification of overheads between fixed and variable is regarded as an unsuitable one for determining whether or not they should be included in the cost of conversion: the dividing line is considered too imprecise. Costs of general management, as distinct from functional management, are excluded unless directly related to current production (as they may be to some extent in smaller companies), but the Companies Act 1985 does allow a reasonable proportion of interest on capital borrowed to finance production costs to be included in the value of stock; however, if this is done the amount must be disclosed (Sch. 4, para. 26).

Net realisable value

Net realisable value is 'the actual or estimated selling price (net of trade but before settlement discounts) less:

(a) all further costs to completion; and

(b) all costs to be incurred in marketing, selling and distributing'.

When stocks are held which are unlikely to be sold within the turnover period normal to the company (i.e. where there are excess stocks), the impending delay in realisation will increase the risk of deterioration and/or obsolescence, and this needs to be taken into account in assessing net realisable value.

Example 8.3 Rising stocks

Let us look at a single-product factory facing a year in which demand is forecast to fall by 30% due to an economic recession:

Production overheads (rent of factory, etc.) = £1 million.
Production capacity 100,000 units per annum.
Variable costs = £10 per unit. Selling price = £25 per unit.
Sales last year 100,000 units.

The management is faced with the decision of whether:

(a) to continue at full production, hoping that demand will pick up sharply the following year if not sooner, and that it possibly won't fall quite as sharply as forecast; *or*

(b) to cut production by up to 30%.

Under SSAP 9, assuming demand does fall by 30%, the figures that will be reported at the end of the year under these two choices will be:

	(a) Full production Units	(b) Production cut by 30% Units
Opening stock	20,000	20,000
Units manufactured	100,000	70,000
	120,000	90,000
Units sold	70,000	70,000
Closing stock	50,000	20,000
	£	£
Fixed costs	1,000,000	1,000,000
Variable costs (£10 per unit)	1,000,000	700,000
Total costs (cost per unit made)	2,000,000(£20)	1,700,000(£24.285)
Sales (£25 per unit)	1,750,000	1,750,000
Cost of goods sold:		
Opening stock (£20 per unit)	400,000	400,000
add Cost of units manufactured	2,000,000	1,700,000
less Closing stock by FIFO method	− 1,000,000(£20)	−485,700(£24.285)
Cost of goods sold	1,400,000	1,614,300
Profit (Sales *less* Cost of goods sold)	350,000	135,700

The danger of rising stocks

Although SSAP 9's requirement to include production overheads in costing finished goods gives a fair picture when stocks are being maintained at prudent levels in relation to demand, their inclusion can produce unduly optimistic profits when a manufacturer leaves production unchanged in periods of lower demand. This is illustrated by Example 8.3.

In practice, the profit from full production would be likely to be reduced by interest charges to finance carrying increased stock, but even so management can bolster profits a great deal in the short term by continuing high production in the face of falling demand. Rising stocks unmatched by rising turnover may give some warning here, and this can be monitored by the ratio Stocks/Turnover (Example 8.4).

Example 8.4   Stocks/Turnover ratio: A. ARENSON

A. ARENSON, the office furniture manufacturer, reported:

Year to 31 July	1972	1973	1974	1975
	£000	£000	£000	£000
Turnover	2,501	4,927	7,675	6,437
Stocks	656	782	1,605	3,305
$\dfrac{\text{Stocks}}{\text{Turnover}}$	26.2%	15.8%	20.9%	51.3%

The strain of rising stocks and falling turnover in 1975 was reflected by a sharp jump in borrowings (despite £750,000 raised by an issue of convertible preference shares), higher interest charges and a very sharp fall in profits:

Amount due to				
bankers	183	217	356	1,110
Interest payable	24	73	141	248
Pre-tax profits	385	661	868	317

Demand was slow to recover, and the company ran into loss in the first six months of the following accounting year.

With CA 1981's requirement to subclassify stocks and WIP, the cause and likely effect of rising stocks is now more easily analysed. For example, suppose we had had two otherwise identical furniture companies, both with exactly the same previous record as Arenson, reporting in 1975 as follows:

	Company A	Company B
	£000	£000
Turnover	6,437	6,437
Stocks		
Raw materials	318	2,232
Work in progress	605	605
Finished goods	2,232	318
	3,305	3,305

There is a great deal of difference between Company A, where stocks of finished goods are clearly excessive, and Company B, which has managed to trim back production in line with sales, and may well have been very shrewd in buying timber and chipboard forward at a time of rapidly rising raw material prices.

Long-term contracts

A *long-term contract* is defined by SSAP 9 as 'a contract entered into for manufacture or building of a single substantial entity or the provision of a service where the time taken to manufacture, build or provide is such that a substantial proportion of all such contract work will extend for a period exceeding one year'.

Shipbuilders, constructional engineers and the like frequently engage in long-term contracts. Because of the length of time such contracts take to complete, to defer taking profit into account until completion would result in the profit and loss account reflecting not a true and fair view of the activity of the company during the year, but rather the results of those contracts which, by the accident of time, were completed by the year end.

It is normal with long-term contracts to have an arrangement under which the contractor receives payment on account on the basis of the 'work certified' by an architect or surveyor. Traditionally, there are two ways of computing the profit to be taken. The 'work certified' is an essential piece of information whichever of the two ways of arriving at the profit to date is adopted.

Under the first method, profit to date is computed as follows:

$$\begin{array}{l}\text{Work}\\\text{certified}\\\text{at balance}\\\text{sheet date}\end{array} - \begin{array}{l}\text{Costs}\\\text{incurred}\\\text{on contract}\\\text{to date}\end{array} = \begin{array}{l}\text{Profit}\\\text{to date}\end{array}$$

The second method takes a proportion of the overall profit expected:

$$\left\{\begin{array}{l}\text{Total}\\\text{contract}\\\text{price}\end{array} - \begin{array}{l}\text{Total costs}\\\text{incurred on}\\\text{contract}\\\text{to date}\end{array} - \begin{array}{l}\text{Total}\\\text{estimated}\\\text{further}\\\text{costs to}\\\text{completion}\end{array}\right\}$$

$$\times \quad \frac{\text{Work certified to date}}{\text{Total contract price}} = \begin{array}{l}\text{Profit}\\\text{to date}\end{array}$$

If the first formula is used it is still necessary to have regard to the costs likely to be incurred in completing the job, for it is clearly wrong to take a profit on the first stage of a contract if the profit is likely to be lost at a later stage. In either case, in considering future costs, it is necessary to allow for likely increases in wages and salaries, likely increases in the price of raw materials and rises in general overheads in so far as these items are not recoverable from the customer under the terms of the contract: inflation can play havoc with the profitability of fixed-price or inadequately protected contracts, as many companies have learned to their cost.

In neither case is it usual to take up the entire profit to date. Some companies take only two-thirds, others only three-quarters. Many multiply by a further fraction:

$$\frac{\text{Amount received to date}}{\text{Work certified to date}}$$

Where the customer is entitled (as is usually the case) to retain, say, 10% of the amount certified as 'retention monies', so as to ensure satisfactory rectification of any defects, the use of this further fraction of, in this case, 9/10ths, has the effect of disregarding that part of the profit appropriate to the amount retained.

The amount reflected in the year's profit and loss account will be the appropriate proportion of the total profit by reference to the work done to date, less any profit already taken up in prior years

---

Example 8.5   Long-term contracts: 'COMMERCIAL CONTRACTS LTD'

'COMMERCIAL CONTRACTS LTD' is engaged in a long-term bridge-building contract.

	£
Work certified to 31 December 1984	1,250,000
Total contract price	2,000,000
Costs incurred on contract to 31 December 1984	1,025,000
Estimated further costs to completion	575,000
Amount received from customer by 31 December 1984	1,125,000
Profit taken on the contract in 1983	45,000

The company takes up three-quarters of the profit earned to date, reduced by the fraction: amount received to date ÷ work certified to date. What profit will be taken up on the contract in 1984?

Using the first formula:

$$\text{Work certified at balance sheet date} - \text{Costs incurred on contract to date} = \text{Profit to date}$$

Profit to date = £1,250,000 − £1,025,000 = £225,000

Of which: ¾ × $\frac{1,125,000}{1,250,000}$ = 67½% will be taken up = £151,875

but £45,000 of this was taken up in 1983, so only £106,875 remains to be taken up in 1984.

Using the second formula:

$$\left\{\text{Total contract price} - \text{Total costs incurred on contract to date} - \text{Total estimated further costs to completion}\right\} \times \frac{\text{Work certified to date}}{\text{Total contract price}} = \text{Profit to date}$$

Profit to date = (£2,000,000 − £1,025,000 − £575,000) × $\frac{1,250,000}{2,000,000}$ = £250,000

Of this £250,000 profit, 67½% will be taken up (as before) i.e. £168,750, less the £45,000 already taken up in 1983 = £123,750.

The difference between the two figures for profit to date is due to the difference between the profit margin on that part of the contract completed to date (£225,000 on £1,250,000 in the first formula = 18%) and that estimated on the contract as a whole (£400,000 on £2 million in the second formula = 20%).

The second formula requires an estimate to be made of future costs and is therefore open to subjective judgement. Results should be viewed with caution if the overall profitability margin is estimated to be higher than the margin to date; i.e. if the second formula allows a higher profit to be taken now than the first formula would allow.

---

on the contracts still on hand. The aim of using a multiplying factor of two-thirds or three-quarters is to ensure that unless the remaining work on a contract is disastrous, some profit remains to be taken when the contract is finally completed. Example 8.5 illustrates the treatment of long-term contracts in the accounts of an imaginary company, 'COMMERCIAL CONTRACTS LTD'.

Requirements of SSAP 9 on long-term contracts

In the past, accounting treatment of long-term contracts has varied enormously from company to company. BOVIS, for example, in its 1972 accounts noted that 'no provision is made for anticipated future losses' and a year later had to be rescued by P. & O. At the other end of the scale companies like JOHN LAING pursued policies of extreme prudence: all losses were taken when they were foreseen, but no account was taken of profits on contracts unfinished at the end of the year.

SSAP 9 requires that 'The amount at which long-term contract work in progress is stated in periodic financial statements should be cost plus any *attributable profit*, less any foreseeable losses and progress payments received and receivable', and the amount of attributable profit included should be disclosed. Attributable profits on contracts are, however, only required to be taken up when 'it is considered that their outcome can be assessed with reasonable certainty before their conclusion'; if the outcome cannot be reasonably assessed, 'it is prudent not to take up any profit', so management is still left with a certain amount of latitude, and the key point to watch for is undue anticipation of profits.

SSAP 9 also requires balance sheets to show how the amount included for long-term contracts is reached by stating:

(a) the amount of work in progress at cost plus attributable profit (i.e. profit or loss taken to date), less foreseeable losses;

(b) cash received and receivable at the accounting date as progress payments on account of contracts in progress.

Thus, if the bridge contract we discussed in Example 8.5 was the only contract of Commercial Contracts Ltd to appear in the balance sheet at 31 December 1984, and if the first formula is used, it would appear as follows:

	£	£
Work in progress, at cost *plus* Profit taken to date	1,176,875	
less Cash received from customer	1,125,000	
		51,875

Chapter 9

DEBTORS

TRADE DEBTORS AND OTHER DEBTORS

Debtors (also known as 'receivables') are a current asset, representing amounts owing to the business.

The balance sheet formats in Schedule 4 of the Companies Act 1985 require debtors to be subdivided into:

(a) *trade debtors* – those arising from the sale of goods on credit,

(b) *amounts owed by group companies* – see Chapter 15,

(c) *amounts owed by related companies* – see Chapter 16,

(d) *other debtors* – for example debts due from the sale of fixed assets or investments, and

(e) *prepayments and accrued income* – for example rent or rates paid in advance.

The amount falling due after more than one year should be shown separately for each item included under debtors (CA 1985, Sch. 4, note (5) to the balance sheet formats). Most companies show a single figure for debtors in their balance sheet, and give details in a note thereto, as illustrated here:

ULTRAMAR *Details of debtors*

Balance sheet

	Note	1983 £ million	1982 £ million
Current assets			
Stocks		370.5	214.4
Debtors	16	330.1	223.5
. . . .			

16. Debtors

	1983 £ million	1982 £ million
Amounts falling due within one year:		
Trade debtors	225.5	140.6
Other debtors	33.9	27.9
Prepayments and accrued income	25.2	14.4
	284.6	182.9
Amounts falling due after one year:		
Indonesian debt service equalisation	30.0	25.2
Other debtors	13.0	15.3
Prepayments and accrued income	2.5	0.1
	330.1	223.5

(A paragraph under 'Accounting Policies' described how the amount for Indonesian debt service equalisation arose.)

Where a company has an unusual type of debtor, a separate subdivision may be shown, e.g. HENLEYS, the motor distributors, with their special deposit arrangements with motor manufacturers, shown here:

HENLEYS *Note to the balance sheet*

Debtors	1983 £000	1982 £000
Amounts falling due within one year:		
Trade debtors	9,607	9,807
Vehicle stock deposits	1,974	1,433
Other debtors	2,098	3,711
Prepayments and accrued income	949	1,568
	14,628	16,519

Vehicle stock deposits comprise amounts held by manufacturers against the general supply of new vehicles, which are consigned to the group without specific payment being required. Vehicles held in this way are available for set-off against the deposits. Deposits are not immediately variable and as such can at any time fall short of, or exceed, the aggregate wholesale value of vehicles held on consignment.

Bad debts and doubtful debtors

The granting of credit inevitably involves some risk that the debtor will fail to pay, that is, will become a bad debt. When a business recognises that a debt is bad, the debt is written off to profit and loss account. That is to say, the balance appearing as 'debtors' falls by the amount of the debt, and 'bad debts' appears as an expense. This expense is normally shown separately in the published accounts only if the amount is material.

In addition, it is normal to set up a 'provision for doubtful debtors'. To do so a charge is made to profit and loss account and, in the balance sheet, the provision for doubtful debtors is deducted from the total debtors. Once again, the provision for doubtful debtors is disclosed separately in the published accounts only if it is material.

A provision for doubtful debtors may be *specific*, that is to say based upon the businessman's estimate of the probable loss, studying each debt in turn; for instance, there is a 10% probability that Smith will fail to pay his debt of £12,100, therefore we must provide £1,210; or it may be *general*, e.g. 2½% of total debtors; or a combination of the two.

The importance of debtors

Companies such as supermarket chains, whose turnover is almost entirely for cash, will have very few debtors; the figure appearing in the balance sheet is likely to be largely prepayments and non-trade debtors, and will have no particular significance. SAINSBURY's, for example, with sales of £2,688 million p.a., showed trade debtors of a mere £1.3 million in its 1984 accounts. At the other extreme are companies whose entire turnover is on credit terms, and very large amounts of working capital may be tied up in debtors. Here the efficiency with which credit accounts are handled, and the timing of the taking of profit where payments are by instalment, are of considerable interest to the analyst.

Debt collection period

The ratio Trade Debtors/Turnover can be used to monitor a company's credit control, as we describe in Chapter 23, and this is possibly a more meaningful measure if expressed in terms of time, as the *debt collection period*:

Debt collection period (in days) =

$$\frac{\text{Trade Debtors}}{\text{Sales (Turnover)}} \times 365$$

It is interesting to compare this ratio in similar companies:

MARLEY *Debt collection period*

	1983 £000	1982 £000
Turnover	500,919	422,490
Trade debtors (under 1 year)	71,354	67,339
Trade debtors (over 1 year)	594	106
Debt collection period	52.4 days	58.3 days

REDLAND *Debt collection period*

	1983/84 £ million	1982/83 £ million
Turnover	914.9	799.1
Trade debtors (under 1 year)	114.8	99.0
Trade debtors (over 1 year)	—	—
Debt collection period	45.8 days	45.2 days

Some companies and analysts take 360 days to the year, or compute in terms of, say, 260 *working* days.

In a seasonal business it is more accurate to compute the collection period on a month-by-month basis, but this is not possible without inside knowledge. Indeed, the analyst can tell comparatively little about debtors unless a significant proportion of debtors are due after more than one year or unless the company discloses more than the minimum information required by law. Among the things which one would like to find out are the following:

1. What is the customer concentration? Is an undue proportion due from one major customer, or from customers in one important industry? Would failure of one or two customers have a material effect upon the company's financial future?
2. What is the age pattern of debtors? Are some unduly old? Is there adequate provision for bad and doubtful debts?
3. Are any of the debts falling due after more than one year very long-term in nature? In the United Kingdom debtors appear at their face value regardless of when they are due.

51

In the United States, if a debt is not due within one year, it may be necessary to discount it, i.e. to take account of imputed interest. Thus, a debt of $1 million due three years hence might appear, taking interest into account at 10%, as $751,300.

Factors affecting the debt collection period

A short debt collection period is, other things being equal, preferable to a longer one; but as with many ratios one has to qualify this general principle. For by restricting credit, and selling entirely for cash, a business can have a zero debt collection period; but if this drives its customers into the arms of competitors it is scarcely an improvement so far as the business as a whole is concerned. Subject to that qualification, any improvement in collection period, since it represents a reduction in overall debtors, means that more capital is available for other purposes, or that there is less need to borrow money from the bank.

At first sight it may seem that an increase in collection period represents a fall in the efficiency of the debt collection section. This is likely to be the case, but it is not necessarily so. The debt collection period may increase (decrease) between one period and another for a number of reasons:

1. If there is a *policy change* with regard to:
    (a) credit terms to existing customers; if, for example, the board of directors, to obtain a valuable order from a major customer, offers two months' credit instead of one;

    (b) the granting of credit; for instance, if potential customers whose credit rating was formerly insufficient for them to be granted credit, are granted credit – for such customers are unlikely to be among the fastest payers.

2. If there is *poor credit management*:
    (a) if credit is given to unsatisfactory customers;
    (b) if the invoicing section falls behind; customers will not pay until they receive an invoice and, in general, pay at a fixed time determined by the date on which they receive an invoice, e.g. at the end of the month in which they receive an invoice;
    (c) if statements are late – some businesses wait until they receive a statement;
    (d) if there is no consistent follow-up of overdue debts, by letter and/or telephone, or even in person.

Why it is important to keep a watch upon collection period

Although it is necessary for most businesses to offer some credit, any unnecessary credit is bad management because it ties up money which (normally) earns no return, and which is subject to increased risk. The customer who is short of money, and who finds he can order things from a company without having to pay for them at the end of the month, tends to place more and more of his orders with that company; if he subsequently goes into liquidation, he is likely to do so owing a hefty amount.

HIRE-PURCHASE AND CREDIT SALE TRANSACTIONS

(Reference: SSAP 21 *Accounting for leases and hire purchase contracts*.)

Definitions

A *hire-purchase transaction* is a transaction in which the *hirer* agrees to hire goods from their *owner* in return for which he pays (usually) a deposit and a series of weekly, monthly, quarterly or yearly payments. The intention is that when the hiring period comes to an end, the ownership of the goods will pass to the hirer, sometimes on the payment of a nominal sum, sometimes with the final instalment; ownership, therefore, does not pass to the hirer until all payments have been made.

A *credit sale* is an outright sale (usually by a retailer) where payment by instalments is agreed in writing as a condition of the sale. Under a credit sale arrangement the property in the goods passes immediately to the purchaser, who becomes the owner of the goods, but payment is required to be made over a period. If the purchaser defaults, the seller can sue for payment but is not entitled to reclaim the goods.

Interest is normally charged by the seller both in credit sale and hire-purchase arrangements; the great difference between them is that in a credit sale the 'purchaser' owns the goods from the outset, whereas in the case of a hire-purchase sale, they do not become his until the final payment is made. Thus the seller cannot reclaim the goods in the case of a credit sale if the purchaser defaults, whereas, subject to the terms of the agreement and the law on hire-purchase, he can in the case of a hire-purchase transaction.

Amounts due under credit sale transactions are

debtors, and normally appear with other trade debtors, though they may be shown separately. In the case of a hire-purchase transaction, there has, strictly speaking, been no sale, and the goods involved are still an asset of the seller; but, adopting the principle of 'substance over form', most companies refer to the item as 'hire-purchase debtors' or 'instalments due under hire-purchase agreements'.

Timing of profit taking

Whether the sale is by credit sale arrangement or on hire-purchase, there are two elements of profit: the profit on the sale of the goods themselves and interest upon the amounts outstanding. There are a number of ways in which these two forms of profit can be spread over the accounting periods involved; but essentially these break down into two:

1. Take all the profit on the sale immediately, and spread only the interest element.
2. Spread both the profit on the sale and the interest over the life of the agreement.

Although method 1 is permissible for credit sales, method 2 is the more prudent. Method 1 is not recommended for hire-purchase, as the goods have not actually been sold.

Where a credit sale is made on truly 'interest-free' terms, there is no interest to spread, though logically there is an interest cost so far as the selling company is concerned. This is not normally taken into account, though it could be, by taking into account imputed interest. But it is always necessary to make provision for collection costs. Such a provision might, for instance, be 10% of the credit sale account debtors outstanding on balance sheet date.

The rule of 78

Finance companies frequently apply the 'rule of 78' in spreading either the interest alone, or the whole profit and interest, over the life of the agreement. This is simply a form of the 'sum of the years' digits method' already discussed in connection with depreciation in Chapter 6. What happens is this: the period of the agreement is set down in months (or it could be weeks in the case of a weekly agreement, or years where payments were on an annual basis), and the sum of the digits represents the sum of $1 + 2 + 3 + 4 \ldots$ to n, where n is that number of months (or weeks or years). It is called the rule of 78 because for a year's agreement, the sum of $1 + 2 + 3 + \ldots + 12$ is 78. Any interest charge is then spread as follows (in this case a year's agreement):

First month 12/78ths of total interest
Second month 11/78ths
Third month 10/78ths
. . .
Twelfth month 1/78th

See Example 9.1.

Some companies use this same method for hire-purchase transactions, but it is generally considered more prudent to spread both profit and interest over the life of the transaction (Example 9.2), rather than to take profit at the outset.

The rule of 78 is a simple, though not totally accurate, way of spreading interest or profit over the period of an agreement. Some companies use more sophisticated techniques, spreading interest or profit by what is termed the 'actuarial method', taking into account interest (at the true effective rate payable) on the balance outstanding period by period.

Example 9.1   Credit sale, method 1: 'VOLUME UNLIMITED LTD'

Hi-fi equipment costing £425 is sold by 'VOLUME UNLIMITED LTD' to S. O. Loudwater for £600, to be spread by means of a credit sale agreement over nine months. Taking into account interest and collection costs of £45, Loudwater is to pay a total of £645, i.e. £71.67 per month, commencing with delivery of the goods on 1 November 1985. Volume Unlimited Ltd prepares accounts to 31 December annually. How much profit will be taken upon Loudwater's agreement in 1985 (assuming he pays two instalments, one on 1 November and one on 1 December) and how much in 1986, the final payment being made on 1 July 1986?

All the profit on selling goods, purchased for £425, for £600 – i.e. £175 – will fall into 1985, the year in which the sale was made, as will the interest for two months, computed as follows:

November 9/45ths of £45 = £9
December 8/45ths of £45 = £8
(since the sum of the digits 1, 2, 3 . . . 9 is 45).

At 31 December 1985 there would appear among debtors seven instalments of £71.67 (£501.69) less a provision for unearned interest and collection costs (£45 − £9 − £8 = £28) = £473.69.

Example 9.2   Hire-purchase, method 2: 'DEFERRALS LTD'

The hire-purchase trading account of 'DEFERRALS LTD' for 1986 is as follows:

Hire-purchase sales	£120,000
less Cost of goods sold	£80,000
Gross profit on HP sales (33⅓%)	£40,000

Receipts from 1986 HP sales	= £36,000
Profit to be taken in 1986	
£36,000 × 33⅓% profit margin	= £12,000
Provision for unearned profit	
carried forward on 1986 HP sales	
= £40,000 − £12,000 = £28,000	

HP sales in 1986	£120,000
less Cash received	£36,000
	£84,000
less Provision for unearned profit	£28,000
Hire-purchase debtors	
(from 1986 sales)	£56,000

If, say, £63,000 is received in 1986 in respect of transactions from 1985; and £42,000 from 1984, when the profit margins were 30% and 35% respectively; the total profit from HP sales to be taken in 1986 would be:

From 1986	£12,000
From 1985 (30% of £63,000)	£18,900
From 1984 (35% of £42,000)	£14,700
Total profit	£45,600

Hire-purchase information given in accounts

A good set of accounts will give quite a lot of information on hire-purchase and credit sale business; e.g. GREAT UNIVERSAL STORES states how the profit is taken and how the interest is brought in, and shows the amount of provisions made and describes what they cover (see illustration below).

Some companies arrange for their credit sales and hire-purchase transactions to be handled by a separate finance company, so that they receive payment for goods at once and thus reduce their requirements for working capital. In these cases, of course, the amounts outstanding are of no concern to the selling company and do not appear in its accounts.

GREAT UNIVERSAL STORES *Information on hire purchase*

	Notes	1983 £000	1982 £000
Current assets			
Stocks		215,664	217,796
Instalment and hire			
purchase receivables		697,960	610,802
Deduct:			
Provisions for deferred profit, finance			
charges and collection costs	1(e)	168,026	147,160
		529,934	463,642
Trade, banking and finance receivables		73,464	72,809
Bank balances and cash		231,752	234,896
		1,050,814	989,143

Notes to the accounts

1. Accounting Policies

(e) Instalment and Hire Purchase Receivables

The gross profit and service charges on goods sold under hire purchase and certain instalment agreements are brought into profit as and when instalments are received. Interest on hire purchase finance and personal loan agreements with a term not exceeding three years is brought into profit on a straight line basis over the period of the agreements. Interest on other personal loan agreements is brought into profit in proportion to the reducing balance outstanding. The provision for deferred profit, service charges and collection costs in the balance sheet represents the unearned proportion of gross profit, finance charges and interest and to a lesser extent covers future costs of instalment collection and commission payable to mail order agents.

FACTORING

Factoring represents the outright sale of a company's trade debtors to a factoring house.

In general, factoring houses offer three facilities:

1. *A sales accounting service*, taking over from the company responsibility for credit control, sales accounting and debt collection.
2. *A guarantee against bad debts*, the factor paying whether or not the customer does. Factoring tends to provide greater protection against credit risks than credit insurance, which is normally limited to a proportion of the debt, say, 70%. The factor charges a commission for these services of around 2%, but much depends upon the nature and volume of the business. Clearly, the service costs more where the business has a large number of smaller accounts, and is in a risky industry, and less where it has few, large, accounts, all of which are companies with household names.
3. *An improvement in liquidity*. The factor assesses the client's business and arrives at an agreed debt collection period. Suppose the client offers 30-day terms, but, in fact, is taking 60 days to collect the average debt. A reasonable assessment might be 45 days. The factor therefore undertakes to make payment 45 days after the invoice is raised, thus improving the liquidity of the client's business by 15 days' debtors, and the factor will doubtless aim to get the average collection period down to below 45 days. If the client wishes the factor will, upon receiving invoices, forward 75–90% of their value immediately, charging interest at, say, 3–4% over bank overdraft rate from that date to the normal collection date (in our example the 45th day).

Factoring can be especially useful to the seasonal business, which does not need to raise the additional money mentioned in (3) above (upon receiving invoices) except at certain times of the year. It is also of advantage to companies with foreign customers. Most factors tend to be either subsidiaries of UK clearing banks or part of an international factoring organisation. In either case, the factor tends to have expert knowledge of the credit standing not only of customers in the United Kingdom, but also of those abroad, whereas the ordinary company has some difficulty running a credit check upon a potential customer overseas.

As explained earlier, most factoring is upon a non-recourse basis, the factor taking the entire credit risk; but it is possible to make other arrangements, especially where debt collection might prove a problem, and the client wishes to handle this himself. In the case of non-recourse factoring, the existence and identity of the factor are both known to the customer. In what is termed confidential invoice discounting (or confidential factoring), the company maintains its own accounting records, and collects the money from customers in the ordinary way; but each time an invoice is raised, a copy is forwarded to the factor, who advances, say, 80% of the value of the invoice. As cheques are received from customers, they are passed to the factor, who banks them, deducts the amount already advanced, plus his charges, and remits the balance. The customer then does not even know of the existence of the factor.

In general, it is impossible from an inspection of published accounts to say with certainty whether or not a factor is involved; but a single sharp reduction in collection period and total debtors outstanding might make one suspect that factoring had been introduced.

Chapter 10

BANKING

Bank facilities

There are three main methods by which a company can borrow money from a bank: by overdrawing on its current account, by loans and by the use of acceptance credits. The bank normally agrees with a company the maximum amount that can be borrowed under each method, and this is called granting a facility. For example, a company that has the bank's permission to run an overdraft of up to £1 million has overdraft facilities for that amount.

What is shown in the balance sheet is, however, not the limit of each facility but the amount the facility is being used at the year end; only the amounts actually borrowed from the bank on the balance sheet date appear in the balance sheet, although some idea of the average amount overdrawn during the year can be gained from the interest charges reported in the profit and loss account. The bank facilities available to a company are not normally published, although broad statements may be made about the company having 'ample overdraft facilities' or being 'well within its bank facilities'.

Schedule 4 of the Companies Act 1985 requires bank loans and overdrafts falling due within one year to be shown separately from those falling due after more than one year. The use being made of acceptance credit facilities is included in 'Bills of exchange payable'.

Overdrafts

The traditional method of clearing bank lending is to allow the customer to overdraw on his current account. It was originally designed to cover fluctuations in the company's cash during the year and gives the company complete flexibility of drawing within a given limit, which is normally reviewed annually.

Bank advances on overdraft are technically repayable on demand and, although this is seldom enforced, the bank when granting overdraft facilities does expect the customer to produce budgets and cash flow forecasts to show the purposes for which the facilities are intended and the plans for eventual repayment. Bank lending on overdraft is traditionally short-term in character, designed to cover fluctuations in working capital requirements rather than to provide permanent capital for the company.

In recent years, however, long-term interest rates have been driven so high by inflation that few finance directors have been willing to commit their companies to long-term debt. Instead they have resorted more and more to borrowing from their banks, where interest on an overdraft is charged at an agreed percentage over the clearing bank's base rate (see below) which they hope will average less than current long-term rates, and where the company is free to reduce its borrowing whenever it wishes. Although it is now quite common for companies to finance a large part of their working capital in this way, clearing banks are usually reluctant to let companies increase their overdraft ad lib, even against a floating charge, preferring their clients to convert any 'hard-core' borrowing that has built up on overdraft into loans (see Bank loans below).

The cost of borrowing on overdraft

The interest a company has to pay on its overdraft is usually set at a given percentage above its bank's base rate, depending on the standing of the customer; a financially stable, medium-sized company might pay a fixed 1½% above base.

The base rate, the datum on which the rates of interest are based, is adjusted up and down to reflect fluctuations in short-term interest rates. Each bank sets its own base rate according to supply and demand and the fluctuations of short-term interest rates, though in practice the clearing banks' base rates keep very much in line with each other.

Fluctuations of the overdraft

As we have said, the overdraft figure given in the balance sheet is the amount the overdraft facility is being used at the year end; as companies normally choose their year end to fall when business is at its slackest, the balance sheet figure is unlikely to be the maximum amount the company has overdrawn during the year.

For example, a company in a seasonal business, with peak sales in the summer, could be expected to build up stocks from early spring and to carry high debtors across the summer. With an annual turnover of say £15 million, an overdraft of £100,000 at its year end (31 December) and £150,000 bank interest paid (reflecting an average overdraft of £1,500,000 during the year, bearing interest on average at 10%), the amount the company was actually overdrawn during the year would be likely to fluctuate with the sales cycle as shown in Example 10.1.

In practice, profit on sales and depreciation on assets would accumulate during the year, steadily improving the overdraft position, but sharp increases would be expected with the payment of dividends and Corporation Tax, and capital expenditure would also have an immediate effect on the overdraft position.

Vulnerability of borrowing on overdraft

Companies which rely heavily on borrowing on overdraft and on floating-rate loans (see below) are vulnerable to rising interest rates, particularly if their profit margins are small, and those which let their overdrafts steadily increase year by year without raising further equity or fixed-interest capital are steadily increasing their risk.

Another hazard of financing on overdraft is that the government can and does from time to time clamp down on bank lending; in addition, the banks are also liable to restrict credit on their own account when they find themselves up against their own overall lending limits or too heavily lent in the particular sector in which the company operates. As credit controls often come when conditions are unfavourable for capital raising, a company which is financed extensively on overdraft can all too easily find its operations severely constrained by its immediate cash position.

Example 10.1   Example of annual fluctuation in overdraft

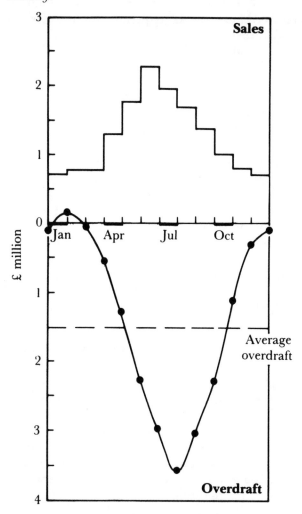

Bank loans

The simplest type of bank loan is one where the full amount is drawn by the borrower at the outset and is repaid in one lump sum at the end of the period. The duration (or 'term') of the loan is seldom more than seven years but, unlike an overdraft, a bank loan cannot be called in before the end of the term unless the borrower defaults on any condition attached to the loan.

Interest charged

Interest is charged either at a fixed rate or, more frequently, at a *floating* rate: an agreed percentage over base rate, or over London Inter-Bank Offer Rate (LIBOR). Where LIBOR is used, an interest period is agreed between the borrower and the bank and the bank then, on the first day of each interest period, determines the rate at which deposits are being offered in the interbank market for the relevant period.

For example, if a rate of 1% over LIBOR and a

three-month interest period have been agreed and the three-month LIBOR rate is 10.7% at the start of the period, the borrower will pay 11.7% for the next three months, and the rate will then be redetermined. Banks frequently allow borrowers to vary their choice of interest period – one month, three months or six months – during the life of a loan.

Drawing and repayment by instalments

Where the borrower doesn't need all the money at once, the bank may allow the loan to be drawn down in tranches (specified instalments). Repayments may also be arranged in instalments, which may often be a stipulation of the lender; banks like to see money coming back gradually to make repayment easier for the borrower and to give early warning of a borrower getting into difficulties over repayment. Details of drawing down and repayment are agreed in advance, together with the rate of interest payable and the security to be given, although any of these features can be altered subsequently by mutual agreement.

Security

Bank loans are sometimes secured on assets acquired by the loan or on other assets of the company, but a floating charge is more usual. If the loan is not secured at all, the company may be required to give a *negative pledge*, i.e. to undertake not to give security to any new or existing creditor or to borrow further amounts under existing security without the bank's prior agreement in writing.

Loan facilities

There is an increasing trend, particularly in European banking, to provide companies with more flexible financing by means of loan facilities. Drawing down (usually with a minimum limit on any one drawing) can be allowed at any time given a little notice, repayment is flexible, and subsequent redrawing may possibly be allowed, but the borrower will be charged for this flexibility by a *commitment commission* payable on any unused portion of the facility for as long as the facility is left open.

FINANCING OVERSEAS INVESTMENT

Prior to 1979, when the Exchange Control Act 1947 was suspended, a UK company wishing to finance direct investment overseas could purchase foreign currency at the current market rate only if its overseas investment satisfied very stringent Bank of England criteria. Otherwise the company either had to purchase foreign currency at a premium through the investment currency market or it had to borrow.

Two special methods of borrowing were developed as alternatives to the direct borrowing of foreign currency: the back-to-back loan and the currency swap.

Back-to-back or 'parallel' loans

The company borrows foreign currency and, in the same transaction, lends an equivalent amount of sterling. As the loans are matched, they are usually netted out against each other, with only the differences due to exchange rate movements being included in the total in the company's bal-

ance sheet, and with details being given in a note (e.g. SLOUGH ESTATES, shown in the previous column).

Netting out avoids the double counting that would otherwise occur if a UK company borrowed sterling to lend on in a back-to-back arrangement.

Currency swaps

An alternative method of lending sterling in exchange for foreign currency is to swap currencies with an agreement to reverse the transaction after a given period. The method has some technical advantages, the main one being that the UK company's sterling loan is secured by the foreign currency, as the subsequent reversal of the swap is conditional upon both parties honouring the agreement.

In a back-to-back loan, if the borrower of the sterling defaults, the UK company's right to set off the foreign currency it had borrowed against the sterling debt would depend on the way in which the loan had been set up, and the law of the foreign country.

Currency swaps normally appear in a note to the accounts.

Interest rate swaps

The primary purpose of an interest rate swap is to protect a company against the impact of adverse

SLOUGH ESTATES *Extract from note on unsecured loans*

	£000
US$ variable interest loan 1986	1,700
Less reciprocal sterling variable interest loan 1986	(2,372)
US$ 4¾% loan 1993	6,887
Less reciprocal sterling 4% loan 1993	(6,993)

fluctuations in interest rates on the interest charge the company has to pay on its floating-rate debt. The company agrees a fixed rate with a bank on a nominal sum for a given period; the company then pays the bank the fixed rate and the bank pays the company the floating rate. For example, REDLAND reported in 1984 that 'During the course of the year Redland signed a number of interest rate swap agreements which have fixed an interest cost of 11½% on $63 million of debt.'

When used in conjunction with a currency swap, it enables a company to lock in at a fixed rate of interest in one currency to cover floating rate interest charges in another currency.

Companies may also use interest rate swaps in the reverse direction to reduce the proportion of their fixed-rate interest charges (e.g. if they take the view that interest rates will fall). In neither case is there any transfer of principal (capital).

BILLS OF EXCHANGE

Definition

A bill of exchange is, briefly, an order in writing from one person (the *drawer*) to another (the *drawee*) requiring the drawee to pay a specified sum of money on a given date. When the drawee signs the bill he becomes the *acceptor* of the bill, and the person to whom the money is to be paid is the *payee*.

The main legislation on bills is contained in the Bills of Exchange Act 1882, and their use in practice is clearly and concisely described in a book, *The Bill on London*, produced by Gillett Brothers, one of the discount houses.

Purpose

The primary purpose of a bill of exchange is to finance the sale of goods when the seller or exporter wishes to obtain payment at the time the goods are despatched and the buyer or importer wants to defer payment until the goods reach him, or later.

In these circumstances A, the supplier of goods to B, would draw a bill of exchange for the goods, which B 'accepts', acknowledging the debt and promising payment at some future date, normally three months ahead. Bills of this type are called *trade bills*.

A can then sell the bill to a third party, C, at a discount to the face value of the bill; and C in turn can endorse it and sell it on to D. In this case if B subsequently defaults, D can claim payment from A, and if A also defaults D can then claim on C.

Alternatively A can retain the bill, which gives a legal right to payment at a given date in the future (the date of maturity), or the bill can be deposited at a bank as a security against borrowings.

Presentation in the balance sheet

If Company A's year ends before the bill has reached maturity, then:

(*a*)   if A still holds the bill, it would be included in debtors; *or*

(*b*)   if A has discounted the bill, it would not appear in the balance sheet, but should be shown as a contingent liability, in case B subsequently defaults on payment.

In Company B's balance sheet the outstanding bill would be shown under creditors as a *bill of exchange payable*.

Discounting

When a bill of exchange is discounted, i.e. sold to a third party at a discount to its face value, this is usually done through one of the discount houses, which will trade it in the money market. The discount on a trade bill depends on prevailing interest rates, on the creditworthiness of the drawer, the acceptor and any subsequent endorsers, and on the nature of the underlying transaction. In the case of a *bank bill*, that is, one where a bank is the acceptor of the bill, or has endorsed it, the discount rate will be less than on a trade bill. The finest rates are obtained in discounting bills drawn against exports or imports and accepted by 'eligible banks' (i.e. those banks whose acceptances are eligible for rediscount at the Bank of England, which include the clearing banks, accepting houses and some other banks with active acceptance business). (*Accepting house*: a member of the Accepting Houses Committee, an association of British merchant banks, whose acceptance business is a material part of their banking business and is approved by the Bank of England.)

Acceptance credits

Many eligible banks (especially the accepting houses) specialise in accepting bills for customers. They provide this type of short-term finance by granting the client an acceptance credit facility up to a given limit for an agreed period, and the client can then draw bills of exchange on the bank as he wishes, provided the running total of bills outstanding does not exceed the prescribed limit (in other words, it is a revolving credit facility). The bank 'accepts' the bills, which can then be discounted in the money market at the finest rate, and the customer receives the proceeds of the sale, less the acceptance commission he has to pay to the accepting house (normally between ⅜% and ½% p.a. for good-quality borrowers). When the bill falls due for payment (usually three months later), the customer pays the bank the full face value of the bill and the bank in turn honours the bill when it is presented by the eventual purchaser. The bank has to honour the bill even if the customer defaults, because it had 'accepted' responsibility for meeting the bill when it fell due.

The acceptance of bills by banks is normally related to commercial transactions, either specifically matched or linked to the general volume of business, so that the bills are self-liquidating.

Unlike an overdraft, the interest on discounted bills is paid *in advance* by the deduction of discount charges from the face value of the bill and, in addition, if the bills have been accepted by a bank, the company will also have to pay the acceptance commission in advance. In spite of these extra costs, variations of interest rates often make the use of acceptance credit facilities cheaper than an overdraft or a bank loan.

Acceptance credits in the balance sheet
The future obligation of a company to provide cash cover to meet bills that have yet to mature under an acceptance credit facility must, if material, be shown separately in a company's balance sheet under creditors as 'Bills of exchange payable' (CA 1985, Sch. 4 formats), as illustrated here:

BOC *Note on net current assets*

CREDITORS: Amounts falling due within one year

	1983 £ million	1982 £ million
Deposits and advance payments by customers	18.6	17.6
Trade creditors	118.0	97.8
Bills of exchange payable	6.3	3.3
Payroll and other taxes . . .		

Points for analysts to watch on bills

The discounting of bills is a traditional method of providing finance for many businesses, particularly importers and exporters, and acceptance credits are a standard form of short-term finance available to companies, so there is nothing inherently wrong with finding 'bills payable' or 'bills receivable' in a company's accounts, but a sharp change in the amounts involved can be a symptom of cash shortage.

Bills payable
If bills are not normally used by the company or in the particular trade, or if there is a marked increase in the total involved, the company may be resorting to the use of bills in lieu of cash to satisfy creditors or to the use of bills to borrow more money.

Bills receivable
A drop from normal levels in bills receivable is also of interest: the company may be discounting bills (selling them at a discount in advance of their maturity date) to obtain cash in order to ease liquidity problems.

Chapter 11

CREDITORS, PROVISIONS AND CONTINGENT LIABILITIES

(References: SSAP 18 *Accounting for Contingencies*; SSAP 21 *Accounting for Leases and Hire Purchase Contracts.*)

Creditors

The two balance sheet formats in Schedule 4 of the Companies Act 1985 present creditors in different ways:

Format 1 shows them under two headings, *Creditors: amounts falling due within one year* and *Creditors: amounts falling due after more than one year.*

Format 2 shows them under a single heading, *Creditors*, in which case the amounts falling due within one year must be shown separately for each item and in aggregate.

Most companies use Format 1, which nets out *Creditors falling due within one year* (also known as Current liabilities), against *Current assets* to produce Net current assets (liabilities). For example:

BEJAM *Balance sheet*

Employment of capital	Notes	1984 £000	1983 £000
Fixed Assets . . .		58,462	51,599
Current Assets . . .		37,092	42,093
Creditors falling due within 1 year	17	(49,121)	(50,121)
Net Current Assets (Liabilities)		(12,029)	(8,028)
Total Assets less Current Liabilities		46,433	43,571
Creditors falling due after 1 year	18	(1,677)	(4,220)
Provision for liabilities and charges		(6,289)	(3,118)
Net Assets		38,467	36,233

Types of creditor

The following items are required to be shown, if material:

(*a*) debenture loans (see Chapter 5);
(*b*) bank loans and overdrafts (see Chapter 10);
(*c*) payments received on account;
(*d*) trade creditors;
(*e*) bills of exchange payable (see Chapter 10);
(*f*) amounts owed to group companies;
(*g*) amounts owed to related companies;
(*h*) other creditors, including taxation and social security;
(*i*) accruals and deferred income.

Details of types of creditor are usually given in notes to the balance sheet, rather than in the balance sheet itself. For example:

BEJAM *Notes to the balance sheet*

17 Creditors falling due within 1 year	1984 £000	1983 £000
Bank loans and overdrafts	600	4,284
Other loans	—	396
Receipts on account	378	431
Trade creditors	28,910	30,883
Bills payable	162	175
Corporation tax	8,091	5,490
Other taxes and social security	928	1,090
Proposed dividend	1,974	1,720
Employee profit sharing scheme	633	409
Accruals and deferred income	7,445	5,243
	49,121	50,121

18 Creditors falling due after 1 year	1984 £000	1983 £000
Bank loans	1,600	2,200
Other loans	—	1,781
Bills payable	77	239
	1,677	4,220

Payments received on account

These arise where a customer is asked as a sign of good faith to deposit money in respect of a contemplated purchase. If the purchase goes through, the deposit becomes a part payment and ceases to be a creditor. Should the sale not be consummated, the deposit would normally be returned, though it could conceivably be forfeited in certain circumstances.

Trade creditors

Trade creditors are people who are owed money for *goods* supplied. The size of trade creditors shows the extent to which suppliers are financing a company's stock.

Other creditors including taxation and social security

Taxation and social security are each shown separately. Taxation due within 12 months will normally include one year's mainstream Corporation Tax (see Chapter 13), ACT on any dividends recently paid, ACT on any proposed dividends, and any foreign tax due.

Accruals and deferred income

An *accrual* is an apportionment of a known or determinable future liability in respect of a service already partly received. Thus, a business paying rent of £6,000 half-yearly in arrears on 30 June and 31 December would, if it had an accounting year ending 30 November, show an accrual of £5,000 (the five months' rent from 1 July to 30 November unpaid at the end of its accounting year). *Deferred income* is money received by the company but not yet earned.

Other items

The following items may also appear under creditors:

Dividends proposed

Under Section 235(1) of the Companies Act 1985, the directors' report must state any amount which the directors recommend be paid by way of dividend. Although the company has no legal obligation to pay these proposed dividends until they have been approved at the annual general meeting, companies always show them as a liability.

Deposits

In addition to deposits in respect of a contemplated purchase (included under *payments received on account*), deposits may have been charged where goods have been despatched in containers, drums, barrels or boxes, to ensure their return. The container, etc., remains part of the stock of the despatching company, until it becomes apparent that it will not be returned, e.g. when the return period has elapsed, when it will be treated as having been sold.

In financial companies, where deposits are a major item, representing money deposited to earn interest, deposits are shown as a separate heading.

Provisions

A 'provision' (as defined by CA 1985, Sch. 4, paras 88 and 89) is either:

(a) any amount written off by way of providing for depreciation or diminution in the value of assets (the amount would normally be deducted from the value of the assets, rather than being shown separately); *or*

(b) any amount retained to provide for any liability or loss which is *either* likely to be incurred, *or* certain to be incurred but uncertain as to the amount or as to the date on which it will arise.

Provisions for liabilities and charges

Under this heading are shown provisions for:

(a) pensions and similar obligations;
(b) taxation, including deferred taxation; *and*
(c) other provisions.

Particulars should also be given of any pension commitments for which no provision has been made (CA 1985, Sch. 4, para. 50(4)(b)). (See also ED 32 *Disclosure of pension information in company accounts*.)

The item taxation will normally only include deferred taxation, as other taxation will be shown under creditors, unless the amount is uncertain.

Other provisions may include provisions for deferred repairs or deferred maintenance with a view to equalising the charge against profits from year to year. For example, the balance sheet of claymining company WATTS, BLAKE, BEARNE shows an amount described as 'Provision for deferred revenue expenditure' for repairs and overburden removal.

Contingent liabilities

A contingent liability is a potential liability which had not materialised by the date of the balance sheet. By their nature, contingent liabilities are insufficiently concrete to warrant specific provision being made for them in the accounts, and none is in fact made.

However, under the Fourth Schedule of the Companies Act 1985 a company must show by way of note or otherwise:

(a) any arrears of cumulative dividends (para. 49);

(b) particulars of any charge on the assets of the company to secure the liabilities of any other person, including, where practicable, the amount secured (para. 50 (1));

(c) the legal nature of any other contingent

OCEAN TRANSPORT & TRADING *Note to 1983 balance sheets*

Contingent liabilities

	Group		Parent company	
	£m			
	1983	1982	**1983**	1982
Guarantees in respect of shipbuilding and other loans and bank overdrafts of Overseas Containers Ltd, its subsidiaries and associated companies	**1.3**	1.8	**1.3**	1.8
Group's share of amount payable if a subsidiary of Overseas Containers Ltd is unsuccessful in resolving a dispute with the Inland Revenue	**4.1**	4.1	**4.1**	4.1
Guarantees on behalf of:				
Subsidiary companies	—	—	**47.0**	33.6
Associated companies	**0.3**	2.2	**0.3**	0.5
Other guarantees, mainly performance bonds	**11.0**	11.8	**—**	—
	16.7	19.9	**52.7**	40.0

Two ships (net book amount £6.1m) have been mortgaged as security for a loan of Overseas Containers Ltd.

---

liabilities not provided for, the estimated amount of those liabilities, and any security given (para. 50 (2)).

Examples of contingent liabilities include:

(*a*) bills of exchange discounted with bankers;
(*b*) guarantees given to banks and other parties;
(*c*) potential liabilities on claims (whether by court action or otherwise);
(*d*) goods sold under warranty or guarantee;
(*e*) any uncalled liability on shares held as investments (i.e. the unpaid portion of partly paid shares held).

The extract above from the 1983 accounts of OCEAN TRANSPORT & TRADING LTD will serve to illustrate this.

Note that the guarantees on behalf of subsidiary companies are nil in the group accounts. Parent companies often guarantee the borrowings of their subsidiaries, but as these borrowings appear in the group accounts as part of the debt of the group, no further liability can arise as far as the group is concerned.

Note also that items concerning Overseas Containers Ltd, which is an associated company of Ocean Transport & Trading, are shown separately from the contingent liabilities of other associated companies because of their material size.

Court actions
There is some reluctance in the United Kingdom to disclose potential liability in actions before the court, though this is normal practice in the United

States and is becoming more common in the United Kingdom. The note from TURNER & NEWALL's accounts illustrated here is an example of this.

TURNER & NEWALL *Note to the 1983 accounts*

The Company and certain subsidiaries are among more than 300 companies named as defendants in a large number of court actions concerned with alleged asbestos-related diseases in the USA and are among a number of defendants to claims in the UK from employees and former employees. Because of the slow onset of these diseases the directors expect that similar claims will be made in future years but the expenditure which may arise from such claims cannot be determined.

The significance of contingent liabilities
In many cases notes on contingent liabilities are of no real significance, for no liability is expected to arise, and none does. Occasionally, however, they are very important indeed, and points to watch for are a sharp rise in the total sums involved, and liabilities that may arise outside the normal course of business. In particular, experience suggests that any contingent liability (e.g. in the form of guarantees) in respect of an investment (e.g. a subsidiary) that has been disposed of can be particularly dangerous. For there is an implication either that the new owners are not prepared to give their guarantee, or that it is unacceptable to the other party – a definite sign of weakness. And to guarantee the liabilities of someone, or some

company, over which one has no control entails some risk. Guaranteeing the borrowings of associated companies may also be dangerous.

Capital commitments

Schedule 4, para. 50 (3) of the Companies Act 1985 requires that, where practicable, the aggregate amounts or estimated amounts, if they are material, of

(*a*) contracts for capital expenditure (not already provided for) *and*

(*b*) capital expenditure authorised by the directors, which has not been contracted for,

be shown by way of note, as the extract below from OCEAN TRANSPORT & TRADING shows.

Such a note provides *some* indication of the extent to which the directors plan to expand (or replace) the facilities of the group, and thus of the potential call upon its cash resources. It should be read in conjunction with the directors' report and chairman's statement and any press announcements by the company, but it is not a particularly reliable guide to cash flows unless it gives some information on timing. It is impossible to tell from the note below how long the various ships to which Ocean is committed will take to build, or when payments will fall due.

Other financial commitments

The Companies Act 1985 requires particulars to be given of any other financial commitments which have not been provided for and which are relevant to assessing the company's state of affairs (Sch. 4, para. 50 (5)). This requirement covers such things as leasing commitments, where the sums involved can be very large indeed, as illustrated by SHELL TRANSPORT AND TRADING's note on leasing arrangements, shown here.

SHELL TRANSPORT AND TRADING *Note to the 1984 accounts*

Leasing arrangements

The future minimum lease payments under operating leases that have initial or remaining terms in excess of one year, and capital leases together with the present value of the net minimum lease payments at December 31, 1984 were as follows:

	Operating leases	Capital leases
	£ million	
1985	606	139
1986	400	106
1987	330	97
1988	242	89
1989	188	79
1990 and after	1,370	401
Total minimum lease payments	3,136	911

· · · · · ·

The note distinguishes between operating leases and capital (finance) leases, which are explained below.

Leases

SSAP 21, *Accounting for leases and hire purchase contracts*, published in August 1984, divides leases into two types, *finance* leases and *operating* leases, and requires quite different accounting treatment for each type. A *finance* lease is defined as a lease which transfers substantially all the risks and rewards of ownership of an asset to the *lessee*. All other leases are *operating* leases.

Finance leases

Prior to SSAP 21 a company could enter into a finance lease instead of borrowing the money to

---

OCEAN TRANSPORT & TRADING LTD *Note on capital commitments, 1983 accounts*

Capital commitments

	£m			
	Group		Parent company	
	1983	1982	**1983**	1982
Capital expenditure for which contracts have been placed but which is not otherwise provided for in these accounts	**43.3**	50.7	**42.5**	39.5
Capital expenditure authorised by the Directors but for which contracts had not been placed at the balance sheet date	**11.3**	0.5	—	—

purchase an asset, and neither the asset nor the commitment to pay leasing charges would appear in the balance sheet. This was known as 'off-balance-sheet financing', which produced 'hidden gearing', as the company had effectively geared itself up just as much as if it had borrowed the money to purchase the asset, except that it had to pay leasing charges rather than paying interest and bearing depreciation charges.

SSAP 21 requires a finance lease to be recorded in the balance sheet of the lessee as an asset and as an obligation to pay future rentals. The initial sum to be recorded both as an asset and as a liability is the present value of the minimum lease payments, which is derived by discounting them at the interest rate implicit in the lease. The method of accounting is illustrated in Example 11.1.

Example 11.1   Accounting for a finance lease

A company acquires a small computer system on a finance lease. Lease payments are £10,000 p.a. for five years, with an option to continue the lease for a further five years at £1,000 p.a. Payments are made annually in advance, i.e. the first payment is made on taking delivery of the computer. The interest rate implicit in the lease is 10%, and the estimated useful life of the system is five years.

The *present value* of the minimum lease payments discounted at 10% p.a. can be calculated using figures from the table *Present value of 1 in n years' time* in Appendix 2:

Payment date	Present value of 1 (from table)	Present value of £10,000 payment
On delivery	1.0	£10,000
In 1 year	0.909	9,090
In 2 years	0.826	8,260
In 3 years	0.751	7,510
In 4 years	0.683	6,830
Present value of minimum lease payments		£41,690

The computer system will thus be recorded as an asset of £41,690 and the liability for future rental payments will also be recorded as £41,690. After the first year:

(a)   the asset will be depreciated over the shorter of the lease term (the initial period plus any further option period, i.e. a total of ten years in this case),

and its expected useful life (five years). Annual depreciation charge on a straight line basis is therefore one-fifth of £41,690 = £8,338, reducing the asset value to £33,352.

(b)   the present value of the remaining minimum lease payments is recomputed. There is no longer a payment due in four years' time (£6,830 in our table above), so the present value of future payments is now £41,690 − 6,830 = £34,860. £6,830 is deducted from the future liability and the remaining £3,170 of the £10,000 payment made on delivery is shown as interest paid.

These calculations would then be repeated each subsequent year:

End of year	Asset value	Remaining payments	Interest charge
1	£33,352	£34,860	£3,170
2	25,014	27,350	2,490
3	16,676	19,090	1,740
4	8,338	10,000	910
5	Nil	Nil	Nil

Operating leases

An operating lease is normally for a period substantially shorter than the expected useful life of an asset; i.e. the *lessor* retains most of the risks and rewards of ownership.

Under an operating lease the lease rentals are simply charged in the profit and loss account of the lessee as they arise. Leased assets and the liability for future payments do not appear in the balance sheet, even though companies can enter into operating leases of several years' length, as the extract from Shell Transport and Trading's accounts illustrated opposite.

Implementation of SSAP 21

Lessee companies are asked to adopt SSAP 21's accounting practices as soon as possible, but are not obliged to do so until accounting periods starting on or after 1 July 1987, so accounts published before the end of 1988 are likely to vary considerably in their treatment of finance leases. Companies are, however, required to disclose an analysis of their obligations under finance leases for each of the next five years from the balance sheet date and the aggregate amounts payable thereafter, for accounting periods beginning on or after 1 July 1984, so this will introduce some initial uniformity.

Chapter 12

TURNOVER, TRADING PROFIT AND PRE-TAX PROFIT

INTRODUCTION

As described briefly in Chapter 1, the profit and loss account, sometimes referred to as the revenue account, is a score-card of how the company has done over the last year (or whatever period is being reported on). It can conveniently be divided into three parts:

(*a*) how the profit (or loss) was earned;
(*b*) how much was taken by taxation;
(*c*) what happened to the profit (or loss) that was left after taxation.

This chapter covers the first part, and the next two chapters will cover the second and third parts.

How the profit was earned

The Companies Act 1985 offers the company the choice of four profit and loss account formats. Formats 1 and 2, shown in Examples 12.1 and 12.2, start with sales invoiced (turnover) and deduct operating costs to produce trading profit; they then add other income and deduct other charges to reach pre-tax profits. Formats 3 and 4, which are rarely used by listed companies, show charges and income separately, and are effectively two-sided versions of Formats 1 and 2.

The difference between Format 1 and Format 2 is the way they show operating costs. *Format 1* breaks down operating costs by function into:

Cost of sales (which will include all costs of production, such as factory wages, materials and manufacturing overheads, including depreciation of machinery)
Distribution costs (costs incurred in getting the goods to the customer)
Administrative expenses (e.g. directors' and auditors' fees, head office expenses)

Format 2, on the other hand, breaks down operating costs by their nature:

Raw materials and consumables
Staff costs
   Wages and salaries
   Social security costs
   Other pension costs
Depreciation and other amounts written off fixed assets
Other external charges
Change in stock of finished goods and work in progress

Example 12.1   Profit and loss account: Format 1

	£000	£000
Turnover		7,200
Cost of sales		3,600
Gross profit (or loss)		3,600
Distribution costs	1,100	
Administrative expenses	900	
		2,000
		1,600
Other operating income		50
[Trading profit]		1,650
Income from shares in related companies		40
Income from other fixed asset investments		5
Other interest receivable		120
		1,815
Amounts written off investments	15	
Interest payable	600	
		615
[Pre-tax profit on ordinary activities]		1,200

In Examples 12.1 and 12.2:

(a) the items in square brackets, 'Trading profit' and 'Pre-tax profit', have been included because they are important to the analyst, although they do not appear in the formats in Schedule 4 of the Companies Act 1985;

(b) the item 'Income from shares in group companies', which would appear in the profit and loss account of the holding company of a group, has been omitted because the profit and loss of a holding company is seldom if ever published (see Chapter 15);

(c) related companies and their contribution to the profit and loss account are described in Chapter 16.

Example 12.2   Profit and loss account: Format 2

	£000	£000
Turnover		7,200
Changes in stocks of finished goods and work in progress		160
Other operating income		50
		7,410
Raw materials and consumables	1,700	
Other external charges	1,120	
Staff costs		
Wages and salaries	2,050	
Social security costs	300	
Other pension costs	120	
Depreciation and other amounts written off tangible and intangible fixed assets	400	
Other operating charges	70	
		5,760
[Trading profit]		1,650
Income from shares in related companies		40
Income from other fixed asset investments		5
Other interest receivable		120
		1,815
Amounts written off investments	15	
Interest payable	600	
		615
[Pre-tax profit on ordinary activities]		1,200

The formats reflect the increased disclosure requirements of the EEC Fourth Directive, as a result of which the information gap which for-merly existed in UK accounts between turnover and profit has disappeared. In the past some companies included value added statements in their accounts to fill the gap, but they are now becoming increasingly rare.

Most retailers follow Format 1; manufacturing companies are divided fairly evenly between Formats 1 and 2, while some use a combination of both. For example, UNILEVER shows cost of sales, distribution and selling costs, and administrative expenses (i.e. Format 1) in the profit and loss account, and then gives a detailed breakdown of raw materials and packaging, staff costs, depreciation, etc. (i.e. Format 2) in a note.

Effect of accounting policies on profitability

Before going on to discuss individual components, it is worth noting three important points of interaction between the profit and loss account and the balance sheet, where abnormal accounting policies can materially alter the reported profits:

1. *Valuation of stock* The higher the value at the end of the period, the lower the cost of goods sold and the higher the profits.

2. *Depreciation* The lower the charge for depreciation in a particular year, the higher the book value of fixed assets carried forward and the higher the profits.

3. *Capitalising expenditure* All expenditure incurred by a company must either add to the value of the assets in the balance sheet or be charged in the profit and loss account. In the sense that it would otherwise be a charge against profits, any amount that can be capitalised will increase profits directly by the amount capitalised at the expense of the profits in future years, when increased capital values will require increased depreciation. Items which are sometimes capitalised include:

(a) research and development;
(b) interest;
(c) starting-up costs.

Research and development
Under SSAP 13, the standard accounting practice on research and development, all expenditure on research and development should normally be written off in the year in which it is incurred. However, where development is for clearly defined projects on which expenditure is separately identifiable and for which commercial success is reasonably certain, companies may if they wish defer charging development expenditure 'to the extent that its recovery can reasonably be regarded as assured'. Deferred development expenditure should be separately disclosed.

Interest

Capitalising interest on a project during construction is a normal and reasonable practice provided interest is not capitalised outside the planned timescale of the project. It would be reasonable, for example, to capitalise interest on a new refinery while it was being built, but not on the cost of the site before work had begun (it might lie undeveloped for years), nor on the overall cost once the refinery was completed but hadn't been put into production because demand for the product had slumped. For example, LADBROKE GROUP's accounting policies on interest charges are as follows:

(*a*) Interest accruing on certain hotel and holiday expenditure and film production to the date of availability for occupancy or exhibition is capitalised.

(*b*) Interest accruing on investment and dealing properties before full letting is capitalised to the extent that it exceeds income receivable, and provided that the capital value of each individual property does not thereby exceed its market value. Once fully let, all income and charges are taken through the profit and loss account.

Policy (*a*) is prudent, but policy (*b*) could raise difficulties if properties remain unlet, or only partially let with income falling short of interest payments. Interest is then capitalised up to 'market value', but market values are very much a matter of subjective judgement, and can fall disastrously, as many property companies discovered in the big shake-out in 1973/74.

Where capital is borrowed to finance the production of fixed and/or current assets, the Companies Act 1985 allows the interest charge incurred during the period of production to be included in the value of the assets, but if it is included, the amount must be separately disclosed (Sch. 4, para. 26 (3)). The annual accounts must state the amount of interest capitalised during the year (*Admission of Securities to Listing*, Section 5, Chapter 2, para. 21(g)). For example:

J. SAINSBURY *Note to 1984 accounts*

Tangible Fixed Assets

· · · · ·

The amount included in additions in respect of capitalised interest incurred in the year amounted to £1.3 million after deducting tax relief of £1.3 million. The capitalised amount brought forward from previous years was nil.

Starting-up costs

The starting-up costs of a new factory, including the costs of removal from old premises, the initial losses of a new unit (e.g. a hotel or supermarket), and the advertising, promotional and other expenses of launching a new product, should normally all be charged to revenue as they are incurred.

Where a company capitalises starting-up costs it may be expanding faster than is prudent, and if the new project fails to live up to expectations the company could run into serious trouble. An extreme example of capitalising starting-up costs is in PINEAPPLE DANCE STUDIOS' 1984 accounts, illustrated below. Had the expenditure incurred by Pineapple's US subsidiary before it started trading been charged to the profit and loss account, a reported group profit of £116,000 after tax would have become a loss of £197,000.

PINEAPPLE DANCE STUDIOS *Extracts from 1984 accounts*

	Notes	1984 £000	1983 £000
Profit and Loss Account			
Profit on ordinary activities before taxation		209	156
Taxation		(93)	4
Profit on ordinary activities after taxation		116	160
Consolidated Balance Sheet			
Intangible assets	13	313	—

Note 13

Expenditure incurred by Pineapple Broadway Inc. prior to its commencement of trade has been carried forward as an intangible fixed asset. This expenditure will be written off over a period, not exceeding five years, commencing with 1984/85, against the revenue to be generated by that operation and is not therefore treated as a realised loss for distribution purposes.

Consequences of abnormal accounting policies

If a company does overstate its profits in the year being reported on, the assets carried forward in the balance sheet will make future profits harder to earn: the opening stock for next year will be the figure for this year's overvalued closing stock, underdepreciated plant will wear out before it has been written off, and capitalised expenditure will inflate capital values, thus reducing the apparent return on capital employed and increasing the provision for depreciation. (Understating liabilities also has the same effect: profits for the year are inflated, but the liability will catch up with the company later on.)

The company's accounting policies, which appear either as 'Note 1' to the accounts, or as a separate statement, should be read carefully to see if there are any unusual features that might affect the company's reported profits. The statement should also point out any changes to policies, and companies are required to report 'any material respects in which any items shown in the profit and loss account are affected by any change in the basis of accounting' (CA 1985, Sch. 9, para. 18(6)(b)). For example, BLUE CIRCLE INDUSTRIES in 1983 reported that the group had discontinued its policy of providing additional depreciation to take account of inflation since the last fixed-asset valuations or since assets were acquired and the results for 1982 had been restated accordingly. The impact of this change had been to increase reported profits on ordinary activities by £20.9m (1982 £17.8m).

Any changes that are not explained, or that increase profits without reasonable accounting justification, should be viewed with caution, and with downright suspicion when 'new and thrusting' management is involved.

We now turn to the individual items on the profit and loss account.

SALES (TURNOVER)

Statutory requirements

Companies are required by the standard formats of the Companies Act 1985 to disclose turnover (i.e. total sales) in their profit and loss account. Turnover is defined as the amount derived from the provision of goods and services falling within the company's ordinary activities (after deduction of trade discounts and before adding VAT and other sales-based taxes, e.g. excise duty; Sch. 4, para. 95). The following information must also be given:

1. If a company carried out *two or more classes of business* during the year which in the directors' opinion differ substantially from each other, it must describe the classes and show each one's turnover and pre-tax profit (Sch. 4, para. 55(1)).
2. If in the year a company supplied *geographical markets* which in the directors' opinion differ substantially, the amount of turnover attributable to each must be stated unless, in their opinion, it would be seriously prejudicial to the interests of the company to do so (Sch. 4, para. 55(2) and (5)).

Stock Exchange requirements

The Stock Exchange's *Continuing Obligations* for listed companies require a listed company to circulate with the annual report of the directors a geographical analysis of turnover *and* of contribution to trading results of those trading operations carried on by the company (or group) outside the United Kingdom and Ireland. However, although companies are required to make shareholders 'aware of significant contributions derived from activities carried out in any one territory', 'No analysis of the contribution to trading results is required unless the contribution to profit and loss from a specific area is "abnormal" in nature'. (*Admission of Securities to Listing*, Section 5, Chapter 2, para. 21.2.)

Fortunately, most companies with extensive overseas operations do give a geographical analysis of trading results and some, like COPE ALLMAN (illustrated overleaf), also include an analysis of assets and of employees.

Analysis of profitability

The analyst can do a good deal of work upon an analysis such as Cope Allman's, calculating various ratios, using them to compare performance between products and between geographical areas, and seeing how they vary from year to year.

Note should also be taken of the directors' report or chairman's statement as, in a good set of accounts, these will contain comment on the reasons for marked changes in profitability, and may indicate future trends.

It can, for example, be calculated from Cope Allman's table that:

(*a*) the average return on assets employed, excluding divested businesses, improved very significantly from 12.9% in 1983 to 21.7% in 1984;

(*b*) operating profit on packaging was only 7.1% of sales in 1984, compared with 8.7% for the group as a whole, but it had improved sharply from 3.9% in 1983;

(*c*) although the turnover and operating profit of amusement machines both fell slightly, return on assets employed rose from 14.8% in 1983 to 16.3% in 1984, due to a sharp reduction in assets employed;

(*d*) sales per employee in 1984 were £26,830 in the United Kingdom, £34,482 in Europe and £78,858 in North America, although this analysis is slightly distorted because the company has analysed turnover geograph-

COPE ALLMAN *Note to 1984 accounts*

1. Segmental analysis

	Turnover 1984 £000	Turnover 1983 £000	Operating Profit 1984 £000	Operating Profit 1983 £000	Assets Employed 1984 £000	Assets Employed 1983 £000	Employees 1984 No.	Employees 1983 No.
(a) activity								
Packaging	100,909	83,115	7,172	3,210	37,648	32,516	2,726	2,814
Amusement machines	28,031	28,808	1,848	2,093	11,301	14,135	1,252	1,456
Engineering	28,157	23,514	4,619	2,667	14,035	15,266	771	770
	157,097	135,437	13,639	7,970	62,984	61,917	4,749	5,040
Divested businesses	5,268	21,787	105	(559)	—	2,299	35	297
Head Office	—	—	(1,287)	(1,252)	(817)	(1,174)	35	57
	162,365	157,224	12,457	6,159	62,167	63,042	4,819	5,394
(b) geographical*								
United Kingdom	88,432	89,856	7,107	3,304	38,468	43,161	3,296	3,654
Europe	42,551	37,789	2,685	1,837	14,924	13,375	1,234	1,277
North America	22,790	14,386	2,665	1,280	8,775	6,021	289	276
Rest of World	8,592	15,193	—	(262)	—	485	—	187
	162,365	157,224	12,457	6,159	62,167	63,042	4,819	5,394

*Turnover is analysed by market; other items are shown by location of business.

ically by market rather than by country of origin, so turnover in 'Rest of World' cannot be attributed to any particular employees;

(*e*) the activity with the highest return on assets in 1984 was engineering, 32.9%, which also achieved the highest operating profit margin on turnover, 16.4%;

(*f*) geographically the highest return on assets was in North America, 30.4%;

(*g*) head office expenses increased marginally, although employee numbers fell by 39%.

These facts can be linked with comments from the report, which should also cover future prospects:

(*h*) 'Packaging. *Cosmetic containers* . . . expected that the improving trend in margins will continue. *Tubes* . . . benefits of development and investment in new capacity. *Closures and containers* . . . principal gains in turnover and profitability in North America [see (*f*) above]. *Plastics distribution* . . . improved performance.' [Packaging looks set for further improvement in profits.]

(*i*) 'the reduction in profits in the amusement machine businesses is more than accounted for by special charges of £0.7m . . . cost of streamlining manufacturing production and of reducing the book value of machines in the

hiring business' [see (*c*) above]. '. . . manufacturing made a profit in the second half after an extended period of losses . . . continued pressure on rental income'. [Profits on manufacturing should increase significantly in 1985, but it will be difficult to do better on hiring.]

(*j*) 'Engineering. *Precision steel strip* . . . record profits mainly due to a very high demand in the USA and favourable dollar exchange rates.' [See (*e*) and (*f*) above; 1984 was an exceptionally good year that may not be repeated.]

(*k*) 'Head office costs include nearly £0.5m redundancy payments and other costs of a move to a smaller head office premises.' [See (*g*) above] 'Head office costs are now at a level almost 40% lower than last year.'

(*l*) 'L. J. Manson retired from the board on 17th October 1983 and M. A. Ashcroft was appointed to the board on that date.' [The old chairman has been replaced!]

Note that Cope Allman's table shows operating profit before the allocation of bank interest and central group expenses: in comparing one company's profitability with that of another it is important to ensure that like is being compared with like, i.e. that the treatment of bank and other interest and central expenses is the same in each case.

TRADING PROFIT

Trading profit does not appear in the formats in the Companies Act 1985, but we have included it because it enables the analyst to calculate two important ratios, Trading profit/Turnover and Trading profit/Capital employed (see Chapter 23).

In Format 1 we define trading profit as turnover *less*:

cost of sales
distribution costs
administrative expenses

plus other operating income.

In Format 2 it is turnover *less* all deductions up to and including other operating charges, *plus* other operating income (see Example 12.2).

As already explained, companies have the choice under the Companies Act 1985 of analysing expenditure (called in the formats themselves 'charges') functionally, i.e. as cost of sales, distribution costs and administrative expenses, or by its nature, e.g. raw materials and consumables, staff costs and so on. Staff costs are defined as wages and salaries, social security costs and pension costs (Sch. 4, para. 94).

The Act does not define cost of sales, distribution costs or administrative expenses.

Cost of sales will represent:
cost of materials consumed;
production wages (both directly on the product or service and those of an overhead nature);
depreciation of production machinery;
production expenses (e.g. rent and rates, light and heat).

Distribution costs will include:
distribution wages (i.e. staff costs of the distribution function);
distribution materials (packaging, etc.);
distribution expenses (e.g. depreciation of motor vans, freight, insurance).

Administrative expenses apparently cover all items not already included in the cost of sales or in distribution costs, and which are not separately disclosed (e.g. as interest) elsewhere in the standard format.

Other operating income will include income from normal operations which does not fall under any other heading, e.g. royalties and rents received. Net income from *rents of land* must be shown separately if it forms a substantial part of a company's revenue (CA 1985, Sch. 4, para. 53(5)).

Disclosure of supplementary information – statutory requirements

Schedule 5 of the 1985 Companies Act requires that the following be shown separately in the profit and loss account or in the notes annexed:

1. *Chairman's emoluments* for each person acting as chairman during the year, unless the duties were wholly or mainly discharged outside the United Kingdom (para. 24).
2. *Directors' emoluments*, including the aggregate amount of pensions and of compensation for loss of office paid to past and present directors (paras. 28 and 29); the number of directors who fall into each band of £5,000, i.e. between £0 and £5,000, £5,001 and £10,000 and so on (para. 25); the number of directors who have waived rights to receive emoluments, and the aggregate amount waived (para. 27).
3. *Employees' emoluments:* the number of employees with emoluments of £30,000 or more, shown in bands of £5,000 (para. 35).

Emoluments of directors and employees working wholly or mainly outside the United Kingdom are excluded.

Most companies combine the information required by items 1 to 3 above into one note, and a few show emoluments both before and *after* tax.

4. *Particulars of staff:* the average number employed during the year, and the aggregate amounts of their (a) wages and salaries, (b) social security costs, (c) other pension costs (CA 1985, Sch. 4, para. 56).
5. *Auditors' remuneration.* This includes expenses (CA 1985, Sch. 4, para. 53(7)). A sharp increase in the auditors' remuneration (i.e. more than merely keeping pace with inflation) may be an indication of accounting difficulties within the company, although the extra work involved in these circumstances can be billed separately as fees for professional advice and thus avoid disclosure or, where a marked increase is shown, the company's problems may have become more conspicuously apparent in other ways. For example in 1974, the year in which FIRST NATIONAL FINANCE CORPORATION plunged from pre-tax profits of about £18 million to a loss of £6 million, the auditors' remuneration jumped 48%, having gone up less than 20% in the previous year.

6. *Hire of plant and machinery:* to be shown if material (CA 1985, Sch. 4, para. 53(6)). There are basically two types of hiring or leasing: the first is where equipment is hired on a temporary basis and can be returned when no longer required (an *operating lease*); the second type is where equipment is leased for its useful life (a *finance lease*, which has to be capitalised in the balance sheet, see Chapter 11). Some companies incur substantial hire charges on finance leases as part of a deliberate policy to reduce the amount of capital tied up in fixed assets and to take advantage of the favourable terms a lessor offers. The lessor is able to offer favourable terms on finance leases because he receives the benefit of the capital allowances on the assets leased, which help to defer his Corporation Tax liability (see Chapter 13).

However, extensive finance leasing may also reflect a shortage of cash – the company resorts to leasing because it can't afford the capital outlay.

7. *Depreciation* and diminution in value of fixed assets (see Chapter 6). In Format 1 depreciation is not shown as a separate item, but in all formats the amount provided during the year will be found in the balance sheet note on fixed assets.

OTHER PRE-TAX ITEMS

Investment income

Statutory requirements
Companies must distinguish in their profit and loss account (or in the notes) between income from quoted investments and that from unquoted investments (CA 1985, Sch. 4, para. 53(4)). Until 1967 it was necessary to distinguish between income from trade investments and other investments, and some companies continue to do this. A *trade investment* is an investment made for a trade reason, rather than purely as a means of earning income. It might, for example, be an investment in a supplier (to help the supplier, to obtain information, or to act as a lever in dealing with him), in a competitor, or in a customer.

Franked and unfranked income
Investment income may be *franked* (dividends paid by another UK company out of profits which have already borne UK Corporation Tax) or *unfranked* (received from a source that has not borne UK Corporation Tax, which includes almost all types of interest received and any dividends from overseas companies). Under SSAP 8, incoming dividends from UK resident companies should be included before tax in the profit and loss account at the amount of cash received or receivable plus the tax credit (see Chapter 13).

Interest paid

The cost of servicing (paying the interest on) all debt is normally allowed to be deducted before profits are assessed for Corporation Tax.

The Companies Act 1985 (Sch. 4, para. 53(2)) requires the disclosure of the interest paid on bank loans and overdrafts, on loans repayable within five years both by instalments or otherwise, and on other loans. Most companies show a single figure in their profit and loss account, giving details in a note which may include some netting out of interest received or other adjustments, as, for example, in the note from RIO TINTO-ZINC's accounts shown here.

RIO TINTO-ZINC *Note on interest payable*

Interest payable	£ million 1983	£ million 1982
Interest paid on borrowings by the Group:		
Loans not wholly repayable within 5 years	120.0	94.7
Loans wholly repayable within 5 years	55.1	46.1
Bank overdrafts	17.8	20.7
Short-term borrowings	5.4	1.6
	198.3	163.1
Less: Amount capitalised relating to projects during construction	28.8	15.4
	169.5	147.7

Profit before taxation

As shown in Examples 12.1 and 12.2, trading profit *plus* income from shares in related companies (see Chapter 16), *plus* income from other investments and other interest receivable, *less* interest payable and any amounts written off investments, leaves the profit before taxation, or 'pre-tax profits'.

Chapter 13

TAXATION

(References: SSAP 8 *Taxation under the Imputation System*; SSAP 15 *Accounting for Deferred Taxation*.)

INTRODUCTION

A UK resident company is liable to Corporation Tax on its income and capital gains, and has to pay Advance Corporation Tax (ACT) when it distributes dividends. If it has income taxable abroad, it will also suffer overseas tax. All this appears in the profit and loss account under the heading 'Taxation'.

VAT, Excise Duty, employee PAYE and other forms of taxation that the company may bear or be involved in are not normally shown, though some companies give supplementary information on their role as unpaid tax collectors; for example, MARKS & SPENCER devotes half a page of its report to taxes it has been obliged to collect during the year, while other companies give details of government charges peculiar to their business (e.g. LADBROKE shows that its operating profit is stated after charging so much 'betting, bingo and machine duties and betting levy').

Schedule 4 of the Companies Act 1985 requires taxation to be shown in *the profit and loss account* under three headings:

1. Tax on profit or loss from ordinary activities
2. Tax on extraordinary profit or loss

3. Other taxes not shown under the above

with notes giving details of the basis of computation, any special circumstances affecting the tax liability, and:

(a) the amount of UK corporation tax,
(b) the extent of double taxation relief,
(c) the amount of UK income tax, *and*
(d) the amount of foreign tax charged to revenue.

The notes may also include details of:

(e) irrecoverable ACT
(f) over/under provision for prior years' taxation
(g) deferred taxation
(h) tax credit on UK dividends received (i.e. on franked investment income)
(i) taxation on share of profit of associated companies (see Chapter 16).

Items (e), (g) and (h) are required by SSAP 8.

TRAFALGAR HOUSE's profit and loss account illustrates a typical presentation of a fairly complex tax charge:

TRAFALGAR HOUSE *Extract from 1984 accounts*

Profit and loss account

	Notes	Year ended 30 September 1984 £000	Year ended 30 September 1983 £000
Profit on ordinary activities before taxation		113,153	79,034
Taxation	6	28,288	18,226

Note 6 Taxation

	1984 £000	**1983** £000
The charge for taxation based on the net profit is arrived at as follows:		
UK corporation tax at 47½% (1983 52%)	2,384	4,199
Less Double taxation relief	1,726	2,145
	658	2,054
Transfer to UK deferred taxation	15,612	10,551
Transfer to overseas deferred taxation	118	783
Tax credit on franked investment income	776	186
Overseas tax	2,469	3,779
Related companies	2,776	986
Petroleum Revenue Tax	7,003	—
Development Land Tax	588	—
Tax over-provided in earlier years	(1,712)	(113)
	28,288	18,226

The UK corporation tax charge for the year has been reduced because of accelerated depreciation and stock relief.

In the *balance sheet* taxation will appear as follows:

1. Under creditors falling due within one year: the amount falling due within one year will normally include one year's mainstream Corporation Tax, ACT on any dividends recently paid, ACT on any proposed dividends, and any foreign tax due.
2. Under creditors falling due after more than one year: companies which traded before April 1965 may not be liable to pay Corporation Tax on the profits of a period until more than one year later (see page 84). Also included may be overdue tax which is in dispute.
3. Under provisions: deferred taxation and any tax where the amount is uncertain.
4. Under assets: ACT paid and payable which has not yet been offset against the company's CT liability (unrelieved ACT is normally offset against deferred tax, and only occasionally appears separately as an asset).

Corporation Tax – the imputation system

Corporation Tax was introduced by the Finance Act 1965 to replace a somewhat complex system under which companies suffered two taxes: Income Tax and Profits Tax. Corporation Tax was subsequently modified from 1 April 1973 by the introduction of the imputation system.

Under the imputation system, whenever a company pays dividends to shareholders, it is required to hand over to the Inland Revenue what is

Example 13.1 Corporation Tax: different levels of dividend distribution

	No dividend £000	*Some dividend* £000	*Maximum dividend* £000
Pre-tax profits	700	700	700
Total Corporation Tax (50%)	350	350	350
	350	350	350
Dividends (net; 10m shares in issue)	Nil	175	350
Retentions	350	175	Nil
Net dividend per share	Nil	1.75p	3.5p
Associated tax credit (30/70ths)		0.75p	1.5p
Gross dividend equivalent	Nil	2.5p	5.0p
Government receives:	£000	£000	£000
Advance Corporation Tax	Nil	75	150
Mainstream tax	350	275	200
Total tax	350	350	350

termed *Advance Corporation Tax* (ACT), which is, *in effect*, the basic rate of Income Tax (*x*%) that would be payable on the dividends if they were grossed up at the basic rate.

The amount of ACT payable is thus a given fraction, $x/(100 - x)$ of the dividend actually paid, where *x*% is the basic rate of Income Tax. For example, if the basic rate of Income Tax is 30%, ACT will be 30/70ths of the actual dividend paid. ACT serves two purposes:

1. It is a part payment of the company's Corporation Tax liability for the period in which the dividend is paid. (The remaining Corporation Tax payable is known as *mainstream Corporation Tax*.)
2. In addition, it is 'imputed' to the shareholder as a *tax credit* which exactly discharges the basic rate UK Income Tax liability on the dividend. So far as the tax inspector is concerned, the shareholder's income from the company is the sum of the (net) dividend plus the tax credit. This sum of the (net) dividend plus the tax credit is usually referred to as the 'gross equivalent', and it is on the gross equivalent that the dividend yield on a share is calculated.

The total amount of tax the government receives from a company operating mainly or solely in the United Kingdom is *normally* independent of the amount of dividends paid, as Example 13.1 shows.

Tax years and rates of tax

The *fiscal* (Income Tax) *year* runs from 6 April to 5 April and is referred to by stating both years, e.g. Income Tax year 1985/86 is the year from 6 April 1985 to 5 April 1986.

The *financial year* (FY) runs from 1 April to 31 March and is referred to by the year in which it *starts*, e.g. financial year 1985 is the year from 1 April 1985 to 31 March 1986. The rate of Corporation Tax for each financial year used to be set in the Budget at the *end* of the financial year, but in March 1984 the Chancellor announced the rate for the past year (FY 1983) and for the *following three years*.

The tax rates since the imputation system was introduced are shown below:

Financial year (FY)	Corporation Tax rate	Basic rate of Income Tax (6 April)	ACT as fraction of dividend
1973	52% (Note)	30%	30/70ths
1974	52%	33%	33/67ths
1975 and 1976	52%	35%	35/65ths
1977	52%	34%	34/66ths
1978	52%	33%	33/67ths
1979 to 1982	52%	30%	30/70ths
1983	50%	30%	30/70ths
1984	45%	30%	30/70ths
1985	40%	30%	30/70ths
1986	35%		

Note: If a company's accounting year falls partly in one financial year and partly in the next, the profits are divided between the two financial years on a time basis and bear Corporation Tax at the appropriate rate for each financial year. The rate of ACT, however, is the rate of ACT at the date of dividend payment (*not* the rate at the date the dividend was declared *nor* the rate in force in the period in respect of which the dividend is being paid).

If a company's taxable profits (income and capital gains) do not exceed £100,000 in a year, its income is subject to a lower rate of Corporation Tax, the *small companies* rate, set at 30% for 1983 to 1986. There is also marginal relief for companies with profits of between £100,000 and £500,000, but this relief will disappear when the standard rate of Corporation Tax falls to 35%.

CORPORATION TAX WITH NO DISTRIBUTION OF DIVIDENDS

Before we get any further involved in the complications of ACT, let us first deal with how the amount of Corporation Tax chargeable to a company is worked out, assuming that the company pays no dividends. This is the calculation of tax and after-tax earnings on what is called the 'nil distribution' basis, i.e. no distribution of dividends.

Inland Revenue's assessment of Corporation Tax

There are several reasons why the tax charge

shown in the profit and loss account may not be 'normal', i.e. may differ from what the layman might expect, namely, pre-tax profits × average rate of Corporation Tax during the company's accounting year. The amount of Corporation Tax payable depends not on the company's pre-tax profit figure, but on the assessment made by the Inland Revenue. The tax charge varies not only because of differences that arise between the taxable profit and the profit shown in the company's accounts (the 'book profit'), but because of differences in rate.

The differences fall into three categories:

1. *Permanent differences*, where expenses are disallowed or income is tax-free or is taxed at a rate other than that of UK Corporation Tax (see page 79).
2. *Timing differences*, where the company may be liable to pay the full rate of tax at some time, but not in the year being reported upon.
3. *Previous years*, where the effect of losses and/or unrelieved ACT carried forward can materially reduce the tax charge for the year (see page 81).

Easily the most important difference in most companies is the timing difference caused by depreciation (in the company's accounts) not being the same as the capital allowances applied by the tax inspector, although timing differences will be greatly reduced by the phasing out of first-year allowances.

Depreciation and capital allowances

Different classes of asset have long been treated quite differently for tax purposes. For some, like commercial buildings, there has never been any form of depreciation, or as the Revenue terms them 'capital allowances'. Others have been treated particularly generously (e.g. plant and machinery), or more harshly than similar assets (e.g. expensive private motor cars).

The rules and rates of allowance are subject to periodic change, depending on whether the government wishes to be seen to encourage, or discourage, capital expenditure.

Until recently, most (but not all) classes of asset on which capital allowances were available were granted in the year of purchase either a first-year allowance (deductible from cost in computing writing-down allowances) or an initial allowance.

Under reforms made by the Finance Act 1984 most first-year and initial allowances are being phased out and will disappear by 31 March 1986, except for business buildings in Enterprise Zones. When the process is complete, only writing-down allowances will be available elsewhere.

The effect of the change is considerable. To take industrial buildings:

	Initial allowance	Writing-down allowance
To 13 March 1984	75%	4% p.a. straight line
14 March 1984– 31 March 1985	50%	4% p.a. straight line
1 April 1985– 31 March 1986	25%	4% p.a. straight line
After 31 March 1986	nil	4% p.a. straight line

Thus a company which incurred expenditure of £500,000 on an industrial building on, say, 1 March 1984 would be able to deduct from that year's profits:

	£
Initial allowance (75%)	375,000
Writing-down allowance (4%)	20,000
	£395,000

whereas if it did so on 1 April 1986 it would be able to deduct only:

Writing-down allowance (4%)	£20,000

The effect of the change is even more marked in the case of plant and machinery which, from 22 March 1972 to 13 March 1984, was generally eligible for a 100% first-year allowance in the year of purchase. The 100% first-year allowance is reduced for expenditure incurred:

	First-year allowance
14 March 1984–31 March 1985	75%
1 April 1985–31 March 1986	50%
After 31 March 1986	nil

and a writing-down allowance is given in subsequent years at 25% p.a. on a reducing balance basis. After 31 March 1986 a writing-down allowance will be available in the year of purchase. because there will be no first-year allowance. Whereas a company which purchased a computer on 1 March 1984 for £400,000 would have been able to deduct the entire cost against profits of the accounting period of purchase, one which did so on 1 April 1986 would be able to deduct only £100,000 in the year of purchase; £75,000 in year 2; £56,250 in year 3; and so on.

Example of a timing difference

A company will have a subnormal tax charge if the capital allowances received for the year are greater than the amount the company provides for depreciation, as Example 13.2 illustrates.

Example 13.2   Depreciation and capital allowances

If a company invested £1 million in plant and machinery in 1978, and used straight line depreciation spread over an anticipated five-year life, the capital allowances and depreciation would have been:

	Capital allowance £	Depreciation £
1978	1,000,000	200,000
1979	Nil	200,000
1980	Nil	200,000
1981	Nil	200,000
1982	Nil	200,000
Total	1,000,000	1,000,000

If the company made taxable trading profits of £1 million in each of the five years and we ignore all other allowances for the purpose of illustration, the Corporation Tax payable at 52% would have been:

	Taxable profit £	Corporation Tax liability £
1978	Nil	Nil
1979	1,000,000	520,000
1980	1,000,000	520,000
1981	1,000,000	520,000
1982	1,000,000	520,000
Total	4,000,000	2,080,000

Had capital allowances been the same as depreciation the figures would have been:

	Taxable profit £	Corporation Tax liability £
1978	800,000	416,000
1979	800,000	416,000
1980	800,000	416,000
1981	800,000	416,000
1982	800,000	416,000
Total	4,000,000	2,080,000

Deferred taxation

In order to remove the effect of timing differences from the profit and loss account, i.e. to allow for deferred tax liability, companies transfer to a Deferred Tax Account a sum equal to the difference between the Corporation Tax actually payable on taxable trading profits and the tax that would have been payable if the capital allowances had equalled the depreciation shown in the company's accounts.

In Example 13.2, the deferred tax would *originate* in 1978 and would be shown in the company's accounts for 1978 as:

Profit and loss account	£000
Pre-tax profits	800
Tax (see Note)	416
Profits after tax	384

Note

Corporation Tax payable	Nil
Transfer to provision for deferred tax	416
Total tax charge	416

The deferred tax thus originated is then added to the accumulated figure for 'deferred tax' in the balance sheet.

In the years 1979 to 1982 the effect of the timing difference would have been *reversed*, in that more tax would be payable than the tax charge shown in the profit and loss account; the transfer would have been from the deferred tax account, reducing the balance in the account to zero at the end of 1982, and the Note in each of those four years would read:

Corporation Tax payable	£520,000
Transfer from deferred tax	£104,000
Total tax charge	£416,000

Accounting for deferred taxation

In 1975 the Accounting Standards Committee proposed to make it obligatory for all companies to account for deferred taxation on all material timing differences, as this is quite clearly the prudent thing to do for two reasons:

(*a*)   the system of capital allowances might change adversely (as it did in 1984);

(*b*)   a company falling on hard times could find itself with an onerous tax charge if it has to cut back heavily on capital expenditure.

However, the proposal met with considerable opposition and, as the result of representations from the CBI and others, it was decided to allow companies to exclude from their provisions for deferred tax 'any tax effects which can be demonstrated with reasonable probability to continue for the future . . . if no liability is likely to arise as a result of reversal of timing differences for some considerable period (at least three years) ahead and that there is no indication that after this period the situation is likely to change so as to crystallise the liabilities' (SSAP 15, para. 28). Where these criteria are not fully satisfied 'it may be appropriate to provide only part of the full potential deferred taxation' (SSAP 15, para. 30), so the scope for differences of treatment from company to company is enormous.

The folly of ignoring the concept of prudence eventually caught up with company accounts when, in the 1984 Budget, the timing of capital allowances was radically altered with the phasing out of first-year allowances. As a result most companies had to make a substantial transfer to their deferred tax account, and in some cases the transfers were very large indeed, as the extracts from the ROYAL BANK OF SCOTLAND's 1984 accounts illustrate:

ROYAL BANK OF SCOTLAND GROUP *Effect of 1984 Budget on deferred tax provisions*

Consolidated profit and loss account

	Note	£m	1983 £m
Profit before extraordinary items		72.4	95.1
Extraordinary items	8		
Profits less losses on disposals		25.1	(1.6)
Provisions required for corporation tax changes		(177.7)	—
Transfer from reserves		177.7	—
Profit attributable to ordinary shareholders		97.5	93.5

Note 8 Extraordinary items

Profits less losses on disposals . . .
Provisions required for corporation tax changes as a result of the Finance Act 1984:
The company and subsidiaries:

Deferred taxation	(102.9)	—
Provision for tax variations on leases	(32.2)	—
	(145.5)	—
Share of associated companies	(32.2)	—
	(177.7)	—

Analysts should be sceptical where after-tax profits have been increased by reducing or omitting provision for deferred taxation, and in these cases it is recommended that a standard tax charge should normally be applied in calculating earnings per share (see page 183).

Methods of accounting for deferred taxation

SSAP 11, which preceded SSAP 15, defined two permitted methods of accounting for deferred taxation:

1. *The deferral method*, where amounts taken to the deferred tax account at the rate of Corporation Tax at the time remain unchanged despite any subsequent changes, so that reversals take place at the same, original rate.
2. *The liability method*, where deferred balances are maintained at the current rate of tax, so

that the balance has to be adjusted when the rate of Corporation Tax changes.

SSAP 11 called upon companies to state which method they were using for deferred tax in their note on accounting polices, although as the rate of tax remained at 52% from 1973 to 1982 it made no difference which was used. Some companies still state which method they use (as in MARKS & SPENCER's 1984 accounts, shown here).

MARKS & SPENCER *1984 accounts*

Deferred taxation is provided on the liability method, unless there is reasonable probability that such liability will not arise in the foreseeable future . . .

SSAP 15 implies that the liability method should be used, in that it requires adjustments to the deferred taxation account resulting from a change in the rate of taxation to be separately disclosed, and major adjustments due to fundamental changes in the tax system to be treated as an extraordinary item. Most companies now use the liability method.

Other uses of the deferred taxation account

In addition to differences between capital allowances and depreciation, timing differences requiring deferred tax treatment also arise over the following items.

Accruals

Certain items of expenditure or income (e.g. debenture interest) are accrued in the accounts but are not included for tax purposes until paid or received. SSAP 15 calls for the provision for deferred taxation on these.

Revaluation of assets

If the surplus on revaluation is written into the accounts, SSAP 15 requires that a provision for taxation should be made out of the revaluation surplus as soon as a liability is foreseen, usually at the time a company decides in principle to dispose of the asset. If a company's year end falls after the decision in principle but before the actual disposal, the provision for taxation would be included in deferred tax, but these circumstances rarely arise.

Asset sales

When an asset is sold, any excess of proceeds over original cost is subject to tax at the rate applicable to capital gains (Example 13.3).

Example 13.3   Sale proceeds exceed original cost

An industrial building which cost £1.3 million is sold in April 1985 for £2.3 million. The gain of £1 million will be subject to Corporation Tax of:

30/40ths of 40% of £1 million = £300,000

Where an industrial building is sold, the proceeds of sale are compared with the tax written-down value; if the proceeds exceed the tax written-down value a balancing charge is made, or if they are less a balancing allowance is given. Balancing charges are added to taxable profits, and balancing allowances are deducted from taxable profits. The balancing charge (or balancing allowance) represents the difference between the sale proceeds (or cost if that is less) and the tax written-down value (see Example 13.4).

Example 13.4   Computation of balancing charge

If the building in Example 13.3 had a written-down value for tax purposes at the time of sale of £0.5 million, the balancing charge would be:

(Proceeds of sale or cost, whichever is the less) – Tax written-down value = £1.3 million − £0.5 million = £0.8 million

and the company's taxable profits would be increased by £0.8 million. Tax on this £0.8 million would be in addition to the tax on the capital gain in Example 13.3.

In the case of plant and machinery (but not assets leased to non-traders, or cars), a 'pool' is maintained of plant available for writing-down allowances. Where such assets are sold, the proceeds of sale (or their cost if less) are simply deducted from the pool; there is normally no balancing allowance or balancing charge. If a company disposes of a building at a profit and purchases another, it can obtain what is known as 'rollover relief' by electing to have the gain arising on the disposal deducted from the cost of the new building rather than paying tax on it (Example 13.5).

Example 13.5   Rollover relief

If freehold premises costing £200,000 were sold for £250,000, and new premises were bought for £375,000, a company could defer payment of tax on the £50,000 gain by electing to deduct £50,000 from the cost of the new premises. However, if the new premises were subsequently sold for, say, £400,000, tax would be assessed on the gain of £400,000 less (£375,000 − £50,000), i.e. on £75,000.

The relief is subject to a number of conditions. SSAP 15 does not normally require provision for deferred tax where advantage has been taken of rollover relief.

Further reasons for 'abnormal' tax charges – permanent differences

Permanent differences, the effects of which are not of course offset by provisions for deferred tax, include the following items:

Disallowed expenses

Some items, such as the cost of entertaining UK customers, are charged by companies to their profit and loss account thus reducing pre-tax profits, but are not allowed as expenses by the Inland Revenue in calculating taxable profits. This causes the tax charge to appear higher than 'normal'.

Franked income

This is income that has already borne Corporation Tax, i.e. dividends received from other UK companies. Franked income is *not* subject to Corporation Tax a second time, which means that companies receiving dividends can pass them straight through to their shareholders, together with the tax credits, without incurring any further tax. Thus the gross value of franked income to a *company* is normally the dividend received grossed up at the Corporation Tax rate rather than at the basic rate of Income Tax.

SSAP 8 requires the sum of dividends plus tax credits to be brought in at the pre-tax level and an amount equal to the tax credits to be included in the taxation charge. For example, if a company's only taxable income was £700,000 in dividends from other companies, together with associated tax credits of £300,000, the profit and loss account would show:

Pre-tax profits	£1,000,000
Taxation	300,000
Profits after tax	700,000

and the apparent tax rate would be 30%.

Capital gains

Unless a company's capital gains are treated as an extraordinary item, the tax payable on them is included in the Corporation Tax charge, but is effectively charged at the Capital Gains Tax rate. Thus if a company's sole taxable profit for the year was £1,000,000 of capital gains made in the normal course of business, the profit and loss account would show:

Pre-tax profits	£1,000,000
Taxation	300,000
Profits after tax	700,000

and the apparent tax rate would be 30%.

Gains and losses on loans

Gains on loans are not subject to Corporation Tax, and losses on loans are not deductible as expenses. For example, if a company issued a loan stock at £99% and subsequently bought it in for cancellation at £95%, neither the £1% loss on issue nor the £5% gain on repurchase would be included in the calculation of the company's Corporation Tax charge.

Losses

Where a company makes a loss, it may carry that loss back for up to two years to recover Corporation Tax previously paid or, failing that, can carry the loss forward indefinitely to offset against future profits. However:

(*a*)   Losses by UK-resident subsidiaries cannot be offset against profits elsewhere in the group unless the subsidiary is at least 75% owned by the parent company. If the loss-making subsidiary is less than 75% owned, the group's tax charge will appear abnormally high, but the losses can be carried forward within the subsidiary and, if and when subsequently matched against future profits, the effect on the group's tax charge will be reversed.

(*b*)   Losses by non-resident subsidiaries cannot be offset against UK profits for tax purposes, but they can be carried forward as in (*a*), with the same effect.

(*c*)   Capital losses, for example the loss on sale of investments, cannot be offset against trading profits.

Stock relief

Stock relief was introduced by the Finance Act 1975 as a temporary measure to stop companies being taxed both unfairly and penally on the increase in value of stocks caused by inflation, then running at over 20%. Subsequently, it was put on a more permanent basis, and in 1981 it was recast to relate the relief to increases in the All Stocks Index rather than to increases in the value of stocks held during a period of account.

With inflation falling to around 5% p.a., the Finance Act 1984 abolished stock relief for any period beginning after 12 March 1984.

Small companies rate

Small companies pay Corporation Tax on income at a lower rate. Up to 31 March 1983 the rate was 38%; it was reduced for the year to 31 March 1984 and subsequent years to 30%. It applies to companies with taxable profits (income and capital gains) up to £100,000, but there is marginal relief where profits fall between £100,000 and £500,000, although this relief will disappear when the standard rate of Corporation Tax falls to 35%.

Chargeable gains realised by a small company are not charged at the small companies rate, but at the full rate. But the amount of the gain is, as with other companies, reduced by a fraction which gives an effective tax charge of 30%.

Under- or over-provision for prior years

SSAP 6 requires that normal adjustments of estimates made in prior years should be included in the profit and loss account (see Chapter 14). This can have a significant effect on the reported profit or loss after tax, as is shown, for example, by the 1982 accounts of UBM, the United Kingdom's largest builders' merchants.

UBM *1982 accounts*

	£000
Loss before taxation	(2,032)
Taxation	1,370
Loss after taxation	662
(Loss) Earnings per ordinary share	(1.6)p

Their note on taxation showed that the tax relief was arrived at after 'Adjustment in respect of previous years (987)'. But for this, the loss after taxation would have been more than doubled and the loss per share would have increased to 4.0p.

Overseas income

1.   Overseas income of non-resident subsidiaries is not liable to UK taxation; it bears only foreign tax. The foreign tax may be at an appreciably lower rate than UK Corporation Tax, particularly in countries such as Ireland, which give foreign companies several years of tax holidays to encourage them to set up subsidiaries there.

2.   Dividends, interest or royalties remitted to the United Kingdom from certain countries, including the United States, may bear a further 'withholding tax'.

3.   Overseas income of a UK-resident company is liable to UK tax whether remitted or not.

4.   Double taxation relief (DTR) is given for overseas tax on income liable to UK tax, so overseas earnings that are remitted to the United Kingdom by overseas subsidiaries normally bear no UK tax if the foreign tax has already been borne at a rate equal to or greater than UK Corporation Tax. If the foreign tax is lower, only the difference is payable in the United Kingdom, but in both cases this is only true for foreign taxes of an income nature (taxes of a capital nature do not qualify for relief). Example 13.6 illus-

trates the way in which double taxation relief is applied:

Example 13.6   Double taxation relief

A UK holding company which does not itself trade has one overseas subsidiary, whose profit and loss account shows:

	£000
Pre-tax profits	1,000
Tax paid at 40%	400
	600
Dividends	400
Retentions	200

The UK holding company's £400,000 dividends are subject to 15% withholding tax (£60,000) on remission, so the UK company actually receives £340,000.

For UK tax purposes the holding company's dividend is grossed up:

	£000
Dividend from subsidiary	400
Associated foreign tax at 40%	266
Gross income from subsidiary	666

UK tax is then calculated:

	£000
Corporation Tax 50% on £666,000	333
less DTR, which is the *lesser* of	
(a) Tax paid on £340,000 net £266,000 + £60,000 = £326,000	326
(b) UK Corporation Tax liability of £333,000	
Tax payable in the UK	7

The UK holding company's profit and loss account would show:

	£000	£000
Pre-tax profits		1,000
UK Corporation Tax	333	
DTR	326	
	7	
Overseas tax	400	
Withholding tax	60	
		467
Profit after tax		533

Effect of previous years

Not many listed companies have substantial accumulated losses and/or unrelieved ACT to carry forward, but when they have the effect on the tax charge can be dramatic. COURTAULDS, for instance, showed UK Corporation Tax of £0.2m in 1984 on a UK operating profit of £79m explaining, in a note, that 'The Group's taxation position has benefited from the effects of UK capital allowances exceeding depreciation charged in the accounts and . . . tax losses to be carried forward to be offset against future profits have decreased during the year to £92.9m (1983 £123.6m).'

Courtaulds also made it quite clear that it had no intention of resuming any provision for deferred tax in the United Kingdom, which it had discontinued making in 1972, and defended its position by showing the tax reliefs it still had available in a note:

COURTAULDS *Provisions for liabilities and charges*

. . .

At 31 March 1984, tax reliefs available for offset against future UK trading profits and deferred tax on related timing differences, both calculated at the future rates of corporation tax proposed in the Finance (No. 2) Bill 1984, are as shown below. The comparative figures at 31 March 1983 have been calculated at 52%.

	1984 £m	1983 £m
UK capital allowances	(53.6)	(64.7)
Other UK and overseas timing differences	7.7	11.1
UK unused tax losses	38.2	64.3
ACT recoverable	57.2	51.9
	49.5	62.6

However, tax reliefs brought forward will eventually get used up, so it is recommended that, in comparing a company like Courtaulds with other companies, the standard rate of Corporation Tax should normally be applied to UK profits.

CORPORATION TAX WITH DIVIDEND DISTRIBUTION

We have so far dealt with factors affecting the amount of tax a company pays if no dividends are paid.

The distribution of dividends affects the company's overall tax liability if:

(a) the distribution is very high,

(b) a large proportion of the company's earnings comes from overseas and bears foreign tax at anything more than a modest rate.

In either case ACT may be unrelieved.

Limitations on the use of ACT

ACT can be set off against Corporation Tax liability on trading and on unfranked investment income. But it cannot reduce the mainstream Corporation Tax (referred to from now on as 'mainstream tax') on income arising in the United Kingdom in any year below a minimum rate of (Corporation Tax rate − basic rate of Income Tax), as illustrated in Example 13.7.

Example 13.7 Unrelieved ACT due to high dividend distribution

In the financial year 1983 tax rates were as follows:

Corporation Tax rate	50%
Basic rate of Income Tax	30%
So, minimum rate of mainstream tax was	20%

In that year, if a company operating solely in the United Kingdom distributed £770,000, considerably more than its profits after tax of £500,000 (perhaps to maintain its dividend in a poor year), it would suffer unrelieved ACT as follows:

	£
Pre-tax profit	1,000,000
Corporation Tax (50%)	500,000
	500,000
Dividends paid	770,000
ACT paid (30/70ths of £770,000)	330,000
Minimum mainstream tax (20%)	200,000
ACT set off	300,000
	500,000
Unrelieved ACT (£330,000 − £300,000)	30,000

ACT is normally set off against the Corporation Tax liability for the year in which the related dividend has been distributed, but any that cannot be used in that year (i.e. is unrelieved) can be carried back for six years (two years for periods ended before 1 April 1984), or carried forward indefinitely.

Irrecoverable ACT

Although ACT can be carried forward indefinitely, SSAP 8 regards it as irrecoverable if its recoverability is not 'reasonably certain and foreseeable', i.e. the carry-forward should normally not extend beyond the next accounting period.

Alternatively, unrelieved ACT can be deducted from that proportion of the balance of deferred tax against which ACT can be set off in the future (*not* deferred tax representing future mainstream tax or tax on deferred chargeable gains). For example, with Corporation Tax at 52%, and an ACT rate of 30%, 22% must remain in charge to meet mainstream liability. Thus if a deferred tax account balance of, say, £119,000 represents tax on:

Deferred chargeable gains on £50,000 at 30%	£15,000
Trading income £200,000 at 52%	104,000
	119,000

then the minimum mainstream tax on the trading income would be £200,000 at 22% = £44,000, leaving the balance of £60,000 (£104,000 − £44,000) as the maximum amount against which unrelieved ACT could be offset (£60,000 = £200,000 at 30%).

If unrelieved ACT is set off against deferred tax it will be deducted from deferred tax in the balance sheet rather than being charged to the profit and loss account, and so will *not* increase the profit and loss account figure for taxation.

Irrecoverable ACT, on the other hand, should be included as part of the tax charge, and the amount should be separately disclosed if material, as shown here in UBM's 1982 accounts:

UBM *Irrecoverable ACT*

Taxation

	1982 £000	1981 £000
United Kingdom:		
Tax (relief) charge on the (loss) profit for the year		
Corporation tax at 52%	(2,244)	1,146
Deferred taxation	(1,516)	(37)
Irrecoverable advance corporation tax	3,142	—
Adjustment in respect of previous years	(987)	(366)
	(1,605)	743
Overseas	235	—
	(1,370)	743
The tax on the (loss) profit for the year has been reduced (increased) by the following items		
Stock appreciation relief	1,302	935
Timing differences between capital allowances and depreciation	1,504	(151)

ACT and relief on foreign tax

Until 1984 any ACT paid by a company which could not be offset against Corporation Tax attributable to UK income was offset against Corporation Tax attributable to foreign income *before* crediting relief for overseas tax. The result was that, if the ACT and the overseas tax credit together exceeded the Corporation Tax liability on the foreign income, the balance of the relief on foreign tax (Double Taxation Relief, DTR) was lost, because DTR could not be carried forward.

The order of set-off has been reversed from 1 April 1984, so that ACT is now offset *after* DTR. As a result, no DTR is lost because of dividend distribution and, as we have said, any unrelieved ACT can now be carried back for up to six years or carried forward indefinitely. Example 13.8 illustrates the sequence of offset.

Net earnings

Net earnings are the same as nil earnings unless the dividend distribution the company makes increases the company's overall tax liability.

In Example 13.8, earnings on a nil distribution basis would be £500,000, but with some dividend distribution the 'net' earnings would be only £480,000 because of £20,000 unrelieved ACT.

Where net earnings differ from nil, it is due to unrelieved ACT being deemed to be irrecoverable.

'Full distribution' earnings

These are the earnings that would be attributable to ordinary shareholders if they were all distributed as dividends; they are expressed at the gross level: dividends plus associated tax credits.

As foreign tax cannot be used as a credit against ACT, the maximum distribution a company can make at gross level (dividends plus tax credits) = Pre-tax profits – Minimum mainstream tax on UK earnings – Foreign tax.

In Example 13.8, 'full distribution' earnings are

£1,000,000 − £0 (no UK earnings) − £400,000 foreign tax = £600,000, made up of £420,000 dividends and £180,000 ACT.

Dividend cover

Dividend cover is the maximum dividend that a company could pay out of profits divided by the dividend actually paid.

Dividend cover with mainly UK operations

The calculation of the cover presents no difficulty when distribution of all the profits does not increase a company's overall tax liability (i.e. when overseas earnings and foreign tax are not significant and the tax charge is reasonably normal). In these cases simply divide the profits after tax, minorities and preference dividends by the ordinary dividends distributed.

Dividend cover in these cases can also be calculated by dividing earnings per share (nil basis) by the dividend per share. (Earnings per share, e.p.s., = profit attributable to ordinary shareholders ÷ number of ordinary shares in issue; see Chapter 14.)

Dividend cover with overseas earnings and foreign tax

Where a large proportion of a company's earnings arises overseas and bears foreign tax (including withholding tax on remitted earnings) at or near to the UK rate of Corporation Tax, dividend cover becomes more complicated because 'full distribution' increases the company's overall tax liability. This is because there is insufficient UK tax liability after DTR against which to offset the ACT that would be payable on full distribution.

In Example 13.8 the dividend paid in *Some*

Example 13.8   The effect of double taxation relief on the offsetting of ACT

Suppose a UK company's earnings all arise overseas and bear foreign tax (including withholding tax on remission) at 40%, UK Corporation Tax is 50% and all earnings are remitted, then with ACT at 30%:

	Nil distribution £000	Some distribution £000	Full distribution £000
Pre-tax profits	1,000	1,000	1,000
Dividends distributed	Nil	280	420
UK Corporation Tax liability	500	500	500
less Double Taxation Relief on foreign tax	400	400	400
CT liability against which ACT can be offset	100	100	100
ACT paid (30/70ths of dividends)	Nil	120	180
ACT offset	Nil	100	100
Unrelieved ACT	Nil	20	80
Total tax paid	500	520	580
Profits after tax (i.e. 'Earnings')	500	480	420
Retained earnings	500	200	None

distribution is only 1.5 times covered, in spite of retentions being more than 70% of dividends paid, because *Full distribution* would cause an increase of £60,000 in unrelieved ACT.

The maximum amount of dividend plus tax credit that a company can distribute out of profits (i.e. the 'gross' dividend under full distribution) is the *lesser* of:

(a) [Pre-tax earnings × (1 − CT rate) − minorities − pref. dividends] ÷ [1 − basic rate of Income Tax], (Note i)

(b) Pre-tax earnings *minus*:
    Minimum mainstream tax on UK earnings (Note ii)
    Foreign tax (Note iii)
    Minorities (grossed up at the standard rate of Corporation Tax)
    Preference dividends (grossed up at the basic rate of Income Tax)

Notes

(i) (a) produces the same answer as e.p.s. ÷ dividend per share.

(ii) Minimum mainstream tax on UK earnings = UK earnings × (Corporation Tax rate − ACT rate).

(iii) The foreign tax should include the withholding tax that would be payable if all overseas earnings were to be remitted to the United Kingdom.

(iv) Franked income plus associated tax credits should be excluded from pre-tax earnings, but should be added back afterwards in both (a) and (b).

Timing of payments of Corporation Tax

Advance Corporation Tax is payable within fourteen days of the end of the quarter in which the distribution is made, and is offset against the Corporation Tax liability for the company's accounting period in which the dividend is distributed (see Example 13.9).

The timing of payment of mainstream Corporation Tax depends on whether the company was trading before 1 April 1965. If it was (the normal case for most listed companies), tax is payable on 1 January of the financial year following the financial year in which the company's accounting

---

Example 13.9   Offset of ACT

A company whose year end is 31 December pays the following dividends for the year 1984:

Sept 84   Interim dividend of 1.4p per share
July 85   Final dividend of 2.8p per share

On the *interim dividend*, ACT of 0.6p per share will be payable within 14 days of 30 September 1984, and will be offset against Corporation Tax liability for the year 1984 (payable 30 September 1985 or later, see below).

On the *final dividend*, ACT of 1.2p per share will be payable within 14 days of 30 September 1985 and will be offset against Corporation Tax liability for the year 1985 (payable 30 September 1986 or later, see below).

In the *1984 accounts* the ACT of 1.2p per share on the final dividend will be provided for as a liability payable within one year, but the company will not be able to offset it against its Corporation Tax liability until 1985.

---

period ended, producing varying intervals:

Accounting period	Tax payable	Interval
1 May 83–30 April 84	1 Jan 86	20 months
1 Nov 83–30 Oct 84	1 Jan 86	14 months
1 Jan 84–31 Dec 84	1 Jan 86	12 months
1 Apr 84–31 Mar 85	1 Jan 86	9 months

These variations in the interval are a carry-over from the position before Corporation Tax was introduced.

Thus for long-established companies with years ending between April and December the Corporation Tax payable in the company's report and accounts can appear in two parts:

(a) Creditors: amounts falling due within one year – i.e. previous year's liability still unpaid, less any ACT on dividends paid in the previous year.

(b) Creditors: amounts falling due after more than one year – liability for the year being reported on, less any ACT on dividends paid in the year being reported on.

In practice, a company with a year ending on 31 December and therefore having mainstream Corporation Tax to pay a year and a day later would probably show it as due within one year.

For companies which started trading after the end of March 1965, Corporation Tax is due nine months after the end of the company's accounting period.

Chapter 14

PROFITS AFTER TAX, EXTRAORDINARY ITEMS, DIVIDENDS AND EARNINGS PER SHARE

(References: SSAP 6 *Extraordinary Items and Prior Year Adjustments*.)

PROFITS AFTER TAX

The unsuspecting layman might think that, once a company had made a profit and deducted tax, all that remained to be done would be to decide how much to pay out to ordinary shareholders and how much of the profit to retain in the business. In some companies it is as simple as that, but, alas, not in many, due to the minor complications of minority and preference shareholders, the major complications of extraordinary items, prior year adjustments and transfers to/from reserves, and the legal restrictions on the distribution of profits (as well as any government dividend restraint in force at the time).

Example 14.1 shows how extraordinary items appear 'below the line' in a profit and loss account – i.e. below the figure for profit attributable to ordinary shareholders, on which earnings per share are calculated. The decision on whether to treat a large item as extraordinary or not can thus substantially affect the apparent profitability of the company and in some cases can actually turn a profit into a loss (or vice versa); extraordinary items are therefore the subject of considerable debate, as we will discuss shortly. The illustration also shows how any prior year adjustment should be included in a separate statement immediately following the profit and loss account (as required by SSAP 6, para. 17).

Minorities

As explained in detail in Chapter 15, minorities

Example 14.1   Extraordinary items in the profit and loss account

Profit and loss account

	£000
Profit on ordinary activities after tax	1,231
less Minorities	68
Profit attributable to shareholders	1,163
Extraordinary items (less tax attributable)	247
Profit for the financial year	1,410
less Dividends	447
Retained profit	963

Earnings per share (see note)	11.16p
Extraordinary items per share	2.47p

Note E.p.s. based on profits of £1,163,000 less preference dividends of £47,000, and 10,000,000 ordinary shares in issue throughout the year.

Statement of retained profits/reserves

	£000	£000
Retained profit for the year		963
Reserves at beginning of year:		
As previously reported	2,742	
Prior year adjustment	(174)	
As restated		2,568
Reserves at end of year		3,531

occur when a group has one or more subsidiaries which are only partially owned by the group. The other (minority) shareholders in the 'partially owned' subsidiary are entitled to a share in the profit or loss of that subsidiary; their share, called 'minorities' or 'minority interests', has to be deducted in arriving at the profit attributable to the group's shareholders.

Preference dividends

Preference dividends, like ordinary dividends, are paid net and carry an associated tax credit. When the imputation system of taxation was introduced the basic rate of Income Tax was set at 30% and the coupons (the rates of dividend) on all UK preference shares were adjusted by statute to 70% of their former value on a once-and-for-all basis.

Thus, for example, a 5% £1 preference share became a 3½% £1 preference share, receiving a dividend fixed at 3½p, plus an associated tax credit dependent on the basic rate of Income Tax at the time of payment of the dividend.

Preference dividends and any arrears of cumulative preference dividends have to be met before any ordinary dividends can be declared.

Profit attributable to shareholders

Profit attributable to shareholders (sometimes called 'profit attributable to the company') is what is left for the shareholders after tax and all other charges have been deducted, but *before* extraordinary items.

It is this figure of attributable profits, less any preference dividends, divided by the number of ordinary shares in issue which gives the earnings per share, i.e. the amount the holder of one share would normally receive if the company distributed all its profits as dividends.

As earnings per share (e.p.s.), which we will

discuss in detail towards the end of this chapter, are a key measure of a company's profitability, the decision on what items should or should not be treated as extraordinary can often make a very significant difference to a company's attributable profits and thus to the e.p.s., as, for example, in the classic case of BURTON GROUP's 1975 accounts, illustrated here.

BURTON GROUP *1975 accounts*

	1975 £000	1974 £000
Profit after taxation	2,384	2,587
Minority interests	(60)	(9)
	2,324	2,578
Extraordinary items	(673)	—
Profit attributable to the holding company	1,651	2,578
Ordinary dividends	1,570	1,618
Balance added to reserves	81	960
Earnings per share	6.34p	7.03p

However, Burton's 1975 profits included £808,000 (1974: £2,993,000) arising from disposals of properties under sale and leaseback (on which there was no tax, due to rollover relief and losses elsewhere), and 1975's extraordinary items represented provisions on unmatched foreign currency borrowings (which were not allowable for tax). Had the sale and leaseback transactions been treated as extraordinary, and the provision for exchange losses on borrowings been treated as a normal expense, then the adjusted figures would have halved e.p.s. in 1975 and would have put the company into loss in 1974, as shown in Example 14.2.

Example 14.2   Effect of treating sale and leaseback as extraordinary in BURTON GROUP *1975 accounts*

	1975 £000	1974 £000
Profit after taxation (as reported)	2,384	2,587
Less: Profit on sale and leaseback	808	2,993
Provision for exchange losses	673	—
Adjusted profit (loss) after tax	903	(406)
Minorities	(60)	(9)
Profit (loss) attributable to the holding company	843	(415)
Ordinary dividends	1,570	1,618
	(727)	(2,033)
Extraordinary items (sale and leaseback)	808	2,993
Balance added to reserves	81	960
Earnings (loss) per share	3.24p	(1.13p)

The treatment of currency adjustments will be dealt with in Chapter 17. Let us now proceed to a detailed discussion of extraordinary items so that the reader can judge for himself whether it was reasonable for the BURTON GROUP to include the profit from sale and leaseback in its normal profits, i.e. 'above the line', or whether it should have been dealt with 'below the line', i.e. as an extraordinary item.

EXTRAORDINARY ITEMS

Conflicting concepts of profit

As the general idea of accounting is many hundreds of years old, one might expect that there would be fundamental agreement among users of accounts as to the basic purpose of the profit and loss account, or income statement as it is normally termed in the United States, but there is not. There are two conflicting views of the basic purpose of the profit and loss account:

(a) the current operating performance concept;
(b) the all-inclusive concept.

Current operating performance concept
Those who advocate the current operating performance concept believe that the profit and loss account should be designed to disclose the earnings of the business which arise from the normal operating activities during the period being reported upon. If this was followed to the extreme, the profit and loss account would include only the ordinary activities of the business during the reporting period; anything extraordinary or relating to prior years, and the effects of accounting changes, would be excluded. A profit and loss account prepared in this way facilitates comparison both with those of the same business for earlier periods and with those of other companies for the current period.

All-inclusive concept
Advocates of the all-inclusive concept, on the other hand, believe that the profit and loss account should include all transactions which bring about a net increase or decrease in net tangible assets during the current period, apart from dividend distributions (which appear in the appropriation section) and transactions such as the issue of shares. The aggregate income shown by such income statements over the life of an enterprise then constitutes a complete historical summary of net income. Advocates of the all-inclusive concept warn that if extraordinary items, the effect of accounting changes and prior period adjustments are charged or credited directly to retained earnings, as they are under the current operating performance concept, there is a danger that they will be overlooked in a review of operating results of several periods.

There has been a shift of opinion towards the all-inclusive concept during the past few years, not only in the United Kingdom but also in the United States and Canada, although none of these countries adopts a pure all-inclusive basis.

SSAP 6 definition of extraordinary items

SSAP 6 uses two confusingly similar terms: extraordinary items and exceptional items. Extraordinary items are defined as:

'Those items which derive from events or transactions outside the ordinary activities of the business and which are both material and expected not to recur frequently or regularly. They do not include items which, though exceptional on account of size and incidence (and which may therefore require separate disclosure), derive from the ordinary activities of the business. Neither do they include prior year items merely because they relate to a prior year.'

The classification of items as extraordinary depends on the nature of the business. For example, most companies would regard the sale of land as an extraordinary item, but REDLAND, whose business involves the continual acquisition and disposal of land (e.g. gravel pits, sold off when worked out), states specifically in its accounts that 'profits from sales of land and property surplus to operating requirements are included in the profit before taxation'.

Presentation of extraordinary items

Extraordinary items (extraordinary income, extraordinary charges and attributable taxation) should be shown separately in the profit and loss account for the year, below the results derived from ordinary activities. If there are extraordinary items, the profit and loss account for the year should include the following elements:

(a) profit on ordinary activities after taxation;
(b) extraordinary items after taxation;
(c) profit for the financial year.

The detailed breakdown required by the formats in the Companies Act is normally given in a note, as in CADBURY SCHWEPPES' 1983 accounts, shown here:

CADBURY SCHWEPPES *Notes to the profit and loss account*

Extraordinary items	1983 £m	1982 £m
Rationalisation costs – UK	13.6	5.8
overseas	6.0	5.3
Closure costs – overseas	4.7	—
	24.3	11.1
UK tax:		
Corporation Tax at 52%	(5.6)	—
ACT recovered	3.3	—
Deferred tax	(2.3)	(1.3)
Overseas tax:		
Tax payable	(0.7)	(0.2)
Deferred tax	(0.8)	—
	18.2	9.6

Importance of extraordinary items

Extraordinary items should be studied carefully for the following reasons:

(a) Treatment of ordinary items as extraordinary (or vice versa) can make a very significant difference to earnings per share.
(b) They may signal important changes in the nature of the business.
(c) They may also give important clues to the quality of management and to the future profitability of the company.

For example, terminal losses written off may indicate:

(a) the capacity of the management to admit their mistakes and/or to face up to changed economic circumstances, and their ability to take action to correct the situation once and for all, rather than devoting a disproportionate amount of management time and other resources into trying to revive dying ducks;
(b) the likelihood of higher future profits as the result of cutting out a loss-maker.

In addition, the chairman's or directors' report and other sources of information (e.g. press reports) should be checked to get a full picture of what lies behind an extraordinary item. For example, the chairman of HEPWORTH CERAMIC, in his 1982 statement, explained in some detail the decision to withdraw from the joint sea-water magnesia operation the company had in Drogheda in partnership with Cement-Roadstone Holdings at a cost of £12m: 'The position of the steel industry in the Western world had altered so dramatically since we decided in 1976 to enter into this venture that it was almost impossible to reconcile or to

believe the change which had taken place in such a short period of time. We could not see, in the short to medium term, any hope of generating profit out of this operation which in addition to being a continual drain on our profitability was also making big calls on us for cash which we did not think we were justified in spending in the present economic climate. This being so, we decided to withdraw from the joint venture, and we have done so.'

It is worth emphasising that one of the main limitations of many companies is the availability of first-class management: if a large proportion of it is devoted to 'salvage operations', the rest of the business is less likely to be run to maximum advantage.

Exceptional items

Items of abnormal size and incidence which derive from the ordinary activities of the business are sometimes called *exceptional items* (a term used but not defined by SSAP 6), and should be separately disclosed above the line (SSAP 6, para. 14). Examples of items which might be exceptional items are: a material profit (or loss) on disposal of a fixed asset and provisions for pension scheme deficits and for plant obsolescence.

Prior year items

Prior year items are items which relate to an earlier year or years. Those which represent the normal recurring corrections of accounting estimates made in prior years should be included in the normal calculation of pre-tax profits and, if material, should be stated in the published accounts.

Prior year adjustments
Only those prior year items which are the result of:

(a) changes in accounting policies, *or*
(b) the correction of fundamental errors,

and are material, are treated as 'prior year adjustments' for the purpose of SSAP 6. Prior year adjustments should not appear in the profit and loss account for the year being reported on, but in the statement of retained profits/reserves.

Restatement of accounts
Prior year adjustments (less attributable taxation) should be accounted for by 'restating prior years', adjusting the opening balance of retained profits accordingly. Where practicable, the effect of the change should be disclosed by showing separately in the restatement of the previous year the amount involved, but restatement in any real sense is comparatively rare. The analyst should therefore ensure that prior year adjustments are

applied to the figures for the prior year or years concerned to obtain a true comparison of the company's results from year to year.

Examples of items needing special treatment (if material) (see also Example 14.3 overleaf)

Prior year adjustments

(a) Change in accounting policy (e.g. change from a method of computing the cost of stock and work in progress including no overheads to one including all production overheads).

(b) Correction of fundamental errors (e.g. a major error in adding up stock figures); these are comparatively rare.

Extraordinary items

(a) Discontinuance of a significant part of a business.

(b) Sale of an investment not acquired with the intention of resale.

(c) Writing-off of goodwill or other intangibles because of unusual events or developments during the period.

(d) Expropriation of assets.

Charge in current year – disclose separately as exceptional

(a) Abnormal charges for bad debts.

(b) Abnormal write-offs of stock and work in progress.

(c) Abnormal expenditure on research and development.

(d) Abnormal losses on long-term contracts.

(e) Most adjustments of prior year tax provisions.

(f) Exchange differences (unless connected with an extraordinary item).

(g) Profit or loss on disposal of a fixed asset (unless the transaction itself is extraordinary for SSAP 6 purposes).

DIVIDENDS

Distribution of dividends

In deciding what profits to distribute the directors of a company should have in mind:

(a) what is prudent in cash terms;

(b) what is prudent from an accounting viewpoint;

(c) what is legally permissible.

Ideally, directors should choose the lowest of these three figures.

In deciding what is prudent in cash terms, directors should weigh up the cost of raising capital in various ways. Is it, for instance, better to borrow (i.e. increase the gearing) rather than ask equity shareholders to contribute more towards the net assets of the company? And, if equity shareholders are to be called upon to provide more, should they be asked to do so by means of a rights issue, in which case each shareholder has the choice of whether to take up, or sell, his rights; or should profits be 'retained', in which case the individual shareholder has no choice?

Unfortunately, the picture is confused by inflation and the present, historical cost, method of accounting. With no inflation (or an inflation accounting system recognised for tax purposes) a company would, in theory, be able to distribute all its profits and maintain its assets in real terms. With inflation most companies need to retain a proportion of their earnings as calculated by historical cost accounting in order to maintain their assets in real terms (but more of that in Chapter 22).

Having decided how much it is necessary to

retain in order to continue the existing scale of operations, and how much should be retained in order to expand, out of profits, the scale of operations, the directors should look at what remains.

Ideally, a company should pay a regular, but somewhat increasing, dividend. For example, from a market point of view, it is preferable to pay: 8.0p; 9.0p; 9.0p; 9.0p; 9.5p; 10.0p; rather than 8.0p; 12.0p; 10.5p; 4.0p; 10.0p; 10.0p; though both represent the same total sum in dividends over the six years, because investors who need steady income will avoid erratic dividend payers, and because a cut in dividend undermines confidence in the company's future. In other words, the directors of a company should think twice before paying a dividend this year which they may not be able to maintain, or setting a pattern of growth in the rate of dividend which could not reasonably be continued for the foreseeable future. For if they do either of these things, they are liable to disappoint shareholder expectations, to damage their market rating and to see their share price slashed if their dividend has to be cut.

Legal restrictions on dividend distribution

Prior to the Companies Act 1980 companies could, in general, distribute profits arising in an accounting period without making good previous revenue or capital losses, and could also distribute unrealised surpluses on asset revaluations.

Companies are now allowed to distribute only the aggregate of accumulated realised profits not previously distributed or capitalised *less* accumulated realised losses not previously written off in a reduction or reorganisation of capital (CA 1985,

Example 14.3   Flowchart of decisions on extraordinary items, exceptional items and prior year adjustments

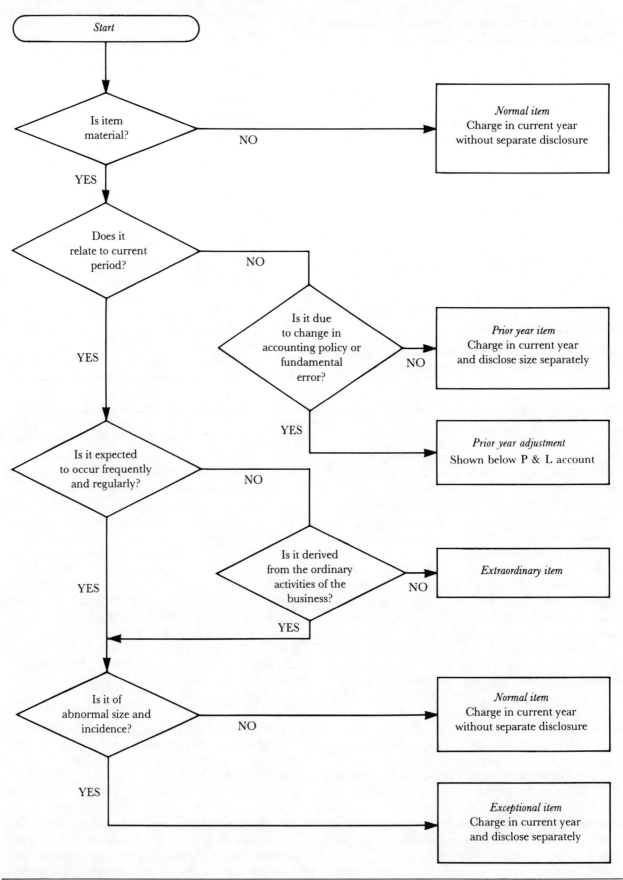

S. 263). The word 'realised' is not defined in the Act, but SSAP 2 says that profits should be included in the profit and loss account 'only when realised in the form of cash or other assets the ultimate cash realisation of which can be assessed with reasonable certainty'.

In addition, a *public* company may pay a dividend only if the net assets of the company after payment of the dividend are at least equal to the company's called-up share capital plus any reserves which are not available for distribution (S. 264(1)). Reserves not available for distribution are defined in Section 264(3) as the sum of:

(*a*)   share premium account;
(*b*)   capital redemption reserve;
(*c*)   accumulated unrealised profits not capitalised *less* accumulated unrealised losses not previously written off in a capital reduction or reorganisation;
(*d*)   any reserve which the company's Memorandum or Articles prohibit being distributed.

This requirement reflects the 'capital maintenance' principle of the EEC Second Directive and means that public companies will, in future, have to cover net losses (whether realised or not) from realised profits before paying a dividend.

Investment companies (a new class of company created by the Companies Act 1980 and defined in Section 266 of the Companies Act 1985 as a UK listed company investing mainly in securities with the aim of spreading investment risk and obtaining the benefit of specialist management *and* which has given notice to the Registrar of Companies) will have the option of paying dividends either on the basis of the capital maintenance section (S. 264) or on an asset ratio test (S. 265). This test requires the investment company's assets after the distribution to equal one and a half times its aggregate liabilities.

Where any company's audit report has been qualified, the auditor must provide a statement in writing as to whether the qualification is material in deciding whether the distribution would be a breach of the Act, *before* any distribution can be made.

Company articles on dividend distribution

Most companies lay down their own rules for dividend distribution in their Articles by adopting Articles 114 to 116 of Table A (the model set of Company Articles given in the First Schedule to the Companies Act 1948); these Articles say:

'114.   The company in general meeting may declare dividends, but no dividend shall exceed the amount recommended by the directors.
115.   The directors may from time to time pay to the members such interim dividends as appear to the directors to be justified by the profits of the company.
116.   No dividend shall be paid otherwise than out of profits.'

Declaration of dividends

Any dividends the directors recommend should be shown:

(*a*)   in the profit and loss account, together with any interim dividend already paid (CA 1985, Sch. 4, para. 51(3));
(*b*)   in the balance sheet as a liability.

Interim dividends can be declared by the directors without reference to the shareholders, but by convention they do not normally exceed half the anticipated total for the year. However, if the latest audited accounts disclose a 'non-distributable' position or if the level of accumulated profits has since fallen significantly, interim accounts must be prepared to justify the payment of an interim dividend (CA 1985, S. 27). Interim dividends appear in the profit and loss account as a distribution, and also in the balance sheet if the company has not paid the interim dividend by the end of the accounting period.

EARNINGS PER SHARE

(Reference: SSAP 3 *Earnings per Share*.)

Earnings per share (e.p.s.) are the amount of profit on *ordinary* activities, after tax and all other charges, that has been earned for each ordinary share and, as such, are a much better measure of the company's performance than profits, which can be boosted by acquisitions paid for by the issue of new shares and by rights issues.

The e.p.s. depend, rather obviously, on the amount of attributable profits (*before* extraordinary items) and the number of shares in issue, thus:

$$\text{e.p.s.} = \frac{\text{Profit attributable to ordinary shareholders}}{\text{Number of ordinary shares in issue}}$$

(see page 183 for details of calculation on a fully taxed basis). What is a little less obvious is that a company's profits may rise without a corresponding rise in earnings per share, because of changes in the issued share capital, as Example 14.4 shows.

The issued share capital of BEJAM was only slightly increased between 1980 and 1984, by

Example 14.4   Comparison of growth in profits and e.p.s.

	1980	1981	Year ending in 1982	1983	1984	Growth p.a. 1980–84
BEJAM (June year end)						
Attributable profits (£m)@	3.97	4.33	5.64	5.76	7.84	+18.5%
Earnings per share	4.1p*	4.5p*	5.8p	5.9p	7.9p	+17.8%
DALGETY (June year end)						
Attributable profits (£m)@	14.2	17.6	20.3	24.0	32.0	+22.5%
Earnings per share	25.1p	24.7p	26.9p	31.0p	41.3p	+13.3%
AGB (April year end)						
Attributable profits (£m)@	1.29	1.66	1.99	2.41	3.30	+26.2%
Earnings per share	7.7p*#	8.2p#	8.4p#	9.4p	10.9p	+ 9.1%

@Profits taxed at standard rate of Corporation Tax
*Adjusted for scrip issues
#Adjusted for rights issues

allotments to employee share schemes, and so the growth in e.p.s. was only slightly less than that of profits. In the same period DALGETY, as well as issuing shares for employee schemes, made several acquisitions for paper (i.e. issued new shares as consideration rather than paying cash), including the acquisition of SPILLERS in October 1979, which increased Dalgety's ordinary share capital by more than 50%. As a result, profits grew very much faster than e.p.s. Finally, AGB's issued share capital nearly doubled between 1980 and 1984, due almost entirely to three 1-for-4 rights issues, made in March 1980, in June 1981 and in February 1983. Profits shot ahead at an average of 26% per annum, but the heavily diluted e.p.s. managed only a modest 9% p.a.

The effect of acquisitions on earnings per share

The fact that an acquisition for paper makes e.p.s. grow at a slower rate than profits does not mean that acquisitions for paper are bad for e.p.s. It all depends on whether the e.p.s. are higher with the acquisition than they would have been without it (Example 14.5 opposite).

Earnings growth by acquisition

Buying earnings cheaply enables a company to boost its e.p.s. when its own earnings are static, or even when they are falling. Suppose in Example 14.5 that the attributable profits of the company were expected to fall the following year to £912,000, despite the recently acquired business performing satisfactorily. The company finds another victim (Example 14.6).

'But,' you may say, 'how did the company in the example manage to get the shareholders of the second acquisition to accept 2.4 million shares for attributable earnings of £468,000, which is 19.5p per share, far higher than the e.p.s. of the acquiring company?' And well may you ask – the secret is in 'market rating'.

Market rating – the PER

The measure of a company's market rating is its Price/Earnings Ratio (P/E ratio or PER), which is the market price of the ordinary share divided by the earnings per share:

PER = Share price ÷ e.p.s.

The PER depends mainly on three things: the overall level of the stock market, the industry in which the company operates and the company's record. In an average market the PER of the average company in an average sector might be around 7 or 8, with high-quality 'blue chips' like BOOTS or MARKS & SPENCER standing on twice the average P/E ratio, while a small company in an unfashionable sector might be lucky to be on a 4 or 5 times multiple, perhaps less if the shares have a restricted market (e.g. large family holdings are closely held), or even lower if the shares are unquoted.

Unfortunately, the introduction of SSAP 15 gives companies considerable scope for subjective judgement in the amount of deferred tax they provide, which, of course, directly affects their reported e.p.s. This makes PERs derived from reported e.p.s. (as published in the *Financial Times* and elsewhere) an unsatisfactory basis for inter-company comparisons, so that most analysts use e.p.s. calculated on a full tax charge to produce comparable PERs. They also estimate a company's profits and e.p.s. for the current year and will quote a *prospective* PER (P/PER) as well as a historical one (see Example 14.7).

Example 14.5   Acquisition for paper

	Existing company	Acquisition	Company post-acquisition
Attributable profits (£)	800,000	200,000	1,000,000
Issued equity (shares)	8,000,000		
Vendor consideration (shares)		1,600,000	
Resulting equity (shares)			9,600,000
e.p.s.	10p		10.4p

In this case 1.6 million shares are issued for a company bringing in £200,000 at the attributable profit level, or 12.5p for each new share, which is higher than the e.p.s. of the existing company, so the e.p.s. of the company, post-acquisition, are improved. Had the acquiring company paid more than 2 million shares for the acquisition, its earnings per share would have fallen.

Example 14.6   Further acquisition

	Present company	Second acquisition	Resulting company
Attributable profits (£)	912,000	468,000	1,380,000
Issued equity (shares)	9,600,000		
Vendor consideration (shares)		2,400,000	
Resulting equity (shares)			12,000,000
e.p.s.	9.5p		11.5p

Prospective PER =

$$\frac{\text{Ordinary share price}}{\text{Estimated e.p.s. for current year}}$$

Example 14.7   Historical and prospective PER

Suppose the fully taxed e.p.s. calculated from a company's latest report and accounts, usually published two to three months after the year has ended, are 8.0p. The analyst is expecting profits to rise by about 27% in the current year, and for there to be a proportionately higher charge for minorities (because one partly owned subsidiary is making a hefty contribution to the improved profits). He therefore estimates that e.p.s. will rise a little less than profits, to about 10.0p. The current share price is 56p, so

Last year's e.p.s.	= 8p	Historical PER	= 7.0
Current year e.p.s.	= 10p	Prospective PER	= 5.6

'Wonder growth' by acquisition

There is nothing fundamentally wrong with improving a company's earnings per share by acquisition, and it can be beneficial all round if there is some industrial or commercial logic involved, i.e. if the acquired company's business fits in with the acquiring company's existing activities or employs common skills and technology, or if the acquirer can provide improved management and financial resources. However, the practice is open to abuse, especially in bull markets.

Enter the 'whiz-kid' (known as a 'gunslinger' on the other side of the Atlantic), who might proceed as follows:

1. Acquire control of a company that has a listing on The Stock Exchange, but little else, e.g. the 'DEMISED TEA COMPANY', known in whiz-kid jargon as a 'shell'.

2. Reverse your shell into an unlisted company, thus giving your victim the benefit of a ready market for his shares and yourself the benefit of a company with real assets.

3. Sell off some of the assets, particularly property that is ripe for development. Don't lose any sleep over the fact that closing a factory throws 200 people out of work, as the office block that will replace it will house twice that number of civil servants in the department recently set up to encourage investment in industry; this 'asset-stripping' process is essential to provide the cash to gain control of your next victim.

4. By now the earnings per share of the 'Demised Tea Company', since renamed 'ANGLO-TRIUMPH ASSETS', have shown remarkable growth, albeit from a very low base (it's very easy to double profits of next-to-nothing), the bull market has conveniently started and the Press has noticed you. You project a suitable image of dynamic young management, talking to them earnestly about the need for British industry

93

to obtain a fair return on assets, and your photograph appears in the financial sections of the Sunday papers. You have arrived.

5. Your share price responds to Press comment, putting your 'go-go' company on a PER of 15 or 20; you continue to acquire companies, but now use shares rather than cash, thus continually boosting your e.p.s., as we have shown.

6. Following Press adulation, you broaden out into TV financial panels, seminar platforms, and after-dinner speeches; the bull market is now raging; Anglo-Triumph features regularly as an 'up stock' in the price changes table on the back page of the *FT* as the PER climbs towards 30. Deals follow apace, and Anglo-Triumph thrusts ahead, acquiring a huge conglomeration of businesses in an ever-widening range of mainly unrelated activities – it may be shoes, or ships or sealing-wax, but it's certainly Alice in Wonderland.

7. The moment of truth. The bull market, after a final glorious wave of euphoria, tops out. Profits in Anglo-Triumph's businesses turn down as little or nothing has been done to improve their management. Asset-stripping becomes politically unacceptable, and the word 'conglomerate' is coined to describe hotchpotch outfits like Anglo-Triumph. Down goes Anglo-Triumph's share price, and with it the market rating; without a high PER the company can no longer boost profits by acquisition, and the game is up.

Whether the whole edifice of Anglo-Triumph collapses completely or becomes just another lowly rated ex-glamour stock depends on the financial structure of the company. If it has geared up (i.e. has built up debt, on which interest has to be paid), and hasn't the cash to service these debts, the company will probably be forced into liquidation unless some sympathetic banker (possibly embarrassed by the prospect of incurring a huge loss if the company goes under) decides to tide things over until 'hopefully' better times.

We must now return to earnings per share, but for further reading on 'fly operators' we would refer readers to Michael Brett's hilariously true-to-life articles in the *Investors Chronicle* on the activities of whiz-kid Mr Rudyard Sharpe, ace of the asset strip and darling of the Sunday share tipsters (*Investors Chronicle* 14 and 21 February 1975) and, in the same vein, fringe banker Mr Cyril Buck of 'FASTBUCK FINANCE' (*IC* 22 February and 29 November 1974) and property developers Messrs Oliver and Arthur Fact (*IC* 17 and 24 January 1975 and *IC* Property Survey of 4 April 1975).

Adjustments to earnings per share – SSAP 3

If a company issues new shares during the year, the e.p.s. for *that year* have to be calculated using the time-weighted average number of shares in issue during the year, and the e.p.s. of *previous years* have to be adjusted to allow for any bonus element in the share issue. SSAP 3 describes in detail the method of adjustment to be used by companies for each type of issue, which are briefly described here.

Scrip (Bonus) issue or share split

Use the year-end figure for number of shares, and apply a factor to previous years' e.p.s. to put them on a comparable basis. For a scrip issue of y shares for every x shares held, the factor is $x \div (x + y)$ and for a split of 1 old share into z new shares it is $1 \div z$ (Example 14.8).

Example 14.8   Scrip issue and e.p.s.

Let us suppose that 'UNIVERSAL TRADERS PLC' is a company whose year ends on 31 December. At the end of 1981 the issued share capital was £4,000,000, of which £1,000,000 was in 3½% preference shares and £3,000,000 was the equity share capital of 12,000,000 ordinary shares of 25p each. No new shares were issued in 1982 and e.p.s. reported in 1982 were 8p: see tabulated accounts opposite, showing adjustments to previous years' e.p.s. required by the issue of new shares in this and ensuing examples.

In 1983 the company made a 1-for-3 scrip issue and profits after tax increased from £1.255m to £1.525m. Earnings per share were 7.5p which, at first sight, appear to be down on the previous year, but 1982's figure of 8p has to be adjusted by a factor of $3 \div (3 + 1)$ to make it comparable with 1983: ¾ of 8p = 6p.

Shares issued in an acquisition

The shares are assumed to have been issued at market price (even if the shares issued, the 'vendor consideration', have been placed at a discount at the time). The weighted average number of shares in issue during the year is calculated and used for working out the e.p.s. (Example 14.9).

Example 14.9   Acquisition issue and e.p.s.

To continue Example 14.8, on 1 April 1984 Universal Traders acquired another company and issued 2 million new fully paid 25p ordinary shares in payment (an acquisition 'for paper').

At the year end, the profits of the new subsidiary for the period 1 April to 31 December 1984 were included in Universal Traders' consolidated profit and loss account and the weighted average number of shares in issue during the year was calculated:

$$\frac{16\text{m for 3 months plus 18m for 9 months}}{12 \text{ months}}$$

= 17.5m on weighted average

Profits at the attributable level came out at £1,400,000 to give earnings per share of 8.0p.

Rights issue

A rights issue is regarded as being partly an issue at the market price and partly a scrip issue (the bonus element); the e.p.s. of previous years are adjusted by the factor appropriate to the bonus element in the same way as a scrip issue (Example 14.10).

Example 14.10   Rights issue (on first day of company's year) and e.p.s.

Let us suppose Universal Traders made a rights issue on 1 January 1985 on the basis of one new share for every 4 shares held at a price of 80p per share, against a market price of 100p on the last day the old shares were quoted cum-rights. The issue would have the same effect as a 1-for-5 at 100p, followed by a 1-for-24 scrip issue. The factor for adjusting the e.p.s. for previous years is thus 24 ÷ (1 + 24), which can be calculated in more complicated cases by the formula:

Theoretical ex-rights (xr) price ÷ actual cum-rights price on the last day of quotation cum-rights

where the Theoretical xr price is, in this case, 1 share at 80p plus 4 old shares at 100p each = 5 shares for 480p = 96p, and 96/100 = 24/25.

If, instead of being made on the first day of the company's year (as in Example 14.10), a rights issue is made during the company's year, the calculation of the bonus element and the factor for adjusting previous years' e.p.s. is just the same but, in addition, the weighted average number of shares in issue during the year has to be calculated (see Example 14.11).

Example 14.11   Rights issue (during company's year) and e.p.s.

If Universal Traders had made its 1-for-4 rights issue on 1 September 1985, then the number of shares at the beginning of the year is adjusted by the reciprocal of the e.p.s. factor and the calculation to find the weighted average is:

$$\left[18\text{m} \times \frac{25}{24} \times \frac{8}{12} \right] + \left[22.5\text{m} \times \frac{4}{12} \right] = 20\text{m shares}$$

which would give e.p.s. of 8.55p rather than 7.6p for 1985.

Adjusting the number of shares in issue during the first 8 months of 1985 by 25/24 allows for the bonus element of the rights issue, i.e. it puts the shares in issue at the beginning of the year on the same basis as the shares in issue at the end of the year.

Fully diluted earnings per share

Where a company has in issue any form of security that does not, at present, rank for ordinary dividends but may do so in the future, e.g. convertibles, deferred or partly paid shares, warrants or options granted, the effect on earnings per share of

---

'UNIVERSAL TRADERS PLC' *Accounts*

Year end 31 December	1982	1983 Scrip issue	1984 Acquisition	1985 Rights issue
	£000	£000	£000	£000
Profit after tax	1,255	1,525	1,745	2,165
less Minorities	260	290	310	420
	995	1,235	1,435	1,745
less Preference dividends	35	35	35	35
Attributable profits	960	1,200	1,400	1,710
add Convertible interest (net)				72
fully diluted attributable				1,782
Ordinary shares in issue	12m	16m	18m	22.5m
1984 weighted average			17.5m	
1985 fully diluted				23.75m
e.p.s reported in 1982	8p	—	—	—
e.p.s. in 1983 and 1984 with 1982 adjusted	6p	7.5p	8.0p	—
e.p.s. in 1985 with prior years adjusted	5.76p	7.2p	7.68p	7.6p
Fully diluted e.p.s.	—	—	—	7.5p

these securities becoming entitled to dividends is called 'full dilution' (see Example 14.12).

Example 14.12   Full dilution of e.p.s.

Suppose that Universal Traders had made a £2 million issue of 6½% convertible unsecured loan stock on 1 January 1985, entitling holders to convert into ordinary shares on the basis of 62½ ordinary shares per £100 nominal of CULS at any time between 1987 and 1992. The calculation of fully diluted e.p.s. allows for the extra 1.25 million shares that would be issued if all the CULS holders converted, and for the annual interest of £130,000 the company would save at the pre-tax level, which has to bear Corporation Tax before being attributable to shareholders. In our example, with Corporation Tax at 45%, fully diluted e.p.s.:

$$\frac{£1.71m + (£0.13m \times 0.55)}{22.5m + 1.25m} = 7.5p$$

SSAP 3 requires companies to show fully diluted earnings per share if dilution reduces the basic e.p.s. by 5% or more. In Example 14.12, 7.5p is less than a 5% drop on the basic e.p.s. of 7.6p, so Universal Traders would not need to report it. Where the dilution is 5% or more, details are usually given in a note rather than in the profit and loss account itself. For example, BRITISH LAND reported basic e.p.s. of 8.1p in 1984 and showed the dilution that would occur on full conversion of the 12% convertible loan stock 2002 in a note:

BRITISH LAND *Note to the profit and loss account*

Earnings per share

Based on 104.03m shares. Fully diluted earnings would be 7.1p based on profit on ordinary activities after taxation adjusted for interest payable on 12% convertible loan stock and on 135.93m shares including those which may be issued on conversion.

Where full dilution involves payments to the company, e.g. warrant-holders exercising their right to subscribe for shares at a given price (the exercise price), the calculation of fully diluted e.p.s. assumes that the company would invest the proceeds of subscription in 2½% Consols.

Adjustments for additional depreciation

Some companies depress their earnings per share by charging additional depreciation on a replacement cost basis in calculating their trading profit; in these cases the analyst needs to add back the additional depreciation charge to put the profits

Example 14.13   Adjusting e.p.s. for additional depreciation: PILKINGTON

In 1984 PILKINGTON reported profit on ordinary activities after taxation and minorities of £23.3m to give e.p.s. of 13.8p, but had included an additional charge for increased cost of replacement and obsolescence of £33.7m. As the additional charge is not an allowable expense for Corporation Tax purposes, it can be added back at the after-tax level:

	As reported £m	Adjusted £m
Profit after taxation	36.7	36.7
Add back additional depreciation		33.7
Adjusted profit after taxation		70.4
Interest of minority shareholders (Note 1)	13.5	25.9
Profit attributable to ordinary shareholders	23.2	44.5
Earnings per share	13.8p	26.4p

Notes

(i) Minority interests are adjusted pro rata to the increase in profits after tax unless the amount of additional depreciation attributable to minorities happens to be known, which is unlikely.

(ii) If adjustments have been made to 'normalise' the tax charge (see Chapter 24), the additional depreciation should be added back at the pre-tax level and the standard tax charge should then be recalculated.

and earnings per share on a basis comparable with other companies (Example 14.13).

Net and nil basis

SSAP 3 requires companies to show net earnings per share in the profit and loss account and to state the amount of the earnings and the number of shares used in the calculation, which is usually done in an accompanying note. Where there is a material difference between earnings per share calculated on the net basis and on the nil distribution basis, because the distribution of dividends has increased the company's tax charge (as described in Chapter 13), the e.p.s. calculated on the nil distribution basis should also be shown on the face of the profit and loss account.

Earnings on more than one class of share

Where there is more than one class of equity share or where some shares are only partly paid, the earnings should be attributed to the different classes of share in accordance with their dividend rights or profit participation.

MOVEMENTS IN RESERVES

Although the effect of most transactions of a company should be reflected in the profit and loss account, there are a number of occasions where transfers are made direct to or from reserves. These include any premium on the issue of shares, unrealised surpluses arising on the revaluation of fixed assets, a general write-off of goodwill, and foreign exchange adjustments (see Chapter 17).

Schedule 4, para. 46 of the Companies Act 1985 requires the source of any increase and the application of any decrease in reserves to be disclosed; this information is normally given either in a statement immediately following the profit and loss account, or in a note to the accounts, as illustrated here:

REDLAND *Note on capital and reserves*

	Group £ million	Redland PLC £ million
Called up share capital		
. . . . .		
Share premium account		
Balance at 26 March 1983	50.5	50.5
Premium arising on shares allotted for cash	0.3	0.3
Balance at 31 March 1984	50.8	50.8
Revaluation reserve		
Balance at 26 March 1983	20.8	2.1
Surplus arising on revaluation of properties	2.6	—
Transfer to profit and loss account	(0.2)	—
Balance at 31 March 1984	23.2	2.1
Profit and loss account		
Balance at 26 March 1983	121.1	67.1
Foreign currency adjustments	0.3	—
Goodwill arising on consolidation of new subsidiaries and associates	(10.0)	—
Transfer to deferred tax	(5.0)	(5.0)
Transfer from revaluation reserve	0.2	—
Retained profit for the year	30.0	19.6
Balance at 31 March 1984	136.6	81.7

Chapter 15

SUBSIDIARIES AND GROUP ACCOUNTS

(Reference: SSAP 14 *Group Accounts*.)

HOLDING COMPANIES, SUBSIDIARIES AND GROUPS

Definitions
(Reference: CA 1985, S. 736.)

A *holding company* is a company which exercises control over another company, its subsidiary company, and is often referred to as the *parent* company.

A *subsidiary company* is a company, control over which is exercised by a holding company by virtue of the fact that the holding company either:

(*a*) is a member of it and controls the composition of its board of directors; *or*

(*b*) holds more than half in nominal value of its equity share capital.

For this purpose *equity share capital* comprises any part of the issued share capital which carries the right to participate beyond a specified amount in either dividend or capital distribution (CA 1985, S. 744). It will include not just the ordinary share capital but all share capital other than non-participating preference shares.

Control involves the power to appoint all or a majority of the board without the consent or concurrence of some other person. (It arises from rights conferred by the Articles, or from voting rights.)

A *group* is a holding company, together with its subsidiary company or companies.

A *wholly owned subsidiary* is one in which all the share capital is owned either by the holding company or by other wholly owned subsidiaries.

A *partially owned subsidiary* is one in which some of the share capital is owned outside the group.

The outside shareholdings are called minority interests.

For an illustration of the use of these terms, see Example 15.1.

Example 15.1   Partially and wholly owned subsidiaries

H is the holding company of a group of companies, and is incorporated in Great Britain.

H holds	100,000 of the 100,000	ordinary shares of S
H holds	7,500 of the 10,000	ordinary shares of T
S holds	5,100 of the 10,000	ordinary shares of U
T holds	1,000 of the 1,000	ordinary shares of V

The H group may be depicted thus:

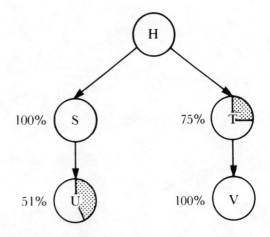

The group consists of:
H's wholly owned subsidiary S
H's partially owned subsidiary T (in which there is a 25% minority)

98

T's wholly owned subsidiary V (which in law is also a subsidiary of H, but colloquially a partially owned sub-subsidiary of H)

S's partially owned subsidiary U (in which there is a 49% minority).

Statutory requirements for group accounts

Where at the end of its financial year a company has subsidiaries, 'group accounts' must be laid before the company in general meeting together with the company's own balance sheet and profit and loss account (CA 1985, S. 229(1)). Group accounts for this purpose normally comprise:

(a) a consolidated balance sheet dealing with the state of affairs of the company and all the subsidiaries to be dealt with in group accounts; *and*

(b) a consolidated profit and loss account dealing with the profit or loss of the company and those subsidiaries.

However, as we shall discuss, alternative methods of presentation are allowed.

Exceptions to consolidation of subsidiaries

Under Section 229(3) of the Companies Act 1985, the directors of a holding company have discretion to exclude a subsidiary from consolidation on any of the following grounds: impracticability, insignificance, disproportionate expense or delay, misleading or harmful effect and dissimilar activities.

In contrast, SSAP 14, para. 21, requires that a subsidiary *should be* excluded from consolidation in the following circumstances (there is no discretion):

1. *Dissimilar activities:* if its activities are so dissimilar from those of other companies within the group that consolidation would be misleading and that it would be better to present separate financial statements.

2. *Lack of control:* if the group does not own share capital carrying more than half the votes, or is restricted in its ability to appoint the majority of directors.

3. *Severe restrictions:* if the subsidiary operates under severe restrictions which significantly impair control by the holding company. For example, the group accounts of BOOKER MCCONNELL do not consolidate the results of some of its overseas subsidiaries, and they explained why in the statement of accounting policies: 'Certain subsidiary companies operate in countries overseas where the amount of profit that may be remitted is restricted or where freedom of action may be limited. In the opinion of the directors, it would be misleading to consolidate these companies and the group share of their results is therefore included in profit only to the extent of remittances received.'

4. *Temporary control:* if control is intended to be temporary.

Where subsidiaries are not consolidated for any of these four reasons, SSAP 14 describes the accounting treatment that should be used in each case (see SSAP 14, paras. 23 to 27).

Group accounts are not required where the company is, at the end of its financial year, the wholly owned subsidiary of another body corporate incorporated in Great Britain (S. 229(2)). In Example 15.1, S would not need to produce consolidated accounts, but T would.

Alternative methods of presentation

Group accounts need not take the form of consolidated accounts for the entire group if the holding company's directors are of the opinion that the same or equivalent information can be better presented to the company's members in some other form, for instance by showing the accounts of each subsidiary separately (CA 1985, S. 229(6)).

The holding company's own balance sheet

Subsidiaries are normally shown at cost less any amounts written off, but some companies show them at their underlying net asset value, i.e. they use the equity method of accounting, which includes them at cost plus the holding company's share of the post-acquisition retained profits and reserves.

The holding company's own profit and loss account

Under Section 228(7) of the Companies Act 1985, the holding company's profit and loss account need not be presented if the consolidated profit and loss account shows how much of the consolidated profit or loss for the financial year is dealt with in the holding company's own accounts and, in practice, one seldom sees the holding company's own profit and loss account.

The company's financial (accounting) year end

Under Section 227(4) of the Companies Act 1985 a holding company's directors must ensure that the financial year of each of its subsidiaries coincides with the holding company's own financial year, unless in their opinion there are good reasons against it. If the financial year of a subsidiary does *not* coincide with that of the holding company the group accounts must, unless the Department of Trade and Industry otherwise directs, deal with the subsidiary's state of affairs at the end of its financial year immediately preceding that of its holding company and with its profit or loss for that financial year (CA 1985, S. 230(7)).

Unfortunately, the Companies Act uses the term 'financial year' here to mean the company's accounting year; the term is normally used to describe the Corporation Tax year, which runs from 1 April to 31 March, as described in Chapter 13. Many companies nowadays arrange for their overseas subsidiaries to end their accounting year, say, three months before that of the holding company, in order to make the task of preparing group accounts easier.

Interests in another company

If a company, A, wishes to obtain an interest in the activities of another company, B, it may do so in three ways:

(*a*) by buying some or all of the assets of company B;

(*b*) by buying some shares in company B;

(*c*) by making a bid for company B.

Buying assets of company B

If company A only wishes to acquire some or all of the assets of company B, it may do so either by paying cash or by paying in shares of company A; the latter is an example of a vendor consideration issue of shares described in Chapter 4. Example 15.2 illustrates the process.

Example 15.2 Acquisition of assets by share issue

Let us suppose that, at 31 December 1985, the balance sheets of A and B were:

	A £	B £		A £	B £
Ordinary share capital	60,000	20,000	Net assets	90,000	32,000
Reserves	30,000	12,000			
	90,000	32,000		90,000	32,000

Suppose A purchases the net assets of B by the issue to company B of 40,000 £1 ordinary shares (valued at par at the time) and that company A considered the assets of company B were 'fair value', i.e. did not need revaluing, then company A's balance sheet would become:

	£		£
Ordinary share capital	100,000	Net assets	122,000
Reserves	30,000	(£90,000 + £32,000)	
		Goodwill	8,000
		(£40,000 − £32,000)	
	130,000		130,000

Goodwill represents the *excess* of the purchase consideration (i.e. the value of the shares A issued to B) over the book value of the net assets purchased.

After A's purchase B's balance sheet would show:

	£		£
Ordinary share capital	20,000	Investment at cost	40,000
Reserves (£12,000 + 8,000 profit on realisation of net assets)	20,000		
	40,000		40,000

B would not automatically cease to exist; it would become an investment holding company.

Had A's shares been listed and had they been standing at, say, 200p at the time, A would only have needed to issue, say, 20,000 £1 ordinary shares, and A's balance sheet after the purchase would have been:

	£		£
Ordinary share capital	80,000	Net assets	122,000
Share premium a/c	20,000	Goodwill	8,000
Other reserves	30,000		
	130,000		130,000

Where goodwill does arise, most companies write it off against reserves (and it is standard practice for analysts to do so in their calculations even when the holding companies do not).

Buying some shares in company B

(*a*) If A acquires 5% or less of the equity of B, A's balance sheet would show the purchase as an *investment* (see Chapter 7).

(*b*) If A acquires more than 5% of the equity of B, the purchaser would still show the purchase as an *investment*, but would be obliged by Section 201 of the Companies Act 1985 to declare its interest.

(*c*) If A acquires 20% or more of the equity of B, and is allowed by B to participate in the major policy decisions of B, usually by holding a seat on B's board, then A should treat B as an *associated company* (see Chapter 16).

(*d*) If A acquires 30% or more of the voting rights of B, or if A in any period of 12 months adds more than 2% to an existing holding of between 30% and 50% in B, then Rule 34 of the Takeover Code obliges A to make a bid for the remainder of the equity of B at a price not less than the highest price A paid for any B shares in the previous 12 months.

Making a takeover bid for company B

Company A may offer the shareholders of B either cash or 'paper' (i.e. shares and/or loan stock and/or warrants of A). If A has already gone over the 30% limit or has added more than 2% in 12 months to a holding of 30–50%, the offer must be in cash or be accompanied by a cash alternative. If the bid results in A acquiring 90% or more of the shares of B that it did not already own, A may force the remaining B shareholders to accept the bid using the procedure laid down in Section 428 of the Companies Act 1985. Example 15.3 illustrates a successful bid, where the excess of the value of the shares issued over the assets acquired appears in the consolidated balance sheet as goodwill on consolidation.

Goodwill on consolidation

Goodwill on consolidation (or 'cost of control') represents the excess of the purchase price over the net assets acquired.

In Example 15.3, had the net assets acquired exceeded the purchase consideration (the market value of the shares issued), the difference would have been termed 'capital reserve on consolidation' or 'surplus arising on consolidation' and would have been shown separately among reserves. Alternatively, had any capital reserve on consolidation existed in respect of another of A's subsidiaries, the goodwill cost of control would normally have been set off against it.

Where a capital reserve on consolidation arises (i.e. when a holding company has paid less than book value for an acquisition), one might well ask whether the assets of the new subsidiary have been overstated, i.e. whether provisions need to be

---

Example 15.3 Acquisition of the entire share capital

Continuing with our example of companies A and B (whose balance sheets were shown at the beginning of Example 15.2), let us suppose that A made a successful bid of 1 share in A for each share of B (with no cash alternative or with the cash alternative underwritten to ensure that A did not have to provide any cash). Thus A acquires the entire share capital of B by the issue of 20,000 £1 ordinary shares in A (standing at 200p each) to the *shareholders* of B, and the balance sheet of A will become:

	£		£
Ordinary share capital	80,000	Net assets	90,000
Share premium account	20,000	Shares in subsidiary at cost	40,000
Other reserves	30,000		
	130,000		130,000

The balance sheet of A does not disclose the underlying net assets of B, simply A's investment in B but, to comply with the provisions of the Companies Act 1985 described earlier in this chapter, company A must also present consolidated accounts. The *consolidated balance sheet of the group* (A and its subsidiary B) simply substitutes the net assets of B for the asset 'Investment in B':

	£		£
Ordinary share capital	80,000	Net assets	122,000
Share premium account	20,000	Goodwill on consolidation	
Other reserves	30,000	(£40,000 − 32,000)	8,000
	130,000		130,000

Had the market value of shares issued exactly equalled the net assets there would have been no goodwill, and in practice most companies write off any difference against reserves in the year of acquisition of subsidiaries.

---

made against stocks or debtors, or further depreciation provided on fixed assets.

There are, however, circumstances where assets, or even cash, can be acquired at below book value; take, for instance, the case of a private company with an issued share capital of £100,000, still held by the handful of shareholders who

originally subscribed at par; the company has sold off all its assets piecemeal, leaving £1.1 million in cash; the shareholders might well decide to sell out for £1 million payable in shares of a listed company in order to avoid any immediate Capital Gains Tax liability.

CONSOLIDATED ACCOUNTS

The consolidated balance sheet

In simple terms a consolidated balance sheet shows all the assets and all the liabilities of all group companies whether wholly owned or partially owned. Where a partially owned subsidiary exists, its shareholders' funds are provided partly by the holding company and partly by the minority interests.

To illustrate the basic principles of consolidated accounts let us take the case of a holding company, 'H LTD', with a partially owned subsidiary, 'S LTD', and imagine that we wish to prepare the consolidated balance sheet for the H Group at 31 December 1985. H paid £340,000 cash for 200,000 of the 250,000 £1 ordinary shares of S Ltd on 1 January 1982, when the balance sheet of S was as shown below.

There are six steps to consolidating the two companies' balance sheets at 31 December 1985, which are also shown opposite.

1. *Ascertain the goodwill cost of control* by comparing the cost to H Ltd of its investment in S Ltd with H Ltd's share of the equity shareholders' funds of S Ltd at the date of acquisition. The goodwill cost of control will be:

	£000	£000
Purchase consideration		340
Holding company's share of ordinary shareholders' funds at date of acquisition:		
4/5ths of Ordinary share capital	200	
4/5ths of Reserves	68	268
Goodwill cost of control		72

    Note the following:

    (a) Any *pre-acquisition profits* of S Ltd which have not already been distributed will form part of that company's reserves, and are thus represented by equity shareholders' funds taken into account in computing goodwill cost of control.

    (b) Any distribution by S Ltd after it is acquired by H Ltd which is made out of pre-acquisition profits (i.e. reserves existing at acquisition) must be credited not to the profit and loss account of H

Ltd as income, but to the asset account 'Investment in S Ltd' as a reduction of the purchase price of that investment. The goodwill cost of control does not change.

2. *Compute the holding company's share of the undistributed post-acquisition profits of the subsidiary.* This equals the holding company's proportion of the change in reserves since the date of acquisition:

    $$\frac{200,000}{250,000} \times (£150,000 - 85,000)$$
    $$= (£120,000 - £68,000)$$
    $$= £52,000.$$

    This, added to the holding company's own reserves, represents the reserves of the group which will appear in the consolidated balance sheet:

    £52,000 + £480,000 = £532,000.

3. *Compute minority interests in the net assets of S Ltd:*

    Minority interests =

    Minority proportion × Net assets (capital + reserves) of S Ltd at balance sheet date.

    The minority interest in the equity shareholders' funds of S Ltd is:

    Minority proportion × Equity shareholders' funds of S Ltd at balance sheet date (31 December 1985)

    $$= \frac{50,000}{250,000} \times £400,000 = £80,000.$$

4. *Draw up the consolidated balance sheet:*
    (a) insert as share capital the share capital of the holding company;
    (b) insert the figures already computed for (i) goodwill (cost of control) (see 1 above) and (ii) minority interests (see 3 above);
    (c) show as 'reserves' the total of the reserves of the holding company and the post-acquisition reserves of the subsidiary applicable to the holding company (see 2 above).

5. *Cancel out any inter-company balances:* the aim of the consolidated balance sheet is to show a true and fair view of the state of affairs of the group as a whole. Inter-company balances (where an item represents an asset of one group company and a liability of another) must be cancelled out since they do not concern outsiders. Thus, if S Ltd owes H Ltd on current account £10,000, this £10,000 will appear as an asset in H Ltd's own balance sheet, and as a liability in that of S Ltd, but it will not appear at all in the consolidated balance sheet.

6. *Consolidate:* add together like items (e.g. add freehold land and buildings of the holding company and freehold land and buildings of the subsidiary) and show the group totals in the consolidated balance sheet. Omit, in so doing, the share capital of the subsidiary, reserves, and the investment in the subsidi-

ary, which have already been taken into account in steps 1 to 3.

It will be seen that only the share capital of the holding company appears in the consolidated balance sheet. The share capital of the subsidiary has disappeared, one-fifth of it becoming part of 'minority interests' while the other four-fifths (£200,000), together with H's share of S's reserves on acquisition (£68,000) and the 'goodwill – cost of control' (£72,000) balance out the removal of H's balance sheet item 'shares in S Ltd' (£340,000).

The consolidated profit and loss account

As explained on page 99, most holding companies avoid the need to publish their own profit and loss accounts by showing the amount of profit or loss they deal with in the group consolidated profit and loss accounts.

'S LTD' *Balance sheet at 1 January 1982*

	£000		£000
Ordinary share capital	250	Fixed assets:	
Reserves	85	Freehold land and buildings	120
		Plant and machinery	146
			266
Ordinary shareholders' funds	335		
7% Debenture	100	Net current assets	169
	435		435

'H LTD' *and* 'S LTD' *Balance sheets at 31 December 1985*

	H Ltd £000	S Ltd £000		H Ltd £000	S Ltd £000
Ordinary share capital	500	250	Fixed assets:		
Reserves	480	150	Freehold land and buildings	150	120
			Plant and machinery	250	180
Ordinary shareholders' funds	980	400		400	300
10% Unsecured loan stock	120	—	Shares in S Ltd	340	—
7% Debenture	—	100	Net current assets	360	200
	1,100	500		1,100	500

'H GROUP' *Consolidated balance sheet at 31 December 1985*

	£000		£000
Ordinary share capital	500	Fixed assets:	
Reserves	532	Freehold land and buildings	270
		Plant and machinery	430
Ordinary shareholders' funds	1,032		700
Minority interests	80		
H Ltd's 10% ULS	120	Net current assets	560
S Ltd's 7% Debenture	100	Goodwill – cost of control	72
	1,332		1,332

Consolidated profit and loss accounts follow the same pattern as described for single companies at the beginning of Chapter 12, except that if the group contains partially owned subsidiaries, the minority interests in the profits of those subsidiaries have to be deducted at the after-tax level.

Continuing with our example of H Ltd owning four-fifths of the £250,000 ordinary share capital of S Ltd, let us suppose that at the beginning of 1986 S Ltd issued 30,000 £1 7% preference shares to a third party as part payment for an acquisition, and that the pre-tax profits and tax charges of H Ltd and S Ltd for that year were:

	H Ltd £	S Ltd £	Total £
Profit before tax	72,000	51,200	123,200
Corporation Tax at 40%	28,800	20,480	49,280
Profit after tax	43,200	30,720	73,920

The combined pre-tax profit, tax and profit after tax will be shown in the group's consolidated profit and loss account.

Calculation of minority interests

The minority interests in the profits after tax of S Ltd will then be computed as follows:

	S Ltd £	Minority interests £
Profit before tax	51,200	
less Corporation Tax	20,480	
Profit after tax	30,720	
less Preference dividends	2,100	2,100
Attributable to ordinary shareholders	28,620 × ⅕ =	5,724
Minority interests total		7,824

It is this sum of £7,824 which will be deducted as 'minority interests' from the profit after tax in the consolidated profit and loss account.

Appropriations of the subsidiary

Suppose, for instance, that S Ltd proposed a single ordinary dividend of 4p for 1986. Then the profit attributable to S Ltd's ordinary shareholders would be appropriated as follows:

	Total £	Minorities £	H Ltd £
Attributable	28,620	5,724	22,896
Proposed dividend of 4.0p per share	10,000	2,000	8,000
Retentions	18,620	3,724	14,896

H Ltd's share of the proposed dividend (£8,000) would also appear, as dividends receivable, in the holding company's accounts, and the two figures would cancel out on consolidation. The dividends payable to minority shareholders (£2,000) would be charged (behind the scenes) against the minority interests deducted on consolidation, and the minorities' share of the retentions (£7,824 − £2,100 preference dividends − £2,000 ordinary dividends = £3,724) added to the consolidated *balance sheet* item 'minority interests'.

The group profit and loss account

Suppose H Group declared dividends of £25,000 for the year. The group profit and loss account would then show:

	£
Profit before tax	123,200
less Tax	49,280
Profit after tax	73,920
less Minority interests	7,824
	66,096
less Dividends	25,000
Retentions	41,096

Retained profit

The group's retained profit of £41,096 would be carried forward partly in the holding company's accounts:

	£
H Ltd profit after tax	43,200
H Ltd's dividends from S Ltd	8,000
less Dividends paid by H Group	25,000
	26,200

The remainder, £14,896, would be carried forward in S Ltd's accounts, being H Ltd's share of S Ltd's retentions.

A few companies show where the retained profits of the group are being carried forward in their profit and loss account, e.g. AUTOMATED SECURITY (HOLDINGS), illustrated opposite, or in their statement of retained profits/reserves.

Alternatively, this information may be given in a note to the accounts.

Unrealised profits on stocks

One group company frequently supplies another company within the group with goods in the ordinary course of trade; indeed, this sort of trading link may often be at the very heart of the existence of the group in the first place. But where one group company has made a profit on the supply of goods to another group company and those goods, or some of them, remain in stock at the end of the accounting year, a problem arises and, although nothing can normally be gleaned from the accounts, the procedure for consolidation is designed to prevent a group's profits being artificially inflated by sales within the group.

AUTOMATED SECURITY (HOLDINGS) *Retained profits: group profit and loss account*

	1983 £000	1982 £000
. . . . .		
Profit on ordinary activities after taxation	4,152	3,061
Extraordinary charges (Goodwill)	1,145	404
Profits for the financial year	3,007	2,657
Dividends	562	419
Amount transferred to reserves	2,445	2,238
The Company	2,489	2,552
Subsidiaries	(79)	(278)
Related companies	35	(36)
	2,445	2,238
Earnings per Ordinary Share	8.22p	7.32p
Earnings per Ordinary Share fully diluted	7.39p	6.52p

Changes in the composition of a group

When a subsidiary is acquired, SSAP 14, para. 29, requires the purchase consideration to be allocated between the underlying net tangible and identifiable intangible assets (e.g. trade marks and patents), on the basis of *fair value to the acquiring company*, any difference representing the premium or discount on purchase; i.e. the acquiring company should revalue the assets of a subsidiary on acquisition, rather than simply adopting the values placed on them in the accounts of the subsidiary.

When a subsidiary is acquired during the accounting period, any pre-acquisition profits must be excluded from the group's results as they are, of course, reflected in the net assets of the subsidiary at the date of acquisition.

The effective date of acquisition (or disposal) of a subsidiary is defined as the *earlier* of (*a*) the date on which consideration passes, *or* (*b*) the date on which an offer becomes or is declared unconditional (SSAP 14, para. 32). Thus, it is no longer acceptable to backdate an acquisition made towards the end of an accounting period so as to increase the apparent profits in the consolidated accounts – as was done by some groups in the past.

There are two principal ways of treating pre-acquisition profits in the consolidated profit and loss account:

1. The pre-acquisition profits of the subsidiary (and its turnover and expenses for the period prior to acquisition) may be excluded completely from the consolidated profit and loss account, and only the post-acquisition profits, turnover and expenses of the subsidiary included; for example, HABITAT MOTHERCARE's accounts for the year that ended in June 1982 simply stated:

HABITAT MOTHERCARE *Accounting policies*

Basis of Consolidation

. . . Following the acquisition of Mothercare plc, these accounts include the results for that company and its subsidiaries for the period from 14th January, 1982 to 25th June, 1982 and the assets and liabilities of those companies as at 25th June, 1982. The comparative figures relate solely to Habitat as it was prior to its acquisition of Mothercare . . .

although Mothercare's sales and profits were running at twice the level of Habitat's at the time.

2. The whole of the subsidiary's pre-tax profit for the year, including the pre-acquisition portion (and the whole year's turnover and expenses), may be included. In this case the holding company's share of the pre-acquisition profits of the subsidiary must subsequently be deducted or pre-acquisition losses added back (e.g. NORCROS, shown below).

NORCROS *Treatment of pre-acquisition and pre-disposal profits or losses*

Profit and loss account

	1981 £000	1980 £000
Group trading surplus	26,670	22,934
Associate companies	1,365	1,008
Investment income	717	705
	28,752	24,647
Interest payable	(6,388)	(5,468)

Operating surplus before taxation	22,364	19,179
Taxation	(8,409)	(8,330)
Operating surplus after taxation	13,955	10,849
Other items less taxation:		
Pre-acquisition/disposal adjustment	(194)	—
Minority shareholders' interest	(2,049)	(1,343)
Surplus attributable to Group	11,712	9,506

. . .

Note on pre-acquisition/disposal adjustment

In respect of subsidiaries acquired in the year:		
Operating surplus after taxation prior to acquisition	78	—
In respect of subsidiaries disposed of in the year:		
Operating deficit after taxation prior to disposal	116	—
	194	—

The second of these two methods is more helpful, since it shows a whole year's turnover and profits, which may then fairly be compared with the assets employed at the end of the accounting period. Furthermore, it provides some indication of the future level of profits of the group as a whole, but it is unfortunately less frequently used than method 1.

Where there is a material disposal, the consolidated profit and loss account should include the subsidiary's profits/losses up to the date of disposal, and should show the gain or loss on the sale of the investment (SSAP 14, para. 31). It is no longer acceptable to consolidate only those subsidiaries which were subsidiaries at the end of the accounting period; i.e. consolidated accounts can no longer leave out the trading results of a subsidiary for the period prior to disposal. Sufficient information should be given to enable shareholders to appreciate the effect on the group's results (e.g. WAGON INDUSTRIAL HOLDINGS, shown in the next column).

In addition, a summary of the effect of acquiring or disposing of subsidiaries during the year should be shown in a footnote to the Source and Application of Funds statement (see Chapter 18), and where a listed company has made a large transaction, shareholders will have been sent a circular giving full details or a copy of the offer document (see Chapter 21).

Sale of subsidiary – Wagon Repairs Limited

On 7 November 1979, the Company sold the whole of the share capital of Wagon Repairs Limited, together with certain properties, for a cash consideration of £4,369,000. The results of Wagon Repairs Limited from 1 April 1979 to 7 November 1979 are included in the Group consolidated profit and loss account and are as follows:

	Period 1 April to 7 November 1979 £000	Year to 31 March 1979 £000
Turnover	3,997	6,308
Profit before taxation	260	468
Profit after taxation	186	449

The Group consolidated balance sheet as at 31 March 1979 excluded the following amounts in respect of Wagon Repairs Limited:

	£000
Fixed assets	1,964
Current assets	3,288
	5,252
Current liabilities	(1,149)
Pension provision	(146)
Net assets	3,957

Further statutory requirements in consolidated accounts

The following disclosure requirements have to be satisfied only in relation to the *holding company*, not to the group:

(a) Remuneration of directors (CA 1985, S. 231). Only the remuneration of the directors of the holding company need be shown, but all their remuneration from the group should be included (e.g. fees they may receive for being directors of subsidiaries).

(b) Particulars of loans to directors and officers (CA 1985, S. 232 and 233).

(c) Employees' emoluments in excess of £30,000 per annum (CA 1985, S. 231).

However, all these requirements have to be met by each subsidiary in its own accounts, which are not normally published but do have to be filed eventually at Companies House.

Information on subsidiaries

Section 231 of the Companies Act 1985 requires that where a company has a subsidiary, its accounts must show:

(*a*) the subsidiary's name;

(*b*) if incorporated in Great Britain, the subsidiary's country of registration (England or Scotland) if different from that of the holding company; if incorporated outside Great Britain, the subsidiary's country of incorporation;

(*c*) the proportion of the nominal value of each class of the subsidiary's share capital held by the holding company.

But information about a subsidiary either incorporated, or carrying on business, outside the United Kingdom, which would be harmful to the business of the company or any of its subsidiaries if made public, need not be disclosed if the Department of Trade and Industry agrees.

Where the required information would be of excessive length, details need be given only of subsidiaries principally affecting the profits or losses and the assets of the group, but in this case full particulars must be annexed to the annual return.

Holdings in subsidiaries held directly by the holding company must be distinguished from those held by another subsidiary.

Subsidiary's holding of holding company's shares

With certain minor exceptions a subsidiary can-not be a member of its holding company (i.e. cannot hold shares in its holding company, either directly or through a nominee), and any allotment or transfer of shares in a company to its subsidiary is void (CA 1985, S. 23).

Where a group acquires a subsidiary that holds shares in the group, the group should cancel them and diminish the amount of the share capital by the nominal value of the shares (CA 1985, S. 146(2)(a)). For example, when LONDON SUMATRA PLANTATIONS, which had a subsidiary which owned shares in HARRISON & CROSFIELD, became a wholly owned subsidiary of Harrison & Crosfield, the shares held by its subsidiary were cancelled:

HARRISON & CROSFIELD *Report of the directors*

Ordinary Share Capital

1,439,989 Ordinary shares of the Company ('the Shares') representing 2.3 per cent of the issued Ordinary share capital have been held by Auxiliary Investments Limited a wholly-owned subsidiary of London Sumatra Plantations PLC, which is now itself wholly-owned by the Company . . . and under the provisions of Section 37 Companies Act 1980 the company cancelled the shares on 30th May 1984. Accordingly the authorised capital of the Company has been reduced by £1,439,989 to £84,190,011 and the issued Ordinary share capital at 30th May 1984 was £60,907,060.

THE INTERPRETATION OF CONSOLIDATED ACCOUNTS

Profitability of subsidiaries

Most listed companies are not particularly forthcoming about the profitability of the various component parts of their organisation, and many do not file the reports and accounts of their subsidiaries at Companies House at the same time as they publish their consolidated accounts.

Thus, while in theory it is possible to deconsolidate strategic parts of the group in order to find out just where the profits are being made, this may not be easy, nor may it be possible at the time the report and accounts of the holding company become available; but the effort involved can be very rewarding, as Example 15.4 shows.

Leaving aside the possibilities of devilling at Companies House, the analyst should look care-

---

Example 15.4 Analysing subsidiaries' performance:
KLEINWORT BENSON

The 1980 accounts of the merchant bank KLEINWORT BENSON showed:

	1980 £000	1979 £000
Profit for the Year after Taxation		
Banking group, after transfer to inner reserves	16,198	9,266

The Chairman's statement mentioned that the contribution of bullion dealers SHARPS PIXLEY, a wholly owned subsidiary, had been 'exceptionally large', but gave no figure for this contribution. Analysts found the actual amount from Companies House:

	1980 £000	1979 £000
Sharps Pixley profits after tax	19,140	2,430

indicating that, but for the exceptionally large contribution from bullion dealing, banking group profits could have taken a nasty tumble in 1980, instead of increasing by almost 75%. It is not, however, correct to net out the bullion dealing profits and deduce that the rest of the banking group made a loss, because the undisclosed transfer to inner reserves could well have been very substantial indeed in 1980.

---

fully at the group's published accounts to see if there are any clues as to the spread of profitability (in addition to those already gleaned from the geographical analysis, discussed in Chapter 12). Worthy of special note are the figures for pre-acquisition profits and minority interests.

Pre-acquisition profits

When a subsidiary is acquired on a known date, and its profits for the whole year are included in the holding company's consolidated profit and loss account and the pre-acquisition profits are subsequently deducted, the apportionment of the pre-acquisition share of the profits is almost always done on a time apportionment basis. It should therefore be possible to compute the profitability of that subsidiary for the year, and to compare it with any forecast made at the time of the acquisition, and with profits it earned in earlier years.

Minority interest

Where most of a group is wholly owned, a clue to the profitability of the partially owned part of the group will be given by minority interests. The figure is of particular significance where the minority interest in the profits varies sharply, as in Example 15.5.

A swing in minorities from profit to loss is especially interesting, for although the chairman's or directors' report will doubtless draw attention to a loss-maker that has been turned round, it may be more reticent about a partially owned subsidiary running into loss.

Transfer prices

A further hazard we should mention in assessing

Example 15.5   Subsidiary performance indicated by minority interests: OWEN OWEN

The Liverpool-based department store company OWEN OWEN's 1980 profit and loss account reported:

	1980 £000	1979 £000
Profit after taxation	1,903	2,287
Profit attributable to minority interests	126	181

while information on subsidiaries showed all except one to be wholly owned, and the partially owned one, G. W. ROBINSON, to be incorporated in Canada. The chairman's report explained that the Canadian subsidiary's shortfall on the previous year was more than accounted for by the loss incurred in a new store during its first full year of trading.

the profitability of individual subsidiaries is that of 'transfer pricing'. When two subsidiaries of a holding company trade substantially with each other or with the holding company (e.g. a manufacturing subsidiary wholesaling through a trading subsidiary), the transfer prices may not always be arm's length prices, and thus the profitability of the business transacted may be slanted towards one subsidiary at the expense of the other. This may be done deliberately to minimise taxation generally, to maximise profits in currencies the group most needs (e.g. for the servicing and repayment of foreign loans), and possibly to hide highly lucrative activities from the jealous eyes of potential competitors.

MERGER ACCOUNTING

(Reference: SSAP 23 *Accounting for Acquisitions and Mergers*.)

When two companies, A and B, come together in a merger effected by a share for share exchange, the *acquisition method* of accounting, as illustrated in Example 15.3, does not satisfactorily reflect a true amalgamation of interests: the assets of B are revalued, any excess of consideration over book value appearing as goodwill; the distributable reserves of B are capitalised; and any excess of the market value of Company A's shares issued over their nominal value has to go into a share premium account.

To overcome these difficulties, the *merger method* of accounting was developed, and was used in several major mergers at the end of the 1960s, including CADBURY with SCHWEPPES and TRUST HOUSE with FORTE. Under merger accounting,

aptly called 'pooling of interests' in the United States, the following occur:

1. The assets and liabilities of both companies are incorporated into the group accounts at book value.
2. The pre-acquisition reserves of Company B are not capitalised, but are available to the group.
3. The shares issued as consideration are recorded at their *nominal* value (so there is no transfer to share premium account).
4. If the total nominal value of the shares issued by Company A is more than the total nominal value of the shares of Company B, the difference is deducted from group reserves. If the total value is less, the shortfall becomes a non-distributable reserve.

Although an early Exposure Draft (ED 3, issued in 1971) advocated merger accounting in certain limited circumstances (e.g. where the merging companies were not too dissimilar in size), the ruling in a subsequent test case, *Shearer* v. *Bercain Limited*, held that, because of Section 56 of the Companies Act 1948, the merger method of accounting was not lawful.

However, the situation was changed by the Companies Act 1981, which contained provisions allowing merger accounting in certain circumstances (see CA 1985, S. 131), and an SSAP on the subject, SSAP 23, was published in April 1985.

Some companies have already taken advantage of the new legislation, for example the ARGYLL GROUP, shown below.

ARGYLL GROUP *Note to the accounts*

	1984	1983
	£000	£000
Total other reserves		
Merger capital reserve	16,924	12,544
Currency translation reserve	1,083	702
	18,007	13,246

Merger capital reserve

On 11 November 1983 the company completed the acquisition of the whole of the issued share capital of Argyll Foods and Amalgamated Distilled Products, and also acquired the minority shareholding in Gulliver Foods and Gulliver Vintners. The Company has followed the merger relief provisions of the Companies Act 1981 and has recorded these investments at the nominal value of the new ordinary shares issued.

The group accounts have been prepared in accordance with the principles of merger accounting and the merger capital reserve in the group balance sheet is set out below:

	£000
Nominal value of 174,823,221 ordinary shares issued to acquire the issued share capital of Argyll Foods and Amalgamated Distilled Products	(43,706)
Nominal value of 6,793,215 ordinary shares issued to acquire the minority interests in Gulliver Foods and Gulliver Vintners	(1,698)
Fair value of 2,449,451 ordinary shares issued to acquire warrants of Argyll Foods and 10 per cent unsecured convertible loan stock of Amalgamated Distilled Products	(3,117)
Cost of original investment in Argyll Foods and Amalgamated Distilled Products	(6,102)
	(54,623)
Issued share capital, convertible loan stock and capital reserves of Argyll Foods and Amalgamated Distilled Products and minority interests in Gulliver Foods and Gulliver Vintners	72,385
Prior year adjustments in respect of goodwill written off	(5,218)
Merger capital reserve at 31 March 1983	12,544
Merger expenses	(983)
Net proceeds from share issues in subsidiaries	4,584
Net transfer from profit and loss account in respect of redemption of preference shares and convertible loan stock in subsidiaries	779
Merger capital reserve at 31 March 1984	16,924

Chapter 16

ASSOCIATED AND RELATED COMPANIES

(Reference: SSAP 1 *Accounting for the Results of Associated Companies*.)

Associated companies

Although loosely used in other contexts, the term 'associated company' is defined for accountancy purposes in SSAP 1:

'A company not being a subsidiary of the investing group or company in which:

(a) the interest of the investing group or company is effectively that of a partner in a joint venture or consortium and the investing group or company is in a position to exercise a significant influence over the company in which the investment is made; or

(b) the interest of the investing group or company is for the long term and is substantial and, having regard to the disposition of the other shareholdings, the investing group or company is in a position to exercise a significant influence over the company in which the investment is made.'

Where the interest of the investing group or company is not effectively that of a partner in a joint venture or consortium but amounts to 20% or more of the equity voting rights of a company, it should be presumed that the investing group or company has the ability to exercise significant influence over that company unless it can clearly be demonstrated otherwise.

Where a company has a holding of 20% or more in another company, but does not treat it as an associated company, a good set of accounts will explain why, e.g. TRUSTHOUSE FORTE.

TRUSTHOUSE FORTE *1984 accounts: Note on investments*

At 31st October, 1984 the Group owned 69% of the equity of The Savoy Hotel PLC ('Savoy') representing 42.3% of the voting rights. The accounts of Savoy have not been consolidated as the Group plays no part in the management or direction of Savoy. The Group's investment in Savoy has been treated as a long-term trade investment and included at cost.

Summary of accounting treatment of associated companies

Consolidated profit and loss account
Turnover: nothing included from associates.
Pre-tax profit: share of associates, shown separately.
Tax: share of associates, shown separately.
Extraordinary items: share of associates, included in the group figure unless material.
Net profit retained: share of associates, shown separately.

Consolidated balance sheet
Unless shown at valuation, the investing group's interest should be shown at *cost*, less amounts written off, plus share of the associated companies' subsequent *retained profits and reserves*.

SSAP 1 also requires separate disclosure of the goodwill element of the cost of associates, loans to and from associates, and any balances representing normal trading transactions (if material).

Equity method of accounting

The treatment of associated companies prescribed by SSAP 1 is sometimes called the 'equity method of accounting'. It is also the method used for subsidiaries in certain circumstances when they are not consolidated (see SSAP 14, para. 24).

Related companies

The Companies Act 1985 defines a 'related company' as any body corporate, other than a group company, in which the investing company 'holds on a long-term basis a qualifying capital interest (i.e. voting equity share capital) for the purpose of securing a contribution to that company's own activities by the exercise of any control or influence arising from that interest' (Sch. 4, para. 92(1)). Where a 'qualifying capital interest' is 20% or more, the company is presumed to be a related company unless the contrary is shown.

The Act requires disclosure of shares held in and loans to related companies, the income from these shareholdings, and amounts owed to and by the related companies.

Holdings in related companies may be carried at cost, or at market value, but most companies regard companies as related only if they hold 20% or more of the voting rights, in which case they normally fall within the definition of an associated company, and are treated as such. For example, BTR describes related companies as 'companies other than subsidiaries where the group has a substantial shareholding and is in a position to exercise significant influence. The consolidated accounts include the group's share of the post acquisition reserves of all such companies.' AUTO-MATED SECURITY (HOLDINGS) simply states in its accounting policies that 'The results of the related companies are dealt with on an equity accounting basis.' But there are exceptions, as THE HIGHLAND DISTILLERIES COMPANY's accounts illustrate:

THE HIGHLAND DISTILLERIES COMPANY *Accounting policies*

Group Accounts
The Highland Distilleries Company plc owns 35.4 per cent of the issued ordinary share capital of Robertson & Baxter Limited and 34.0 per cent of the issued share capital of its subsidiary, Dunard Insurance Group Limited. These companies are related companies under the definitions laid down in Schedule 1 paragraph 91 of the Companies Act 1981 but are not, in the opinion of the Directors, associated companies within the definitions laid down in Statement of Standard Accounting Practice No. 1 because, as Robertson & Baxter Limited and Dunard Insurance Group Limited are the subsidiaries of another company, the Highland Distilleries Company plc is not in a position to exercise significant influence over their policies. Dividends received are included in Group profits.

To summarise, associated companies are also by definition related companies, but related companies are *not* associated companies if the investing company:

(*a*) is not in a position to exercise significant influence, *and/or*

(*b*) holds less than 20% of the equity voting rights.

As both (*a*) and (*b*) are comparatively rare, the terms 'associated company' and 'related company' are generally regarded as virtually synonymous, and at least one company has even regarded them as interchangeable within the same set of accounts:

CRODA *Notes to the 1983 accounts*

Note 8 Transfer to (from) reserves

	1983 £000	1982 £000
. . . . .		
In associated companies	455	91

Note 11 Investments

	Shares in related companies £000
. . . . .	
Share of retained profit	455

Value of investments in associated or related companies

It is easy to see why SSAP 1 calls for more information about associated companies. Before the SSAP was introduced, it was not uncommon to find major trade investments carried at their original cost, although they were yielding a substantial income and were clearly worth much more than the balance sheet showed. For example, in the extracts from GUINNESS's accounts (illustrated overleaf), in which investments in related companies are stated under the equity method of accounting (i.e. are treated in the same way as associated companies), they are shown at a value of £59.2m [E]. Prior to SSAP 1 they could have been carried in the balance sheet at cost totalling, listed and unlisted, a mere £3.4m [G], although the share of profits from them in 1984 was £16.5m [A].

Presentation of information on associated or related companies

Guinness's accounts provide a good example of the treatment of associated or related companies. The share of profits appears on the face of the

GUINNESS *Extracts from 1984 accounts*

Consolidated profit and loss account

	Text ref.	1984 £m	1983 £m
Trading profit		64.9	61.7
Exceptional items		4.0	10.3
		60.9	51.4
Share of profits of related companies	[A]	16.5	15.8
Net finance charges		7.0	8.4
		70.4	58.8
Taxation on profit on ordinary activities (Note 7)	[B]	25.1	20.7
Profit on ordinary activities after taxation		45.3	38.1

Note 7 Taxation on profit on ordinary activities

		1984	1983
Holding and subsidiary companies' current taxation		17.9	14.1
UK deferred taxation		0.7	1.1
		18.6	15.2
Related companies – share of taxation	[C]	6.5	5.5
		25.1	20.7

Consolidated balance sheet – fixed assets

		1984	1983
Tangible assets		280.3	237.1
Investments (Note 16)	[D]	65.7	52.8
		346.0	289.9

Note 16 Investments

		1984	1983
Investments in related companies (Note 17) stated under the equity method of accounting	[E]	59.2	49.0
Other investments		6.5	3.8
		65.7	52.8

Note 17 Investments in related companies [F]

Shares at cost, less goodwill written off:

		1984	1983
Listed – Overseas: market value £35.3m (£27.1m)	[G]	1.1	1.1
Unlisted		2.3	2.6
Share of post acquisition reserves – listed		37.5	27.9
– unlisted		18.2	17.3
Loans		0.1	0.1
		59.2	49.0

The following table analyses the attributable profit before taxation and post acquisition reserves of related companies resident in each territory:

	Profit before taxation		Reserves	
	1984 £m	1983 £m	1984 £m	1983 £m
United Kingdom	1.7	1.7	3.4	3.2
Republic of Ireland	1.9	1.9	12.7	12.5
Africa	12.9	12.2	39.6	29.5
	16.5	15.8	55.7	45.2

Of the dividends declared by related companies £4.8m (£5.0m) [H] is attributable to the Group and includes £4.6m (£4.1m) from listed companies.

The retained earnings of certain African companies are subject to dividend and exchange control restrictions. Attributable post acquisition reserves include non-distributable reserves of £27.9m (£19.2m).

consolidated profit and loss account as a separate item [A], but the share of the tax charge appears only in a note [C].

It is worth noting that, whereas in consolidated accounts the tax charge which appears [B] includes the entire tax charge of the holding company and all its subsidiaries, the amount included for associated companies is only the holding company's share of tax of associated companies. Similarly, the profit before tax of the group is the entire profit of the holding company and its subsidiaries, but *only the holding company's share* of profit of associated companies is shown.

In the group balance sheet, Guinness follows the normal practice of including the group's interest in associated/related companies in a single figure for Investments [D], with a breakdown between investments in related companies and other investments in a note [E], and details of cost and the share of post-acquisition reserves in a further note [F]. This note also contains a fairly rare example of a geographical analysis of investments in related companies, details of dividends [H] and a warning note about exchange controls in certain African countries.

Some companies with investments which would otherwise qualify as associated/related companies prefer not to treat them as such if they are in countries which restrict the remittance of dividends, e.g. HARRISON & CROSFIELD:

HARRISON & CROSFIELD *Note on other investments*

Investments at 31st December 1983 include the following material holdings in excess of 10% of equity capital:

. . . .

Malayalam Plantations (India) Limited	40%

The balance sheet amount of investment in India represents . . . . the Group's interest in the net assets of Malayalam Plantations (India) Limited, . . . In view of remittance restrictions this investment is not treated as a related company. The directors are of the opinion that the present value of the Group's interest is not less than the balance sheet amount.

Extraordinary items, retentions and reserves

The notes to Guinness's accounts also contain details of extraordinary items that are material [I] and of retentions [J] as required by SSAP 1, and explain the increase from £49.0m to £59.2m that took place in the value of investments in related companies during the year:

GUINNESS *Further extracts from 1984 accounts*

Note 8 Extraordinary items		£m
Disposal, closure and reorganization costs		6.3
Related companies' extraordinary items	[I]	3.5
		9.8

Note 17 Changes in related companies	
At 1 October 1983	49.0
Exchange adjustments	1.8
Disposals	(0.3)
Increase in net assets (Note 29)	8.7
	59.2

Note 29 Reserves – Related companies		
At 1 October 1983		45.2
Exchange adjustments		1.8
		47.0
Retained earnings	[J]	1.7
Surplus on revaluation of properties		7.0
		55.7

From this information we can work out what happened to Guinness's £16.5m share of related companies' profits in 1984:

		£m
Taxation	[C]	6.5
Dividends	[H]	4.8
Extraordinary items	[I]	3.5
Retained earnings	[J]	1.7
		16.5

Drawbacks of SSAP 1

Although companies now disclose much more information on substantial and influential investments in other companies than they did before SSAP 1, the equity method of accounting does give the more imaginative members of the business community a great deal of scope for 'dressing up' their accounts. They do so by making marginal adjustments to their holdings:

Example 16.1   Dressing up accounts under SSAP 1

Year 1: Holding Company A holds 19.95% of the voting equity of Company B. Company B makes pre-tax profits of £10m, but distributes only £1m of dividends.

Result: Contribution to Group A's pre-tax profits is £285,000 (£199,500 dividends and £85,500 associated tax credits).

113

Year 2: Group A has increased its holding in Company B to 20.1%, has obtained board representation, and has adopted equity accounting. Company B's profits and dividends are the same as in Year 1.

Result: Group A will include its share of the now associated or related Company B's pre-tax profits of £2,010,000, an increase of more than 600%!

Year 3: In a rising market, Company B's shares are now standing at twice 'cost plus share of subsequent retained profits and reserves'. Group A wants to dress up its balance sheet, so it changes its accounting policy to show its holding in Company B at valuation (i.e. market price).

Result: The balance sheet amount shown for Group A's investment in associated or related companies doubles.

Year 4: Company B makes losses. Group A wants to avoid including its share of these losses in its profit and loss account, so the holding company either sells a shade more than 0.1% of the voting shares of Company B or takes its man off Company B's board.

Result: Group A's profit and loss account includes only dividends (if any) received from Company B, as B is no longer an associated or related company.

Similar manoeuvres can take place at the 50% level in order, for instance, to turn a 51%-owned subsidiary that is heavily borrowed into a 49%-owned associated company whose borrowings don't appear on the investing group's balance sheet (although they will appear as a contingent liability of the group if the holding company has guaranteed them). This trick can do wonders for the investing group's gearing, but it is only 'fair' if the group is no longer responsible for the borrowings of its former subsidiary, i.e. if it hasn't guaranteed them.

In order to bowl out this sort of window dressing, the analyst should check:

(*a*) for any changes in the group's accounting policy on associated or related companies;

(*b*) for any companies that have either become or ceased to be associated or related companies during the year;

(*c*) under Contingent Liabilities, for any guarantees of associated or related company borrowings.

If this sort of thing is found to be going on, we would advise you not to trust the management unless you are sure that any changes are entirely innocent.

Chapter 17

FOREIGN EXCHANGE DIFFERENCES

(Reference: SSAP 20 *Foreign Currency Translation.*)

The problem of variable exchange rates

Until relatively recently, companies with overseas subsidiaries or associates had little difficulty in producing group accounts: most exchange rates were fixed and, although minor differences arose due to the cost of *conversion* (the process of exchanging money in one currency into money in another currency), the adjustments were trifling and *translation* (the process of expressing accounts kept in one currency in terms of another currency for the purpose of consolidation) was simple, except where major devaluations occurred.

With the advent of floating exchange rates, the treatment of overseas accounts has become a major problem, in particular over the rate (or rates) of exchange to be used in translating the profit and loss account and balance sheet items of foreign subsidiaries and associates into sterling when producing consolidated accounts. The choice lies between:

(a) the *closing rate*: the spot rate of exchange at the balance sheet date;
(b) the *average rate* of exchange during the period; *and*
(c) the *historical rate*: the spot rate of exchange at the date of the transaction.

Various methods of translation use different combinations of these rates.

The development of a UK accounting standard

Foreign currency translation is a difficult area and three exposure drafts were needed to develop an acceptable SSAP on the subject, SSAP 20, which was published in April 1983.

SSAP 20 is concerned with:

(a) *individual companies* which enter directly into business transactions denominated in foreign currencies, *and*
(b) *groups* which conduct foreign operations through subsidiaries, associated companies or branches whose operations are based in a country other than that of the investing company, and whose accounting records are maintained in a currency other than that of the investing company.

Individual companies

When a company enters into transactions denominated in a foreign currency (i.e. a currency other than that in which the company's accounts are kept), SSAP 20 requires that they should normally be translated at the rate ruling at the date of each transaction, i.e. at the spot rate.

In the annual accounts of the individual company:

(a) non-monetary assets, e.g. plant and machinery, will already be carried in the accounts in the company's reporting currency, having been translated at the time of acquisition;
(b) monetary assets and liabilities denominated in foreign currencies should be translated at the closing rate;
(c) all exchange differences should be reported as part of the profit or loss for the year (unless resulting from extraordinary items), e.g. differences arising from variations in exchange rates between the dates of invoicing in a foreign currency and the dates of payment.

Example 17.1 illustrates the treatment of four simple transactions involving foreign currency:

Example 17.1   Treatment of foreign transactions by an individual company

Able PLC is a UK company whose accounting year ends on 31 December. During the year, Able:

		Rate of exchange
(i)	Purchases hock from a West German company, Weinburger GmbH, on 31 October for DM50,000	£1 = DM4.0
	Pays Weinburger GmbH on 30 November	£1 = DM3.8
	Goods remain in stock at 31 December	
(ii)	Sells cider to Pomme et cie, a French company, for FFr120,000	£1 = FFr12.00
	Debt remains unpaid at 31 December	
(iii)	Borrows on long-term loan from a Swiss bank SFr1,000,000 on 1 April	£1 = SFr4.00
(iv)	Purchases plant and machinery from a US company for $480,000 on ·15 September	£1 = US$1.20
	Pays on 30 September	£1 = US$1.10

On 31 December exchange rates are:

£1 = DM3.75
£1 = FFr12.50
£1 = SFr3.00
£1 = US$1.30

The company maintains its bank account in sterling and buys or sells foreign exchange as needed on the spot market.

Under SSAP 20 the transactions of Able will be treated as follows:

(i) The purchase will be recorded at the rate ruling on 31 October, £1 = DM4.00. The hock will appear in stock at a book cost of £12,500 and the eventual cost of sales will also be £12,500.
When the account is paid, the rate has fallen to £1 = DM3.8, so it is necessary to pay £13,158 to buy the necessary currency.
An exchange loss of £658 will be charged to the profit and loss account for the year.

(ii) The sale is translated at the rate ruling at the date of the transaction, £1 = FF12.00 = £10,000. At the end of the year, the debtor is a monetary item and translated at the closing rate, £1 = FFr12.50 = £9,600.
The resulting exchange loss of £400 will be charged to the profit and loss account for the year.

(iii) The loan will initially be translated at the transaction rate of £1 = SFr4.00, i.e. as £250,000. At the year end the loan will be translated at the closing rate £1 = SFr3.00, i.e. as £333,333.

The exchange loss of £83,333 may be treated as 'financing' and disclosed separately as part of 'other interest receivable/payable and similar income/expense'.

(iv) The fixed asset will be translated at the transaction rate of £1 = $1.20, i.e. as £400,000. The asset will continue to appear at this cost unless it is revalued. Depreciation will be charged on £400,000. Payment for the machine will take (at £1 = $1.10) £436,364. The loss of £36,364 will be charged to the profit and loss account for the year.

In Able PLC's statement of accounting policies, the treatment of these purchases and sale would be explained in a note similar to that in CHURCH's accounts, illustrated below.

CHURCH *Extract from note on accounting policies*

Foreign Currencies

Assets and liabilities at the balance sheet date . . . are translated to sterling at the rate of exchange ruling at the balance sheet date.

Exchange differences arising on trading during the year are taken into account in arriving at the profit before taxation.

Group accounts

Under SSAP 20, the *'closing rate net investment method'* should normally be used in preparing consolidated accounts. Under this method:

(a) *Balance sheet* items should be translated into the currency of the holding company at the 'closing rate' (the spot rate on the balance sheet date). Differences arising from the retranslation of the opening *net investment* at the closing rate should be taken to reserves.

The *net investment* is the holding company's proportion of the subsidiary or associated company's share capital and reserves. (Long-term indebtedness between members of the group should be treated as part of the net investment.)

(b) *Profit and loss account* items should be translated using either the average rate for the accounting period or the closing rate. Any difference between translation at the average rate and the closing rate should be taken to reserves.

The rate used can make a considerable difference to the reported profit; for example, if a West German subsidiary made a profit of DM14 million during a year in which the rate of exchange fell from DM4.2 = £1 at the beginning of the year to DM3.5 = £1 at the end of the year, averaging DM4.0 = £1 because most of the fall occurred in the last three months, on an average basis the group accounts would include West German profits of £3.5 million; on a closing rate basis they would include £4 million.

If the closing rate method is used, no difference will arise between the balance sheet and the profit and loss account. If the average rate is used there will be a difference which, under SSAP 20, should be recorded as a movement on reserves. The method used should be stated in the accounts, as BLACKWOOD HODGE illustrates here:

BLACKWOOD HODGE *Extract from note on accounting policies*

Foreign Currencies
Profits and losses of overseas subsidiaries are translated into sterling at the average rates ruling during the year. Assets and liabilities are translated into sterling at the rates ruling at the balance sheet date. The resultant exchange differences are shown as movements on reserves.

(c)   *Holding company's foreign exchange borrowings:* where these have been used to finance equity investment in foreign subsidiaries or associates *in the same currency*, differences arising on their translation (at the closing rate) due to currency movements during the period may be offset against differences arising from the retranslation of the opening net investment in (a) above.

In countries with very high rates of inflation it may be necessary to revalue fixed assets in the local currency before translating them at the closing rate, as the accounts of the printing group MCCORQUODALE illustrate:

MCCORQUODALE *Extract from note on accounting policies*

Foreign currency translation
All assets and liabilities expressed in foreign currencies have been translated into sterling at the rates of exchange ruling at the balance sheet date . . .
The local currency profits of the Brazilian associated company are arrived at after charging depreciation based upon the value of fixed assets after their upward restatement for inflation in accordance with local official indices. Over time, these indices broadly correspond to the rate of decrease in the purchasing power of the Brazilian cruzeiro.

The temporal method
Where, and only where, the trade of a subsidiary is a direct extension of the trade of a holding company, e.g. a subsidiary acting purely as a selling agency in a foreign country, the temporal method of translation should be used:

(a)   all transactions should be translated at the rate ruling on the transaction date or at an average rate for a period if this is not materially different;
(b)   *non-monetary assets should not normally be retranslated* at the balance sheet date;
(c)   monetary assets and liabilities should be retranslated at the closing rate; and
(d)   all exchange gains and losses should be taken to the profit and loss account as part of the profit and loss from ordinary activities.

Current UK practice

Realised differences
Most companies deal with realised differences above the line, but some treat major losses as extraordinary items. The WEIR GROUP, for instance, borrowed DM55 million against two promissory notes in April 1970 and used the proceeds (£6.3 million) mainly for investment in the United Kingdom. Then, as the pound fell year by year, the company made a series of provisions to cover the increase in the sterling equivalent of the debt, treating the provisions as extraordinary items (i.e. below the line) and, when in 1975 the loan was repaid early, WEIR also treated the terminal loss as an extraordinary item. As the figures from the accounts (overleaf) show, the sums involved were significant in relation to pre-tax profits.

The overall loss of around £3.6 million on a £6.3 million loan was even more significant because it was not allowable for Corporation Tax purposes.

Weir presumably borrowed Deutschmarks at 7¼% because interest rates were lower in Europe, but although the company may have been extraordinarily unlucky with the weakness of sterling, the borrowings were made in the normal course of the company's business, and so the treatment of the losses as extraordinary items is open to question. However, Weir did realise how vulnerable the unmatched loan made them, and negotiated early repayment in 1975 instead of 1979: as the sterling/DM rate subsequently fell to less than half that of 1970, early repayment saved the company from a further loss of at least £3 million.

Unrealised differences
Almost all UK companies translate their fixed assets at the closing rate and deal with unrealised surpluses and unrealised deficits direct to reserves, but there is less uniformity in the presentation of information. Some companies, like

WEIR GROUP *Treatment of losses on foreign currency borrowings*

Year end Dec	7¼% DM Loan Value in balance sheet	Extraordinary items on loans P & L account	Reported pre-tax profit
	£	£	£
1970	6,301,919	–	1,652,161
1971	6,588,799	(273,364)	2,320,727
1972	7,323,569	(751,278)	2,549,492
1973	8,814,103	(1,530,671)	2,957,302
1974	9,717,314	(903,211)	3,023,816
1975	–	(167,786)	6,205,402

HEPWORTH CERAMIC illustrated below, include an overall figure for exchange adjustments in a statement on retained profits or movements on reserves directly below the profit and loss account, with a detailed breakdown in a supporting note; other companies only show differences on exchange piecemeal in various notes, which is less helpful: the analyst has to scratch around to discover the extent of exchange differences, and even then may not get a full picture.

HEPWORTH CERAMIC *Details of exchange adjustments*

Statement of retained profits

		1983 £000	1982 £000
Profit and loss account at 1st January		80,350	88,109
Profit (loss) retained		6,592	(13,139)
Exchange adjustments	Note 8	4,057	5,502
Goodwill written off		(66)	(122)
Profit and loss account at 31st December		90,933	80,350

Note 8   Exchange adjustments

	1983	1982
Tangible assets	3,211	3,823
Investments	181	95
Working capital, creditors and provisions	2,695	3,472
Finance debt	(1,532)	(1,486)
Cash at bank less bank overdrafts	(498)	(402)
	4,057	5,502

Quarterly and half-yearly figures
Companies which use year-end rates in translating profit and loss account items create a problem in quarterly and half-yearly figures, since the closing rate cannot be known until the year is over, and the quarterly and half-yearly profits have to be retranslated later. Comparable figures present further problems; for example UNILEVER translates quarterly results and comparative figures for the previous year at the closing rate for the previous year. As a result, the report for the first quarter of 1984 showed operating profit for the first quarter of 1983 at £150m, although the report for the first quarter of 1983 had shown it at £165m.

Taxation

The position with regard to overseas activities is complicated by the problems of taxation. Unless a profit or loss item falls within the scope of a tax schedule dealing with income subject to Corporation Tax, or arises from the disposal of an asset in such a way as to be within the computation of a capital gain, then the profit is not taxable, and no relief is available in respect of any loss.

In particular, losses on repayment of foreign borrowings are not allowable for tax purposes. Some companies, including ICI, have overcome this difficulty by channelling foreign currency borrowings through a separate finance company subsidiary; there is no distinction between capital and revenue losses in a banking-type operation so foreign exchange losses show up as revenue losses and qualify for full tax relief.

What the analyst should study

Because of the variety of ways in which UK companies may treat foreign exchange differences, the accounts of companies with substantial foreign interests or overseas borrowings need careful study.

A suggested sequence to follow is to start with the statement of accounting policies, to see what method the company uses to deal with foreign exchange differences, and then check the following:

1.   The profit and loss account and reserves, to

see what differences have been taken below the line (either separately or as extraordinary items) and what have been taken direct to reserves. In addition, the amount due to exchange differences taken above the line may sometimes be disclosed.

2. Loans – to establish the extent of overseas borrowings, their change in value in sterling terms, and the degree to which they match the countries in which overseas operations are conducted. Unfortunately this may not always be possible, because companies are not *compelled* to disclose a breakdown of their borrowings (or their cash) – an omission from the Companies Acts which has not been remedied by SSAP 20. Where operations are in politically risky areas, local borrowings may help avoid the company being left with debts that still have to be honoured elsewhere in the event of the assets they financed being confiscated.

3. Fixed assets, to see what exchange differences have been credited or debited.

4. Current assets, to look for large amounts of cash. These may indicate:

(*a*) profits from overseas operations which the company cannot transfer out of the country of origin because of local exchange control regulations, *or*

(*b*) profits earned in low-tax areas and held there to avoid the UK tax that would be payable on remission, *and/or*

(*c*) overseas profits being held overseas for further investment outside the United Kingdom.

Finally, one should keep an eye open for mention of foreign currency in the chairman's statement, the directors' report and elsewhere.

Unmatched overseas borrowings

By far the most dramatic impact that currency fluctuations have had on the profitability of UK companies in recent years has been the effect of unmatched borrowings (borrowings in one country's currency to invest in another country). Companies have sometimes had little choice in the matter – for example with capital investment in France, where the French have insisted that foreign capital should finance foreign investment

---

RTZ *Exchange losses on long term loans*

Consolidated profit and loss account		1983 £ million		1982 £ million
Net profit on ordinary activities attributable to RTZ shareholders		172.5		103.5
Earnings per ordinary share	59.31p		38.44p	
Exchange losses on long term loans (note 9)		(25.2)		(9.4)
Extraordinary items		(35.1)		(20.1)
Net profit after extraordinary items and exchange losses on long term loans		112.2		74.0
Dividends paid and proposed		54.9		41.7
Retained profit for the year		57.3		32.3

Note 2   Currency translation
Accounts of overseas companies in foreign currencies are translated into sterling at the quoted rates of exchange at the year-end. Exchange differences on translation of net assets and on matching foreign currency long term loans are dealt with through reserves. Exchange differences on other foreign currency long term loans are dealt with in the profit and loss account.

Note 9   Exchange movements on long term loans

	1983 £ million	1982 £ million
The amounts included under exchange losses on foreign currency loans, after deducting outside shareholders' interests, are as follows		
Realised losses on repayment	(6.8)	(6.2)
Provision for losses on outstanding loans, less provided in previous years	(31.3)	(21.2)
Share of exchange losses of related companies	(5.6)	(5.2)
Adjustment for losses included as part of the exchange adjustment on translation of net assets	18.5	23.2
	(25.2)	(9.4)

in their country – but in most cases unmatched borrowings have been entered into voluntarily by companies that have sought the lower interest rates prevailing in stronger-currency countries. As the lower interest rates (broadly reflecting the lower expectations of inflation) benefit the borrower's profitability in the short run then it seems only reasonable, when the difference catches up in the form of a provision for or loss on repayment, that it too should be reflected in the profit and loss account, but this has seldom been the case to date.

WEIR GROUP, described earlier in this chapter, provides a good example of the costliness of borrowing in a strong currency to finance operations in a weak-currency country; the effect can involve very substantial write-offs, as the example of RTZ, shown on the previous page, illustrates. Note that RTZ takes exchange losses on its long-term loans after profit attributable to shareholders, i.e. below the line, to avoid reducing earnings per share – which we find hard to justify.

Chapter 18

SOURCE AND APPLICATION OF FUNDS STATEMENTS

(Reference: SSAP 10 *Statements of Source and Application of Funds.*)

Purpose

Traditionally, published accounts have comprised:

(*a*) a balance sheet providing a statement of the financial position at the end of a company's accounting year, together with 'corresponding figures' showing the position at the end of the previous year (which is, of course, the same as the position at the beginning of the year being reported upon);

(*b*) a profit and loss account showing, in particular, the amount of profit retained in the business from that year.

It is today widely accepted that, apart from share capital issued or redeemed and any revaluation of fixed assets, the profit and loss account (together with the statement of retained profits/reserves) should explain all changes in shareholders' funds between one balance sheet date and the next, including prior year adjustments and items such as preliminary expenses which are allowed to be charged direct to reserves. It thus provides a link between successive balance sheets.

The profit and loss account does not, however, bridge the gap between each item in successive balance sheets, which can only be done by a note on the individual item (e.g. fixed assets) or by a source and application of funds statement, sometimes called a funds flow statement or more simply a funds statement. In the United States such a statement is called a statement of changes in financial position, which is precisely what it is: a statement explaining the balance sheet changes which occurred during the period.

Current practice

Source and application statements have for some years been prepared externally by investors and analysts seeking a more detailed understanding of company reports and accounts. During the 1960s there was a strong trend in the United States and Canada towards the inclusion of funds statements as part of the annual accounts, and this is today general practice there.

In the United Kingdom the practice of including funds statements in reports and accounts grew steadily during the 1960s and 1970s, and is now mandatory under SSAP 10 for most companies.

At this stage we should perhaps point out that where a company itself prepares a funds statement it *may* make use of facts and figures not otherwise available to the external analyst, and this can be a useful source of additional information. For example, in 1984 BEJAM's report and accounts contained the following information:

BEJAM *1984 Report and Accounts*

Report of the Directors

During the year the Company disposed of its 50% interest in the associated company Meatpack Hampshire Limited to a new company headed by the existing management of Meatpack.

Note on Investment in related companies

	Share of net assets £000
Disposal	(895)

Source and Application of Funds statement

Proceeds from sale of shares in related company	365

It was therefore possible to deduce that BEJAM had sold its 50% interest in Meatpack Hampshire for rather less than half asset value. It was also of interest that the contribution from related companies had turned from a loss of £198,000 in 1983 to a profit of £158,000 in 1984, so the disposal of the Meatpack interest at an apparently 'give-away' price may have been a very shrewd move on the part of the company.

In this chapter we will look at two separate aspects of funds statements:

(a)   the requirements of SSAP 10;
(b)   the interpretation of source and application statements, including how to estimate the likely requirements for funds in the future.

The requirements of SSAP 10

Companies with a turnover of £25,000 or more per annum must include a statement of source and application of funds both for the period under review and for the corresponding previous period.

Normal layout
No standard form of statement is prescribed, but the appendix to SSAP 10 gives examples in the following format:

Source	Funds generated from operations; Funds from other sources.
Application	Dividends, tax, fixed assets;
Increase/	
decrease	
in working capital	Showing finally the increase/decrease in net liquid resources.

This format is broadly followed by most companies, though with many variations, particularly over where to start. 'Retained earnings' used to be the traditional starting point before SSAP 10, but as funds statements now have to include dividends paid, the latest point at which a statement can start is 'Profits after tax'. The examples given in the appendix to SSAP 10 suggest including both dividends and tax by beginning with 'Profit before tax'. This is the normal starting point (as illustrated by AUTOMATED SECURITY (HOLDINGS)'s well-presented statement opposite) but a few companies, ICI for example, start right back at 'Trading profit' and thus include interest payments too, so this is the first point to check when studying a funds statement: where does it start?

Treatment of minorities
Where the accounts are those of a group, SSAP 10 requires the funds statement to be 'so framed as to reflect the operations of the group'. The examples in SSAP 10 achieve this by beginning with the item:

Profit before tax and extraordinary
items, *less* minority interests   £xxx

and then adding back

Minority interests in the retained
profits of the year   £xxx

Alternatively, some companies do not deduct minority interests, but show 'Dividends paid to minorities' as an application of funds, but the net effect is just the same: retentions on the part of minorities are left in as a source of funds.

Associated and related companies
Associated and related companies are an entirely different matter. The holding company does not control the funds of associated or related companies, so they are not treated as part of the holding company's funds. However, the profit and loss account of the holding company does include its share of the profit of associated and related companies as part of the profit before tax; some of this may have been remitted by way of dividends paid to the holding company (and thus is a source), and some may have been retained by the associates. This latter part has to be deducted as an adjustment not involving the movement of funds:

Profit retained in associated companies   £xxx

'Netting off'
SSAP 10 recommends (though does not specifically require) that there should be a minimum of 'netting off', since netting off tends to mask the significance of individually important figures.

There is, for instance, a vast difference between A and B in the following:

	Company A	Company B
Purchases of fixed-asset investments	£56,000	£488,000
less Sales of fixed-asset investments	4,200	436,200
	51,800	51,800

if the portfolio of investments at the beginning of the period was £468,100. For A the movement during the period represents a minor increase in the portfolio, whereas B suggests almost a 100% change. But both would appear on a 'netting off' basis as an application of £51,800.

Profit on disposals
The accounting standard does not specifically require the profit or loss on the sale of an asset to be shown. Some companies, like Automated Security (Holdings), do show 'Profit on disposal of tangible fixed assets' and 'Proceeds of disposal of tangible fixed assets' as two separate items, but

others show only a single figure for 'Disposals'. In these cases the profit or loss can usually be calculated from information given in the note on fixed assets, as we illustrate from Automated Security (Holdings)'s 1983 accounts in the next column.

If the profit (loss) comes out at zero, then it is almost certain that it has been included in the depreciation charge. If Automated Security (Holdings) had done this, the depreciation charge would have been increased by 515 to 3,785, and the item 'Loss on sale of fixed assets: 515' would have been omitted. Where a company has sold fixed assets at a profit the depreciation charge will, of course, be reduced.

AUTOMATED SECURITY (HOLDINGS) *Disposal of assets*

Note on Tangible fixed assets	*Total*
Cost or valuation	£000
. . . .	
Disposals	(3,207)
Depreciation	
. . . .	
Disposals	(2,545)

The calculation is then:	£000
Proceeds from sale of fixed assets	147
less Net book cost	
(Cost – depreciation)	662
Profit (Loss) on disposal	(515)

AUTOMATED SECURITY (HOLDINGS) *Statement of source and application of funds*

	1983 £000	1982 £000
Source of Funds		
Profit on ordinary activities before taxation	4,396	3,241
ITEMS NOT INVOLVING THE MOVEMENT OF FUNDS		
Increase in advance rentals	457	1,359
Development expenditure	—	56
Depreciation	3,270	2,956
Goodwill written off	(1,145)	(367)
Loss on sale of fixed assets	515	415
FUNDS GENERATED FROM OPERATIONS	7,493	7,660
FUNDS FROM OTHER SOURCES		
Proceeds from rights issue (less expenses)	—	8,265
Increase in loans	885	315
Proceeds from sale of fixed assets	147	100
Proceeds from share placings	3,978	—
TOTAL INFLOW	12,503	16,340
Application of Funds		
Purchase of fixed assets	9,821	7,097
Taxation paid	235	135
Dividends paid	488	335
Purchase of investments	1,845	295
Repayment of loans	946	645
Movements in working capital (see below)	2,639	111
TOTAL OUTFLOW	15,974	8,618
Movement in Net Liquid Funds	(3,471)	7,722
MOVEMENTS IN WORKING CAPITAL		
Increase in stocks	440	962
Increase in debtors	1,022	121
Increase in short term loans	726	—
Increase/(Decrease) in creditors	451	(972)
	2,639	111

Purchase or disposal of a subsidiary

Under SSAP 10, a source and application statement may either reflect the purchase or disposal of a subsidiary as a single item, or reflect the effect in each item in the statement. In either case SSAP 10 encourages companies to provide a breakdown of the figure for Acquisitions at the bottom of the source and application of funds statement, for example, LRC INTERNATIONAL's 1983 accounts, illustrated here:

LRC INTERNATIONAL *Details of an acquisition*

Source and Application of Funds

Source of Funds

. . . .

Application of funds

. . . .

Analysis of the acquisition of Tynecolour (Holdings) Limited

	£000		£000
Net assets acquired:		Discharged by:	
Fixed assets	716	Cash paid	959
Goodwill	674	Shares issued at	
Stocks	163	market price	30
Debtors	357	Net borrowings at	
Creditors	(209)	date of	
Deferred taxation	(245)	acquisition	467
	1,456		1,456

The interpretation of source and application statements

A funds statement may be useful to a chairman at an annual general meeting, or to an analyst when confronted by an investor asking embarrassing questions such as:

> Where did all the profits go?
>
> If those are the profits, why wasn't it possible to pay a larger dividend?
>
> How come, when there has been a loss, that a dividend can still be paid?
>
> What happened to the proceeds of the recent rights issue?
>
> What happened to the proceeds of disposal of a major fixed asset (e.g. freehold property)?
>
> In the case of a group growing rapidly by takeovers for paper (shares or loan stock), how did the company pay for these new subsidiaries?

However, a funds statement, or a series of funds statements, may also be of use to an analyst trying to trace movements over several years, to identify the trends in liquidity and to estimate the likely need for funds in the future.

Interpreting an imaginary funds statement

Example 18.1 shows the funds statement from an imaginary set of accounts for 1984, together with a projected statement for the year ending 31 December 1985. Each line is numbered for ease of reference (S for source, A for application, while the line numbers in the table on 'Other information' at the bottom refer to other pro-formas in Chapter 24).

Let us look at this information in conjunction with comments gleaned from the chairman's report.

Changes in net liquid funds (Line A 12)

The improvement in 1983 was due mainly to the sale of a subsidiary (Line S 21) and to the low tax paid (Line A 1).

In 1984 the fall in net liquid assets was due mainly to the purchase of a subsidiary for £4 million in February 1984 (Line A 5) being paid for in cash (no new shares were issued, Line S 15), only part of which was financed by an increase in loans of £3 million (Line S 17), the remainder being funded by deferred tax and an increase in overdraft.

Chairman's comments as an aid to forecasting liquidity

IEC's turnover went up by more than £10 million in 1984, but pre-tax profits increased by only £377,000. The chairman commented in his report that turnover in the first three months of the current year was 27% up on the corresponding period in 1984 but that, although all divisions are currently trading profitably, increased costs and strong competition are continuing to put pressure on margins. Despite currently adverse trading conditions, the board of IEC has every confidence in the future prosperity of the company, and is continuing the capital investment programme initiated in 1983 so as to be ready to take maximum advantage of the economic upturn when it comes. In addition, the chairman announced that, since the year end, a further acquisition had been made, the consideration being £500,000 in cash.

Using last year's figures, current trading conditions and anything we can glean from the chairman's comments on this year's prospects, let us now try to project 1985's sources and applications for the IMAGINARY ENGINEERING COMPANY. Of course, any attempt to project the future financial position of a company without the detailed and up-to-date information available within that company is bound to be rough and ready, but it will indicate whether the company is growing healthily, remaining static or heading for cash problems.

IEC's projected funds statement for 1985

Line S 1 1984's improvement included 11 months' contribution from the £4m acquisition; as margins

Example 18.1   Funds statement: 'IMAGINARY ENGINEERING COMPANY' ('IEC')

Line*	Year ending 31 December	1983	1984	1985 Projected
	Source	£000	£000	£000
S 1	Profit before tax *less* minorities	6,247	6,624	7,000
S 2	Extraordinary items	(203)	—	
S 4	Depreciation	3,650	3,741	3,800
S 6	Minority retentions	298	327	330
S 14	**Generated from operations**	9,992	10,692	11,130
S 15	Issue of shares	—	—	
S 17	Increase in Loans	—	3,000	
S 18	(Decrease in Loans)	—	—	(650)
S 19	Disposal of fixed assets	802	758	775
S 21	Sale of subsidiaries	740	—	
S 23	**Source total**	11,534	14,450	11,255
	Application			
A 1	Tax paid	1,947	2,927	3,100
A 2	Dividends	1,780	1,958	2,154
A 4	Purchase of fixed assets	4,890	3,880	4,380
A 5	Purchase of subsidiary	—	4,000	500
A 11	Increase (Decrease) in Working Capital	1,277	2,263	2,545
A 12	Increase (Decrease) in Net Liquid Funds	1,640	(578)	(1,424)
	Application total	11,534	14,450	11,255
	Other information			
112	Debt/Equity ratio	64.1%	82.8%	
106	Acid test	0.82	0.61	
1	Turnover (£000)	32,705	42,857	
110	Working capital ratio	21.7%	22.3%	
	Capital commitments:			
	Authorised (£000)	5,186	5,801	
	Contracted (£000)	1,296	1,480	

*For an explanation of the line numbers, see the pro-forma analysis charts in Chapter 24.

are still under pressure there is little scope for further improvement, say £7.0m at most for 1985.
Lines S 4, 6 and 19 No evidence of marked change.
Line S 17 High Debt/Equity ratio (line 112) leaves little scope for further borrowing.
Line S 18 £650,000 convertible unsecured loan stock remaining unconverted at last date for conversion 31 Dec 1984, is due for redemption on 31 Dec 1985.
Line A 1 Assuming tax paid in 1984 represented tax at 46.8% on 1983 profits, and that tax paid in 1985 will be at a similar rate on 1984 profits.

Line A 2 The company is likely to increase dividends by the same amount as last year, i.e. by 10%.
Line A 4 The expenditure on fixed assets in past years has been roughly equal to the capital commitment that has been let to contract plus half the authorised expenditure. The chairman has said that the investment programme is continuing, so

using the same lead time, £1.48m plus ½ × £5.801m = £4.380m.
Line A 5 The cost of the current year acquisition announced by the chairman.
Line A 11 A 27% increase in turnover and a normal working capital ratio of 22% will mean an increase in working capital in 1985 of 0.27 × £42.857m × 0.22 = £2.545m.

These figures require a balancing item of £1.424 million in Line A 12 to make the 1985 Application total equal the Source total, meaning that the company is likely to have a decrease in net liquid funds in 1985 of around £1.4 million to £1.5 million on the present evidence.

However, as the 'Acid test' ratio (Line 106) has already fallen to a very low level, a further increase in the overdraft looks undesirable. The most likely solution, to restore the imbalance caused by the £4 million acquisition made for cash in 1984, aggravated by substantial increases in the working capital requirement, is for IEC to make a rights issue (Line S 15) in 1985, and one might well ask why part of the consideration for the £4 million acquisition was not made in paper.

Limitations of funds statements

A source and application statement is a record of historical facts. It will record expenditure upon additional plant and machinery, but can express no opinion upon whether the expenditure was necessary, or will be profitable. Similarly, it may show an expansion of stocks (or debtors), but it will not tell us whether this was due to:

(a) poor stock or production control;
(b) inability to sell the finished product; *or*
(c) a deliberate act of policy, because of a feared shortage of supply, a potential price rise, or the need to build up stocks of a new model (or product) before it is launched.

And, in the case of increased debtors, it will not tell us whether it is the debtors who are slow to pay, or the credit policy which has changed; or whether they merely represent the expansion of turnover. It will show how new capital was raised, but not whether it was raised in the best way, nor indeed whether it really needed to have been raised at all or if it could have been avoided by better asset control.

Source and application of funds statements do not usually tell us the following:

(a) Where the money is. In the case of a multi-national group, exchange controls or the tax situation may make it impossible or undesirable to remit some funds to the United Kingdom.

(b) How much more the company can borrow from its bankers. A fall in liquidity may be perfectly in order where a company has made arrangements with its bankers to cover just that eventuality. On the other hand, a company compelled by its bankers to reduce the scale of its operations may show a satisfactory improvement in liquidity, while being crippled by its inability to expand, or possibly being unable to maintain its existing plant properly.

As we have seen in our example of estimating the future fund requirements of the Imaginary Engineering Company, we had to draw on other information from the chairman's statement and from the accounts, and to use ratios (which we will describe more fully in Chapter 23) in order to help us interpret and project the company's flow of funds. Therefore, although a source and application statement is often very handy for giving quick answers to questions about where the money came from and where it went, it is most useful when read in conjunction with all the other information available.

Chapter 19

HISTORICAL SUMMARIES

Variations in form and content

Although a historical summary of the salient features of company accounts is not compulsory, it was requested by the Chairman of The Stock Exchange, London, in a letter to companies in 1964, and over 90% of top companies now provide some form of historical summary. Most companies choose either a five- or ten-year period, but there is no uniformity of content. AARONSON BROS., for example, show only five basic items in their 'Five-year record' (illustrated below).

Many companies go much further than this; BUNZL, for instance, provides 23 items, filling a whole page of the accounts (see overleaf), while some companies include interesting information on their particular type of business (e.g. BEJAM: number of stores and new stores opened during the year, together with the square footage of the average store); others, like ALLIED LYONS, give two or three pages of comparative figures.

Unlike Bunzl, most companies present their summaries with columns chronologically from left to right, which makes studying them much easier, except possibly for Arab investors.

Difficulties of interpretation

Among the difficulties facing the shareholder or analyst who tries to interpret a five- or ten-year summary are the following:

Inflation

Whereas pre-war it was reasonable in Britain to suppose that a pound today was the same as a pound last year and would be the same as a pound next year, rapid inflation has made this concept of a stable currency (referred to in the United States as the 'uniform dollar concept') unsustainable. A pound in 1984 was not the same as a pound in 1983, 1982, 1981 or 1974. To read a ten-year record as though it was is to obtain a false picture, and can be just as misleading as the company chairman who makes much of yet another year of record profits when they have advanced a mere 5% compared with a 15% or 20% rate of inflation. On the other hand, to try to allow for the changing pace of inflation over a ten-year period is very difficult, as we will discuss in Chapter 22.

Changes in accounting bases

Changes in accounting practices can make a signi-

AARONSON BROS. *Group 5-year record*

	1980 £000	1981 £000	1982 £000	1983 £000	**1984 £000**
Turnover	55,433	61,764	71,564	80,351	**89,390**
Shareholders' funds	15,583	15,578	15,688	16,434	**17,684**
Net profit before taxation and minority interest	1,961	543	950	2,010	**3,818**
Earnings/(Loss) per ordinary 10p share	3.43p	(0.76p)	1.74p	5.36p	**10.37p**
Dividend per ordinary 10p share	4.20p	1.20p	1.20p	2.10p	**4.20p**

---

ficant difference to the figures a company publishes; e.g. SSAP 15, published in October 1978, altered the basis for providing for deferred tax from full provision to 'foreseeable future', which sharply increased the shareholders' funds in many companies as provisions for deferred tax which were no longer required were credited to reserves; SSAP 15 also reduced the tax charge for a company in years, from 1978 onwards, in which its capital allowances exceeded the charge for depreciation.

In addition, most companies change their accounting ideas, either expressly or unknowingly, over a long period. Unless the figures for earlier years are revised, or a note drawing attention to the change in basis is included in the five- or ten-year statistical summary, readers may be misled. Thus, a company may in earlier years have operated on the basis that research and development expenditure should be written off in the year in which it was incurred, but may now capitalise it, i.e. carry it forward as an asset whenever the benefits of the expenditure can reasonably be foreseen. Clearly, neither the figures in the profit and loss account in earlier years, nor those in the balance sheet, are comparable with the figures of later years.

BUNZL *Group 5-year summary*

	1983 **£000**	1982 £000	1981 £000	1980 £000	1979 £000
Turnover	**540,546**	361,504	245,652	169,526	229,783
Trading profit	**18,190**	10,748	8,090	8,428	11,545
Share of profits of associated companies	**2,712**	2,513	2,846	2,767	3,309
Interest and dividends receivable	**1,580**	1,804	1,999	1,368	1,307
Interest payable	**(5,157)**	(2,376)	(1,342)	(1,415)	(2,502)
Profit on ordinary activities before taxation	**17,325**	12,689	11,593	11,148	13,659
Tax on profit on ordinary activities	**(7,266)**	(5,305)	(4,655)	(3,919)	(5,263)
Profit on ordinary activities after taxation	**10,059**	7,384	6,938	7,229	8,396
Profit attributable to minorities	**(975)**	(527)	(822)	(531)	(735)
Profit for shareholders	**9,084**	6,857	6,116	6,698	7,661
Extraordinary items	**(641)**	(2,676)	(1,042)	(4,109)	(4,974)
Profit for the year	**8,443**	4,181	5,074	2,589	2,687
Dividends paid and proposed	**3,071**	2,358	2,095	1,893	1,720
(total including tax credit)	**4,387**	3,368	2,993	2,704	2,457
Dividends per share	**11.00p**	9.00p	8.00p	7.23p	6.57p
(total including tax credit)	**15.71p**	12.86p	11.43p	10.32p	9.38p
Earnings per share	**33.8p**	26.2p	23.4p	25.6p	29.3p
Shareholders' funds per share	**247.5p**	254.1p	255.7p	240.2p	200.2p
Net assets employed					
Fixed assets (excluding associated companies)	**48,564**	44,972	38,126	38,727	42,292
Associated companies	**12,385**	10,264	12,267	10,783	9,617
Net current assets and other liabilities	**13,830**	14,484	23,307	19,344	3,549
Net assets	**74,779**	69,720	73,700	68,854	55,458
Financed by					
Shareholders' funds	**70,431**	66,593	66,946	62,901	52,416
Minority interests	**4,348**	3,127	6,754	5,953	3,042
	74,779	69,720	73,700	68,854	55,458

Note
Figures for 1979 include Bunzl & Biach AG.

Changes in basis may arise without any positive decision having to be made on the part of the company. For instance, the major changes to capital allowances and to the rates of Corporation Tax made in 1984, together with the abolition of stock relief, will make the year-on-year comparisons of after-tax items very difficult for the next few years. Similarly, in the past, the comparability of turnover for some companies has been affected by the change from Purchase Tax to VAT, while others have been affected by changes in the rate of Excise Duty.

Changes in the composition of the group
Where a group either grows or contracts, comparability is bound to be affected. Most groups do

not strip out the effect of companies no longer being part of the group, nor do they include additions to the group for the whole period, but only from the date of acquisition.

Use of ratios

Thus, while a five- or ten-year summary can be very helpful, its limitations in times of high inflation and the adjustments which need to be made because of changes in accounting bases and in the composition of the group mean that it should be treated with caution. However, some companies do go to considerable trouble to make the figures as comparable as possible, and explain adjustments in footnotes.

It is sometimes possible to avoid some of these difficulties by using ratios; the current ratio and quick ratio and the collection period (Debtors/turnover) are comparable year by year, for example. But this is not true of all ratios. For instance, profit margin (Trading profit to sales ratio) is affected in historical cost accounts by stockholding gains and by the charging of depreciation only on the basis of historical cost, while Earnings per share are, of course, directly affected by inflation, since earnings are expressed from year to year in pounds of different vintages, while the number of shares in issue is unaffected by inflation.

The key ratios

Despite all the difficulties we have discussed, the company's own historical summary does provide a readily accessible picture of the company's progress over past years, and should therefore be used when the analyst cannot afford the time and effort involved in preparing the detailed summary we advocate in Chapter 24; two key ratios to look at are Earnings per share and Shareholders' funds per share.

Earnings per share
E.p.s. are of prime interest to the investor. Very few companies are as helpful as RTZ in providing

e.p.s. expressed in 'constant pounds' (see extract from RTZ's 10-year financial summary overleaf, in which e.p.s. are shown in 1983 pounds), but a crude adjustment can quite easily be made to allow for the effect of inflation by the use of the Retail Price Index (see Appendix 3). The method is as follows:

(a) Give the base value of 100 to the first earnings per share and scale the remaining e.p.s. figures in the series being adjusted.
(b) Place the average RPI for the period below each e.p.s. figure.
(c) Give the base value of 100 to the first RPI figure and scale the remaining RPI figures in the series.
(d) Divide (a) by (c) and multiply by 100 to obtain an inflation-corrected series of the e.p.s. growth (or decline) from base 100.

Example 19.1 below shows this method in practice, based on figures from the BUNZL summary opposite.

Thus an apparent fall in e.p.s. of about 20% between 1979 and 1981 was, in real terms, a fall of about 40%, and an apparent increase of 15.4% in the four years was a real fall of 23%.

The fall in the value of money has had a diabolical effect on e.p.s. over the last ten years: not only are profits each year overstated due to the historical cost method of accounting, but the e.p.s. can appear to rise encouragingly when, in real terms, they are falling.

As we have mentioned, a few companies do include figures adjusted for inflation; for example, RTZ's ten-year record (see overleaf) shows e.p.s. and dividends adjusted by the Retail Price Index to express them all in terms of 1983 pounds.

Net asset value per share (n.a.v.)
The n.a.v., called 'Shareholders' funds per share' in BUNZL's 5-year summary, is the ordinary shareholders' funds (excluding goodwill and any other intangible assets) divided by the number of ordinary shares in issue (see Example 19.2 overleaf).

Example 19.1   Adjustment of e.p.s. for inflation: BUNZL

Year ending 31 December	1979	1980	1981	1982	1983
Earnings per share	29.3p	25.6p	23.4p	26.2p	33.8p
(a) E.p.s. to base 100 in 1979	100	87.4	79.9	89.4	115.4
(b) Average RPI for year	223.5	263.7	295.0	320.4	335.1
(c) RPI to base 100 in 1979	100	118.0	132.0	143.4	149.9
(d) Real growth in e.p.s. $= \dfrac{(a)}{(c)} \times 100$	100	74.1	60.5	62.3	77.0

Note: Where a company's accounting year is not the calendar year, the RPI for the month in which the company's half year ends can be used as an approximation for the average RPI for the year.

Example 19.2   Calculation of net asset value per share:
BUNZL

		£000
(a)	Issued *ordinary* share capital at 31 December 1983 (Note 1)	7,114
	Reserves	63,317
	Ordinary shareholders' funds (OSF)	70,431
	less Goodwill and other intangible assets (Note 2)	122
(b)	Net tangible assets attributable to ordinary shareholders	70,309

(c) Number of 25p ordinary shares in issue
$= (a) \times 4$ (Note 3) $= 28,456,000$

Net asset value per ordinary share (n.a.v.) $= \dfrac{(b)}{(c)} = 247.1\text{p}$ (Note 4)

Notes:
1. Issued ordinary share capital = issued share capital *minus* any issued preference capital (none in BUNZL's case).
2. Although BUNZL's accounting policy on goodwill is the normal one of writing off the excess of cost over net tangible assets at the date of acquisition against reserves at the time of acquisition, the group includes patents and trade marks in its balance sheet as intangible assets, showing them at cost less accumulated depreciation and writing them off by equal annual instalments over ten years.
3. To obtain the number of ordinary shares in issue at the end of the year (*not* the average number given in the accounts for calculating e.p.s.), multiply the issued share capital by 100p and divide by the nominal value of the ordinary shares.
4. The n.a.v. for 1983 given in BUNZL's 5-year summary is 247.5p rather than 247.1p because the book value of intangible assets has *not* been deducted in calculating 'Shareholders' funds' (i.e. net tangible assets attributable to ordinary shareholders).
5. A quick way to calculate n.a.v. straight off the balance sheet is:

$$\frac{(b)}{(a)} \times \text{nominal value of ordinary share,}$$

but make sure that the issued share capital does not include any preference capital and that any goodwill is deducted from ordinary shareholders' funds.

The progression over the years shows how much profit is being ploughed back into the company to help earnings grow, and is a much better indicator than overall figures for assets employed or for shareholders' funds, which can be boosted by acquisitions for paper. The n.a.v. can, of course, be boosted by upward revaluation of assets, particularly of property, which is usually the cause of any sharp jump in n.a.v. that is larger than the year's e.p.s. less the dividend per share, i.e. is larger than any change that could be caused by retained earnings. Unless a company is making losses, any fall in the n.a.v. is almost always due to extraordinary items, i.e. amounts written off below the line.

RTZ *Extract from financial summary 1974–1983*

£ million	1974	1975	1976	1977	1978	1979	1980	1981	1982	**1983**
Earnings per ordinary share										
As reported (note 1)	27.08p	15.10p	31.37p	31.70p	39.38p	57.64p	59.72p	39.21p	38.44p	**59.31p**
In 1983 terms (note 2)	85.55p	38.40p	68.45p	59.72p	68.48p	88.36p	77.64p	45.56p	41.13p	**60.67p**
Dividends per ordinary share	4.97p	5.42p	8.00p	9.50p	11.50p	15.00p	16.00p	16.00p	16.00p	**18.00p**
Gross equivalent to UK shareholders										
As reported (note 1)	7.55p	8.34p	12.19p	14.26p	16.65p	21.43p	22.85p	22.85p	22.85p	**25.71p**
In 1983 terms (note 2)	22.12p	19.60p	24.87p	25.95p	27.97p	30.86p	28.33p	25.36p	24.06p	**25.71p**

Notes

1 Appropriate adjustments have been made to the earnings per ordinary share to allow for the effect of the rights issues made in 1975 and 1983, and for 1978 in respect of the change in accounting policy on deferred tax.

2 The amounts shown in 1983 terms have been calculated by converting the reported amounts (as amended under note 1) to 1983 pounds by reference to changes in the United Kingdom retail price index. For earnings per ordinary share the change is measured between the average index for each year and that for December 1983, and for the gross equivalent of ordinary dividends the change is measured between the average index for December of each year and that for December 1983.

Chapter 20

DIRECTORS' REPORT, CHAIRMAN'S STATEMENT AND AUDITORS' REPORT

THE DIRECTORS' REPORT

Contents

The contents of the directors' report fall broadly into three categories:

1. *Information required by law* – the statutory requirements – a mass of information some of which is obvious from the accounts anyway, some of which is of comparatively little interest to the analyst (but appears to have been motivated by political considerations, e.g. contributions for political purposes), but some of which may be of vital interest and importance to anyone interpreting the accounts, e.g. the review of the year and likely future developments.
2. *Information required by The Stock Exchange*, which we described in Chapter 3, some of which overlaps the statutory requirements.
3. *Voluntary information* – additional information and commentary which the company wants to include: this is usually concerned with the events of the past year, current trading and future plans and prospects.

The voluntary information is normally contained mainly or wholly in the chairman's statement or review of the year, leaving the directors' report chiefly a catalogue of compulsory details; but if there is no chairman's statement, and there is no compulsion for a chairman to report separately from the board of directors, any voluntary information will be included in the directors' report. In this chapter we will assume that there is a chairman's statement, and we will deal with voluntary information under that heading later in the chapter.

Statutory requirements

Under the Companies Act 1985, a directors' report must give the following information:

(a) the *principal activities* of the company and its subsidiaries, and any significant change (S. 235);
(b) a *fair review* of the development of the business during the year, together with an indication of likely *future developments* and of *research and development* activities (S. 235 and Sch. 7, paras 6(b) and (c));
(c) the names of the *directors* and details of their interests (shareholdings) (Sch. 7, para. 2);
(d) particulars of significant changes in *fixed assets* (Sch. 7, para. 1);
(e) details of company's *own shares* acquired by the company during the year (Sch. 7, Part II);
(f) *important events* affecting the company which have occurred *since the end of the year* (see also post balance sheet events, page 136);
(g) details of *political or charitable contributions*, if over £200 in the year (Sch. 7, para. 3).

Listing requirements

As described in Chapter 3, the Continuing Obligations of listed companies require them to circulate certain information with the annual report; this information is usually contained in the directors' report, but may appear separately or in notes to the accounts. Items of particular interest are:

(a) a geographical analysis of turnover of operations outside the United Kingdom and

Ireland, and of their contribution to the *trading results* if 'abnormal';

(b) holdings, other than by directors, of 5% or more of any class of voting capital;

(c) whether or not the company is a 'close company'.

Control of the company

It is always worth checking whether a small company is a 'bid prospect', e.g. an acquisition-minded company has a substantial holding, as this can explain why the company's share is looking overrated or 'expensive' in comparison with other similar companies.

On the other hand, if the company is a close company (i.e. under the control of its directors or of five or fewer persons – see Chapter 2), or if the directors' interests are substantial although not controlling, the dividend policy is likely to be conservative, because dividends paid to the directors or controlling shareholders will be heavily taxed in their hands. In addition, growth will probably be limited to ploughing back profits, because directors or the controlling shareholders are unlikely to be in a position to take up their entitlement in a rights issue, and because acquisitions for paper would also dilute their control.

However, if the principal director shareholder is nearing retirement, with no obvious successor (check list of shareholders for family names of the next generation, and remember that new issue prospectuses give directors' ages), then an agreed bid could well be in store.

The board of directors

Although many companies are built up primarily through the efforts of a single person, a one-man band is a potentially dangerous situation. He's going to present a succession problem in due course, and what would happen if he had a heart attack tomorrow? And if he's egocentric, he may surround himself with yes-men and come an awful cropper with his company.

We would therefore prefer a top management team: it is, for example, preferable not to combine the posts of chairman and managing director, and to have a separate finance director, and to have at least five board members. We would be unhappy, for instance, with the statement of one chairman/MD: 'Apart from overall control of the Group's affairs, I shall have particular responsibility for financial control, and investigating possible acquisitions by the company.'

We like the inclusion of a few non-executive directors, provided they are of a healthily independent disposition, devote sufficient time to the company to have a good grasp of its affairs (i.e. they must know what's going on), are prepared to make a stand/resign if they disagree on important issues, and bring some relevant experience to the boardroom.

Having checked the composition of the board and the management structure, let us now have a look at the chairman's statement, not only for what it says but also for what we can read between the lines.

THE CHAIRMAN'S STATEMENT

Sequence of study

It is difficult to lay down a set of rules as to the best order in which to study a report and accounts, and each individual will develop his own method (one stockbroker tells us he always goes straight to the directors' holdings to see if they are reducing their holdings!), but we think it is useful to start by glancing at the chairman's statement and the directors' report to see whether anything has occurred which would invalidate a straightforward comparison between one year and another. If, for instance, a major acquisition took place at the beginning of the year under review, almost all operating and financial ratios are likely to have been affected. This does not mean that the ratios are useless: simply that the analyst must bear in mind the change in composition of the group every time he compares one ratio with another.

Having then studied the accounts (a process we will discuss in detail in Chapters 23 and 24) and

having examined any analysis given of turnover and pre-tax profits between classes of business and any geographical analysis of turnover and trading results outside the United Kingdom, the reader will now have a good idea of how the company has fared in the past year, but little idea why (except in the context of happening to know that it was a good, average or bad year for the industry or industries in which the company operates), and little idea of how the company is likely to do in the current year and beyond. It is to the chairman's statement that we should look for this information.

Contents

In companies which believe in keeping shareholders well informed, the chairman's statement will usually contain comment on:

(a) overall trading conditions during the period, current climate and general outlook;

Example 20.1   *Estimating current year profits:* 'POLYGON HOLDING COMPANY LTD'

Activity	Industrial climate	Chairman's remarks	Previous year £m	Reported year £m	Estimate of current year £m
Building	Continued recession	'Further decline inevitable'	1.0	0.8	0.5–0.6
Paper	Cyclical upturn	'Marked improvement'	2.2	1.8	2.4–2.8
Bookmaking	One of the UK's few growth industries	'Continued progress'	1.0	1.2	1.4–1.5
Plastic extrusions	Demand flat	'Market share increasing but lower margins'	0.6	0.75	0.6–0.8
Interest charges	Rates down 2%	'Improvement in liquidity likely'	−0.8	−1.0	−0.8
		Pre-tax total	4.0	3.55	4.1–4.9

(*b*) the performance achieved by each activity, current trading and future prospects;

(*c*) special items of interest (e.g. closures and new ventures);

(*d*) company strategy and plans for the future.

We find it's useful to read through the whole statement underlining key phrases and points of interest as we go, before getting down to any detailed analysis.

Estimating current year profits

A rough estimate of profits for the current year can be constructed (by each activity separately reported) by quantifying the chairman's comments, bearing in mind prevailing conditions and prospects for the industry concerned; for example, 'POLYGON HOLDING COMPANY LTD' (Example 20.1).

The chairman may also give some overall view, e.g. Polygon Holding's turnover in the first three months of the current year has been 22% higher than the same period last year, the paper division's order-book is now four months, compared with one month last year, and, despite constant pressure on margins and the increasing ineptitude of government, the outlook for the group is encouraging. 'Outlook encouraging' sounds to us like a 20–25% increase in pre-tax profits, i.e. to £4.3–£4.5 million, pointing to the middle of the range we constructed division by division.

Other points to bear in mind in making a profits estimate are these:

1. Loss-makers discontinued will not only eliminate the loss but should, in addition, improve liquidity (and thus reduce interest charges, assuming there is an overdraft). But have all terminal losses been taken?

2. Most new ventures, branches, factories, depots, etc., are doing well if they break even in their second year of operation.

3. What is the chairman's previous record? Has he been accurate – cautious – unduly optimistic – erratic? Have past assurances of better times ahead been unfulfilled?

4. Remember, too, that one of the chairman's most important jobs is to maintain general confidence in the company, so he is likely to concentrate on the good points and only dwell briefly or remain silent on the weaker aspects of the company. Here it is a good idea to jot down questions, even if the analyst or shareholder is unlikely to have the opportunity of putting them to the company, because it helps to establish what the chairman hasn't revealed and whether any unexplained area is likely to be significant. A good question to ask oneself is 'What are the company's main problems, and what is being done about them?'

5. Beware of vague statements, such as:
   (*a*) 'Turnover in the first ten weeks of the current year has exceeded the corresponding figure for last year.' It may be 1% ahead in value because of inflation, but a 4% drop has occurred in volume.
   (*b*) 'Unforeseen difficulties have occurred in . . . and a provision of £1.3 million has been made.' Unless there is some indication of the likely overall cost of overcoming these difficulties, or of abandoning the activity altogether, the company should be assumed to have an open-ended loss-maker on its hands.

Longer-term prospects

The chairman of a company should be continually looking to the future and, unless he and his board have good sound ideas on where the future growth in profits is likely to come from, and are steering the company in that direction, then above-average profits growth is unlikely. Although there must, of course, be some restrictions on what a chairman discloses about plans for the future, because of competition, he will usually include some indication of where he thinks the company is going in his annual statement.

A good past growth record is clearly encouraging (a no-growth company is likely to stay a no-growth company unless the management or the management's attitude changes), but what indications are there of future growth? Possibilities to look for are the following:

1. *Better margins on existing business.* This is an unreliable source of growth unless the company *either*

    (*a*) has some very strong competitive advantage, such as patents or lucrative long-term contracts, *or*

    (*b*) has spent large sums of money building up brand images and carving out market share, and is now beginning to reap the benefits,

    and even then the profits growth will only last until the patents expire, the long-term contracts run out and the brand images tarnish.

2. *Further expansion of existing activities within the United Kingdom.* Is there any scope for this, or is the company in a position like BOOTS or MARKS & SPENCER, with a store in every town of any size, or like PILKINGTON, with 90% of the UK glass market?

3. *Diversification within the United Kingdom.* This was BOOTS' answer to its saturation problem with chemist shops: it widened the range of goods sold to include records and tapes, hi-fi, cameras, binoculars, even sandals. BOOTS was using its retailing expertise in wider product ranges, rather than going into some totally unrelated activity, and there does need to be some logic in diversifications or they can come very badly unstuck.

4. *Acquisition within the United Kingdom.* Has the company got a successful record of acquisitions, or would this method of growth be new to it (and therefore more risky)? This was part of PILKINGTON's solution for further growth; it diversified through fibreglass into insulation, boosting the process by acquisition.

5. *Exports.* Is the product suitable for export, or would transport costs make competitiveness overseas unlikely or impossible (e.g. bricks)? Does the company export already, is it a significant amount, and is it growing? The chairman may report that 'exports are 80% up on last year', but if this is an increase from 0.1% to 0.18% of turnover, it is hardly thrilling, and one should be wary of the chairman whose efforts to paint a rosy picture involve misleading statements like that, which should in honesty be qualified by some phrase like 'albeit from a very low base'.

6. *Are there opportunities for overseas growth*, like MARKS & SPENCER opening stores in Europe, or PILKINGTON putting down float glass plants overseas, either on its own or in joint ventures, or by licensing the process to foreign glass manufacturers? There are, however, a good many hazards in opening up operations abroad, apart from the initial expense: different business ethics and practices, language, law, accounting and tax systems, and so on. For manufacturing abroad, cost levels and exchange rates may change over time, so that what today looks a good investment may prove otherwise in years to come if the cost of living rises faster in that country than elsewhere.

7. *Is the company spending money on, and attaching importance to, developing new products?* This is particularly important for pharmaceutical companies; BEECHAM, for instance, in 1984 reported £55.2 million spent on research and development, representing 10% of the pharmaceutical product group's turnover.

    Although any manufacturing company that *isn't* developing new products is almost certainly going downhill, it is also bad news if the chairman is always eulogising about new products that never come to anything: the company's track record on product development should be checked.

8. *Is the company ploughing profits back?* Profits in most industries cannot expand beyond a given point unless the asset base (needed to support the trading needed to generate the profits) is also expanded. There is a limit to gearing up, while acquisitions and rights issues don't necessarily enhance e.p.s.: only steady ploughback gives scope for steady growth in e.p.s.

In the context of future growth, it is also worth checking press cuttings for stories on the company, which often contain glimpses of the company's thoughts on the future (see Chapter 21 on McCarthy's press cutting service).

Information on the quality of management

Returning to the business of assessing the strength of the management, perhaps the most encouraging facet is when the chairman admits to a mistake or to being caught wrong-footed, and reports what is being or has been done about it. A classic example comes from the 'rag trade': the chairman's statement for WEARWELL in 1976, a year in which trading results had fallen from £1 million profit to £28,000 loss on turnover down from £7.1 million to £6.2 million and with over £½ million in terminal losses, contained the following comments:

WEARWELL *Extracts from chairman's report, 1976*

. . . in 1973 we operated what was basically a cash and carry operation. [In 1974 and 1975 the company made two acquisitions for cash and we] found ourselves in the business of building up stock and financing customers for considerable periods . . . sales not as buoyant as expected . . . liquidity difficulties in the opening weeks of 1976 . . . instituted immediate measures, namely:

1. Closure of the mail order supply business which has required the financing of substantial stocks.

2. Cutting out much of the credit business with chain stores.

3. The waiver by directors of a substantial part of their salary entitlement together with a waiver of between 94.0% and 99.9% of their total entitlement to the interim dividend.

4. Strenuous efforts were made to liquidate stocks.

. . . your company operates now only in the cash and carry type business which is where your management has proved its expertise.

We are glad to say that Wearwell's drastic action paid off. The company just managed to get out of the red in 1977, and from then on pre-tax profits grew steadily; five years later the chairman, Asil Nadir (of POLLY PECK fame, the group which Wearwell subsequently joined) was able to report pre-tax profits in excess of £4 million.

Wearwell's shareholders also had a bumpy ride: from an Offer for Sale price of 30p (adjusted for subsequent scrip and rights issues) in July 1973 they saw the ordinary share price fall to a low of 8p in November 1976, and received no dividends at all in 1977 and 1978. But in the longer run they were amply rewarded both as to

---

Example 20.2 WEARWELL *Graph of share price 1973–82*

Source: Datastream.

income (1982 dividends totalled 2.75p net per share), and in capital terms, as the graph of Wearwell's share price during the first ten years of its life as a listed company illustrates (Example 20.2).

In contrast, the chairman of a housebuilding company reported proudly in 1974 that 'notwithstanding all these problems [the three-day week, the shortage of mortgage funds, rising interest rates and increases in building costs] your company increased its turnover to a new record level'. The turnover had risen from £25.4 million to almost £44 million on an equity base of less than £2 million net of goodwill and after writing £8.7 million off the value of the land bank, now in the books at a mere £24.4 million plus £23.4 million work in progress. Apart from the feeling that the chairman was steering his company straight for the eye of a financial typhoon, and his avoidance of mentioning the year's pre-tax loss of £6.3 million in his statement, there were a number of fairly conspicuous danger signals scattered around the report:

(*a*)   The notice of the AGM included a resolution .to appoint a top London firm of accountants

to be joint auditors with the existing provincial firm of auditors.

(*b*)   The directors' report contained a little paragraph on 'financial arrangements', which revealed that the group's bankers had agreed to 'roll up' interest on group borrowings.

But perhaps the most telling fact was an omission: the group's habit of including a historical summary (which in the 1973 accounts had shown turnover since 1966 advance from £½ million to £23.7 million and pre-tax profits progressing over the same period (£000): 142   259   427   621   1,020   1,538   2,844   7,002) had been discontinued! The fall into loss in 1974 was too painful to face. Liquidation followed quite shortly afterwards.

In this context, John Argenti's book *Corporate Collapse* demonstrates that any company that goes on doubling its profits year after year will, in all probability, eventually meet disaster. An underlying reason for this is that a company producing such meteoric profits is probably very highly geared, and is thus highly vulnerable to any marked downturn.

POST BALANCE SHEET EVENTS

(Reference: SSAP 17 *Accounting for Post Balance Sheet Events*.)

It might be thought that, since a company's report and accounts reflect the state of affairs at the balance sheet date, events arising after that date would be excluded, but this is not entirely the case: post balance sheet events (events occurring between the balance sheet date and the date the accounts are approved by the board) should be reflected or disclosed if they are important (CA 1985, Sch. 7, para. 6).

Types of post balance sheet event

SSAP 17 distinguishes between two types of post balance sheet event:

(*a*)   *Adjusting events*, which provide additional evidence of conditions existing at the balance sheet date, e.g. the insolvency of a debtor. The accounts should be adjusted accordingly, but separate disclosure is not normally required.

Where any subsequent events indicate that the 'going concern' concept should not have been applied to the company or to a material part of it, the accounts should also

be adjusted accordingly.

(*b*)   *Non-adjusting events*, which concern conditions which did *not* exist at the balance sheet date. The events should be disclosed together, if practicable, with an estimate of the financial effect.

Disclosure is usually made in the directors' report (e.g. ENGLISH CHINA CLAYS' disclosure of an acquisition, shown opposite), or in a note to the accounts (e.g. BAT INDUSTRIES' acquisition of EAGLE STAR, illustrated opposite), and if the event is of major importance, further details will be given elsewhere; BAT, for example, devoted two whole pages in its report to a write-up on Eagle Star, and gave an indication of its profitability and net asset value in its *Review of the Year*. Alternatively, if a large number of events have occurred since the balance sheet date, a separate document may be included with the report and accounts; this was the course adopted by THOMAS BORTHWICK with its 1980 accounts, to report the details of a whole series of acquisitions and disposals, some of which had taken place after the company's year end.

ENGLISH CHINA CLAYS *Extract from directors' report for year ended 30th September 1984*

Acquisition

On 19th December 1984 the Company acquired the whole of the issued share capital of Edwin H. Bradley Holdings Ltd and its subsidiaries, a private group of companies based in Swindon. The consideration for the acquisition was £51m, paid in cash.

The main activities of Bradley are the manufacture and sale of concrete products (including Bradstone reconstructed stone which enjoys a very high reputation in the trade) to the building industry and the DIY market from factories in Wiltshire and Gloucestershire, both supplied from their own aggregate source, and Yorkshire and Lincolnshire; and the development of private housing estates and commercial properties principally in Wiltshire and neighbouring counties.

Window dressing

One method of improving the appearance of a company's accounts is to borrow short-term money, perhaps just overnight, in order to bump up liquidity at the balance sheet date, a trick that was particularly popular amongst fringe bankers in the early 1970s.

SSAP 17 endeavours to preclude this and similar types of cosmetic operation by requiring the disclosure of 'the reversal or maturity after the

BAT INDUSTRIES *Note on balance sheet and extract from review of the year for 1983*

Post balance sheet events

Acquisition of Eagle Star Holdings PLC – on 18 January 1984 BAT Industries' recommended offer to acquire the entire issued share capital of Eagle Star Holdings PLC became unconditional.

The consideration payable for the shares amounts to £968 million. Details regarding Eagle Star are given on pages 10, 11 and 15.

Review of the year (page 15)

The acquisition of Eagle Star in January 1984 is not reflected in these Group results, but some measure of its future contribution is given by its results for the year ended 31 December 1983, which showed an increase in pre-tax profits of 33 per cent, to £90 million. A review has been carried out of the net assets acquired which indicates that their value more than supports the purchase consideration.

year end of transactions entered into before the year end, the substance of which was primarily to alter the appearance of the company's balance sheet'.

This requirement may not prevent this type of window dressing, but it should discourage auditors from being party to deliberate deceptions.

THE AUDITORS' REPORT

(References: Companies Act 1985, S. 236 and 237; *Auditing Standards and Guidelines*.)

Appointment of auditors

Every company is required to appoint at each annual general meeting an auditor or auditors to hold office from the conclusion of that meeting until the conclusion of the next AGM.

Auditors' access to information

Under the Companies Act 1985 it is an offence for a director or company secretary to give false or misleading information to auditors, and auditors of holding companies have the right to obtain information about subsidiary companies which they themselves do not audit.

The auditor has a right of access at all times to the books and accounts and vouchers of the company and to require from the officers of the company such information and explanations as he thinks necessary for the performance of his duty. He has the right to attend any general meeting, and to be heard thereat on any part of the business of the meeting which concerns him as auditor.

Scope of the report

The auditors are required to report to the members (i.e. to the shareholders) whether in their opinion the profit and loss account and the balance sheet, and any group accounts, have been properly prepared in accordance with the Companies Act 1985 and all relevant SSAPs, and give a true and fair view of the profit and state of affairs of the company or group.

If they are of the opinion that proper accounting records have not been kept, or that the accounts are not in agreement with the books, or if they are unable to obtain all the information and explanations necessary for their audit, they must state the fact in their report; i.e. they must qualify their report.

Qualified audit reports

Auditing Standards and Guidelines (published by the Institutes of Chartered Accountants and the Chartered Association of Certified Accountants) distinguishes between what may be termed a 'clean' audit report and one which is 'qualified', and recommends the form of words to be used in qualified reports in different circumstances.

This can be very helpful to the reader in interpreting the significance of an audit report, provided he or she understands the 'standard jargon', so it is well worth explaining the auditing rules in some detail:

Clean report   In a 'clean' report the auditors will say in an 'opinion paragraph' that, in their opinion, the financial statements give a *true and fair view*, without any qualification. (*Financial statements* embrace the balance sheets, profit and loss accounts, statement of source and application of funds, notes and other statements, which collectively are intended to give a true and fair view of the financial position and profit or loss – SSAP 14, para. 10.)

Qualified report   If the auditor is unable to give a clean report 'he should qualify his report by referring to all *material* matters about which he has reservations. All reasons for the qualification should be given, together with a quantification of its effect on the financial statements if this is both relevant and practicable.' The Standard goes on to emphasise that 'a qualified audit report should leave the reader in no doubt as to its meaning and its implications for an understanding of the financial statements' – although whether this always happens, or whether it is always possible, is open to question.

In addition, when a report is qualified, Section 273(5) of the Companies Act 1985 requires the auditors to state in writing whether the qualification is material for the purpose of determining whether the dividend distribution contravenes other sections of the Act (see auditors' report on TRAFALGAR HOUSE, opposite).

Categories of qualified report
There are two categories:

(a) *uncertainty* – where there is an uncertainty which prevents the auditor from forming an opinion on a matter; *and*
(b) *disagreement* – where the auditor is able to form an opinion on the matter but this conflicts with the view given by the financial statements.

Each category is then further subdivided according to whether the subject matter of the uncertainty or disagreement is *fundamental* (so important and significant 'as to undermine the view given by the financial statements taken as a whole'), or is only *material*. In each case recommended wording is given for the *opinion paragraph*, as shown in Example 20.3.

Example 20.3   Recommended wording for the opinion paragraph

Material uncertainty	: 'subject to'
Fundamental uncertainty	: 'unable to form an opinion as to' (called a 'disclaimer of opinion')
Material disagreement	: 'except for'
Fundamental disagreement	: 'do not give a true and fair view' (called an 'adverse opinion')

Examples of qualified reports

Uncertainty qualifications include:

(a) limitations in the scope of the audit due to lack of information; and
(b) inherent uncertainties, i.e. events which have not yet been concluded: major litigation and investigation (e.g. MINET HOLDINGS auditors' report, illustrated below), long-term contracts, and closures being carried out but not yet completed.

Where an auditors' report refers to specific paragraphs or notes in the financial statements, these should also be checked, as they can often be far more revealing than a tactful auditors' report. For example, the second paragraph of Minet's auditors' report makes much less exciting reading than Note 8 to Minet's financial statements.

MINET *Report of the auditors and Note to the financial statements*

To the members of Minet Holdings PLC

1 We have audited the financial statements on pages 26 to 41 in accordance with approved Auditing Standards.
2 As explained in note 8 to the financial statements:
 (a) investigations and negotiations arising from certain reinsurance arrangements for various syndicates are still in progress;
 (b) following a detailed review of the current situation, a further charge of £5.68 million has been made as an extraordinary item.
3 Subject to the adjustments, if any, that may have been required had the matters in paragraph 2 been determined, in our opinion the financial statements, which have been prepared under the historical cost convention, give a true and fair view of . . .

Neville Russell
Chartered Accountants

Note 8   Extraordinary item
Richard Beckett Underwriting Agencies Limited (the agency) (formerly PCW Underwriting Agencies Limited)

The investigations commenced in 1982 by Inspectors appointed by Lloyd's and the Department of Trade respectively have continued. Full co-operation has been given to these inquiries. No report has as yet been published by the Department of Trade. The Group has continued to provide substantial financial and administrative support to the agency.

The agency's investigation has also continued and is now nearly complete. It shows that various former directors of the agency, together with other individuals, derived an improper personal benefit from certain reinsurance arrangements in connection with syndicates for which underwriting was arranged by the agency and its associated company, WMD Underwriting Agencies Limited. Legal proceedings have been commenced against the persons concerned.

The investigation has also revealed that net reinsurance premiums equivalent to £38.9m are involved. The investigation team has so far located and secured assets valued at approximately £26.2m controlled from Gibraltar. Recovery of this money is being strenuously pursued. Furthermore, negotiations are taking place with various parties with the objective of returning the balance at the earliest possible moment.

Following a detailed review of the current situation, a further charge has been made of £5,680,000, which is in addition to the charge for the year ended 31st December 1982 of £1,136,000, before taxation relief of £116,000. No tax relief on this year's charge has been anticipated, but tax credits may arise in later years from set-off of allowable expenditure against future underwriting agency income.

Two former employees have brought actions for wrongful dismissal against the agency, which has been advised that these actions are unlikely to be successful. It is also possible that other claims may be made by and against the agency.

Disagreement qualifications cover:

(*a*)   unjustified non-compliance with SSAPs and/or inappropriate accounting policies (e.g. TRAFALGAR HOUSE's auditors' report);

(*b*)   disagreement on facts or amounts, or on the way in which they have (or haven't!) been disclosed; *and*

(*c*)   non-compliance with legislation.

TRAFALGAR HOUSE *Disagreement qualification in auditors' report*

To the Members of Trafalgar House Public Limited Company
We have audited the accounts and notes on pages 17 to 33 in accordance with approved Auditing Standards. As explained in note (2), two ships purchased during the year have been treated as sterling assets. In our opinion these assets should be denominated in US

dollars. As a consequence fixed assets are understated by approximately £12 million which should be added to reserves to match exchange differences of £12 million on related loans charged to reserves.
Except for these adjustments in our opinion the accounts and notes give a true and fair view of . . .
In our opinion, the matter referred to in the second paragraph above is not material for the purpose of determining, by reference to these financial statements, whether the dividends paid and proposed in respect of the year ended 30th September 1984 would be in contravention of Section 43 of the Companies Act 1980.

TOUCHE ROSS & CO.,
Chartered Accountants

Fundamental qualifications – the disclaimer of opinion and the adverse opinion – are the extreme forms of qualification, and should be regarded as measures of last resort. Auditors will therefore avoid them whenever humanly possible, so the reader should be on the lookout for 'borderline cases'. For example, the auditors' report on DUNLOP's 1983 accounts (illustrated) implied that the group might be having some difficulty in finding finance for its future needs, and Note 21 to which it referred revealed the seriousness of the situation. A major refinancing and capital reorganisation was announced less than 12 months later.

The key words to watch for are *going concern*. When the auditors feel obliged to say that the accounts have been prepared on a 'going concern' basis, it means that there is some doubt about it, usually that the group or company's bankers haven't (yet) agreed to continue to provide financial support.

DUNLOP *Qualified auditors' report*

To the members of Dunlop Holdings plc
We have examined the accounts of Dunlop Holdings plc set out on pages 14 to 36 and the information . . .

The accounts have been prepared on a going concern basis; as indicated in Note 21, the directors and the company's bankers are working constructively together on measures which they believe should ensure the availability of finance for the group's future needs.

In our opinion, subject to adequate finance being available, the accounts give a true and fair view . . .

ERNST & WHINNEY
Chartered Accountants

Note 21   Debentures and Loans

	Total loans	
	1983 £m	1982 £m
. . . . .	**268.3**	305.1
Less: amounts falling due within one year	**207.4**	39.1
Total amounts falling due after more than one year	60.9	266.0

Note: the increase of amounts falling due within one year from £39.1 million at 31 December 1982 to £207.4 million at 31 December 1983 reflects the fact that more of the group's borrowings were technically repayable on demand.

The company and its principal bankers are working constructively on measures to ensure the availability of finance for the group's future needs. These measures include the granting of security to unsecured lenders.

Materiality

The explanatory note in the auditing standard on qualifications is pretty woolly: 'In general terms a matter should be judged to be material if knowledge of the matter would be likely to influence the user of the financial statements . . . materiality may be considered in relative or absolute terms.' However, in a similar context, SSAP 3 (earnings per share) is rather more specific: 'the fully diluted earnings per share need not be given unless the dilution is material. Dilution amounting to 5% or more of the basic earnings per share is regarded as material for this purpose.'

It might therefore be argued that an auditor need not qualify his report if the amount involved would not alter the bottom line of the profit and loss account by 5% or more; for example, the note on tangible fixed assets in Trafalgar House's 1984 accounts included the following paragraph:

'To the extent that the Group does not amortise freehold and long leasehold buildings owned and occupied as business premises, including hotels, there would have been an additional depreciation charge of £500,000 (1983 £850,000) based on an average life of 40 years.'

Although this was in contravention of SSAP 12, the auditor's report was not qualified on this count, on the grounds that the sum involved was not material: the net profit of the group after taxation was over £80 million.

Emphasis of matter

In general a clean report should not make reference to specific aspects of the financial statements, in case it is misconstrued as a qualification. If, however, the auditor wishes to draw attention to anything he consideres important, for example an unusual (but appropriate) accounting policy, he should do so in a *separate* paragraph, using suitable wording, e.g. 'We draw attention to . . .', and should *not* refer to it in the opinion paragraph. Thomson McLintock's audit report on the COOKSON GROUP illustrates this well.

COOKSON GROUP *Auditors' report; emphasis of matter*

To the Members of Cookson Group plc

We have audited the financial statements on pages 18 to 34 and 39 in accordance with approved auditing standards. . .

The Group values certain metal and mineral stocks on the base stock and LIFO methods in the manner explained in the accounting policies on page 18. We agree with the use of these procedures although they are not in accordance with the recommendations in Statement of Standard Accounting Practice No 9.

The financial statements have been prepared under the historical cost convention as modified for the major related companies by the revaluation of fixed assets. In our opinion these financial statements give a true and fair view . . .

Thomson McLintock & Co
Chartered Accountants

Delay in publication

One final and rather obvious point about auditing: it often takes longer if the company is in difficulties, so any delay in publishing the annual report and accounts is usually a bad sign; The Stock Exchange likes to see them issued within six months of a company's year end, and failure to do so is comparatively rare among listed companies (see page 144 for details of the period currently allowed by the Companies Act 1985 for laying and delivering accounts).

Chapter 21

OTHER SOURCES OF INFORMATION

Investors and analysts should recognise that the annual report and accounts of a company represent only a part, albeit a key part, of the total information available to them, and they should not neglect other sources. For convenience the other sources can be divided into:

(*a*) information the company provides, *and*
(*b*) external information.

INFORMATION PROVIDED BY THE COMPANY

The main sources of information from the company itself, apart from the annual report and accounts, are:

(*a*) half-yearly (and in a few cases quarterly) reports;
(*b*) prospectuses;
(*c*) circulars;
(*d*) company newsletters and magazines;
(*e*) catalogues and sales information literature;
(*f*) annual meetings;
(*g*) company visits.

Half-yearly reports and quarterly reports

The EEC directive on Interim Reports requires each listed company to prepare a report on its activities and profit and loss during the first six months of each financial year. This report must *either* be sent to shareholders *or* be inserted in two national daily newspapers not later than four months after the end of the period (see The Stock Exchange's *Admission of Securities to Listing*, Section 5, Chapter 2, paras. 24 and 25).

In addition to providing information on the first six months, interim figures can and should be used subsequently in conjunction with the full year's figures to detect changes in trends in the second half (see Chapter 23).

Interim statements are not audited and it is possible that the stringent look which is given to the balance sheet at the end of the year, and the consequent making of adequate provisions, does not occur at the half-year. This tends to mean that exceptional and extraordinary items are somewhat more likely to be included in the second half of a year than in the first half.

Prospectuses and listing particulars

When a company offers shares or debentures for sale to the general public it is obliged in law to issue a prospectus; the Third Schedule to the Companies Act 1985 lays down the items which a prospectus must contain.

When a company 'goes public' – that is, when its shares gain a listing on The Stock Exchange (see Chapter 3) – its prospectus has to include all the information required for listing (see The Stock Exchange's *Admission of Securities to Listing*, Section 3, Chapter 2: 'Contents of Listing Particulars'), and so the prospectus is about the most comprehensive document a company ever produces about itself. The normal layout used is as follows:

1. Details of the offer, share capital and indebtedness.
2. Details of the company's directors, secretary, auditors, financial advisers, solicitors, bankers and stockbrokers.
3. Description of the company, giving:
   (*a*) an introduction and a brief history;

(b) a comprehensive description of its business;

(c) information on the management and staff;

(d) details of the company's premises;

(e) use of the proceeds of the issue (where any new shares are being issued);

(f) the earnings record, with a forecast for the current year's profits and intended dividends;

(g) the company's plans and prospects for the future.

4. The accountants' report, containing a table of the last five years' profit and loss accounts and source and application of funds statements and the latest balance sheet.

5. Various statutory and general information on share capital and options, on the Articles of Association, on subsidiary and associated companies, directors' interests and service agreements, taxation clearances, material contracts, and any pending litigation.

On other occasions of shares being offered to the general public either directly, as in a secondary offer for sale of existing shares already listed (e.g. the government's £550 million sale of BRITISH AEROSPACE shares in May 1985), or indirectly, as in a rights issue of new shares of a company whose existing securities are already listed, much less information is required; nevertheless, the prospectus of a secondary offer or the circular letter to shareholders produced for a rights issue can be useful sources of up-to-date information on a company.

Circulars on acquisitions and realisations

Section 6 of The Yellow Book divides transactions into four classes, as shown in Example 21.1.

When a listed company makes a Class 1 transaction (i.e. equivalent to 15% or more of the existing company), shareholders have to be sent a circular giving full details; alternatively, if the company is making a takeover bid, they can be sent a copy of the offer document, provided the offer document includes all the information required for circulars on acquisitions (as contained in Section 6 of The Yellow Book). In either case the information provides the analyst with useful details of any major additions to or realisations of the company's assets.

Example 21.1   Criteria for classification of transactions

Class	Size of acquisition or disposal	Criteria in relation to the company which is acquiring or disposing	Stock Exchange requirements
1	Value of assets	15% or more of company's assets	Company must make an announcement to the Company Announcements Office and to the Press *and* send circular to shareholders (obtaining their consent if either of the first two criteria is 25% or more) *or* publish listing particulars (only if no consent required)
	or Net profit before tax	15% or more of company's net profit before tax	
	or Consideration given	15% or more of company's assets	
	or Equity capital issued	15% or more of equity capital previously in issue	
2	Not Class 1 but bigger than Class 3		Company must make an announcement to the Company Announcement Office and to the Press
3	Value of assets	less than 5% of company's assets	No announcement required unless listing is being sought for securities given in consideration
4	Transactions which involve, or involve an associate of, a director, past director, substantial shareholder or past substantial shareholder		Quotations Department must be consulted beforehand; a circular to shareholders and their consent in general meeting normally required unless transaction is very small

Circulars also have to be sent to shareholders for Class 4 transactions (those involving a director or substantial shareholder, past or present); these can be of considerable interest if the transactions are large and/or if there is any question of sharp practice, but the majority are fairly mundane, produced mainly to ensure that shareholders' interests are scrupulously protected.

Where there is a very substantial acquisition or reverse takeover, it must be subject to shareholders' approval, and the acquiring company will normally be treated as a new applicant for listing (see para. 7 of Chapter 1 of Section 6 of The Yellow Book).

Documents issued in a contested bid

When the management of a company defends a bid, it has to make the best possible case for the company's continued independence and, in doing so, it will often be rather more forthcoming about the company's future plans and prospects than it normally is in the annual report. Analysts may therefore find it worth reading any documents that a company has issued in successfully contesting a bid. It is also interesting to see whether a company subsequently lives up to any rosy picture it may have painted of its future at the time of the bid.

Company newsletters and magazines

An increasing number of companies now produce a house magazine or newsletter for employees, and many produce a 'report to employees' summarising the company's results for the year, often presenting the information in charts or diagrams. These publications can be very helpful in giving the analyst (as well as the employee) a better feel for the company, and they may contain information that is *not* included in the accounts.

Companies producing an annual newsletter or report to employees may also send copies to shareholders to ensure that information given to employees is also made available to the shareholders, but where newsletters are published more frequently or where a large group has several subsidiaries, each of which has its own separate newsletter, they are unlikely to be distributed to investors. If the analyst can lay his hands on them he may gain a better insight into the various activities of the company and pick up facts that are not generally available.

Catalogues and sales information literature

The shareholder or analyst who really wants to know a company should study its catalogues and sales literature for evidence of pricing policy, marketing ability, and changes in product range, quality or design.

Failure to adapt to changing circumstances is an early sign of sleepy management. Innovation may be essential if the company is to keep moving – but not every management is capable of thinking up new ideas and of putting them into practice. Promotional literature on new products can sometimes indicate the potential for success.

Annual General Meeting

When all is going well, annual meetings tend to be sparsely attended. This is a pity, because they provide an opportunity for shareholders to seek and obtain further information about their company.

The usual business of an AGM is:

(*a*) to receive the report and accounts;
(*b*) to declare a dividend;
(*c*) to elect directors;
(*d*) to appoint auditors;
(*e*) to transact any other ordinary business.

Any ordinary shareholder may attend the AGM and speak. Normally his best opportunity to obtain information is upon the motion considering the accounts. If the information he seeks is reasonable (e.g. not of a confidential nature or likely to be of more value to the competition than to members) and he does not obtain a satisfactory answer, he should press the point and state publicly his dissatisfaction. He may find he has more support than he expects.

Generally, directors are prepared to answer all reasonable questions when times are good, but become guarded when the situation is unsatisfactory. If this occurs, the individual shareholder may find that he can obtain the information during informal discussion after the meeting.

Company visits

Companies differ widely in their attitude to company visits by analysts and/or shareholders. Most major companies welcome the interest of both and arrange from time to time group visits at which plans and prospects are discussed in depth, and those interested are able to seek further information.

Those actually making visits should ask themselves the following:

(*a*) Is there any evidence of cut-back, of falling sales and growing stocks or of maintenance delayed to save cash?

(*b*) Is the workforce contented – or are labour relations uneasy?

(*c*) Do they look efficient – or is there a general atmosphere of chaos?

(*d*) Do they appear forthcoming, or are they hiding something?

It is also worth asking management whether it is experiencing any difficulties: good management is usually prepared to talk about the problems facing the company, and to explain the action being taken to overcome them.

Finally, always ask about the competition: the replies will help to show whether the management has a practical and realistic attitude to the business environment in which it operates, and may well provide the analyst with useful information about other companies in the industry. We well remember on one company visit, in reply to a question about a competitor, the chairman simply remarked 'that company is structured for disaster'. The competitor went bust a year later.

EXTERNAL INFORMATION

There is a vast range of external information useful to the analyst who wishes to make a study in depth of a particular company, group or industrial sector. Useful sources include:

(a)   the Registrar of Companies;
(b)   Extel Cards;
(c)   ICC Datacards;
(d)   *The Hambro Company Guide*;
(e)   Macmillan's;
(f)   McCarthy Information Services;
(g)   Finsbury Data Services;
(h)   Datastream;
(i)   .Key Notes;
(j)   the Economist Intelligence Unit;
(k)   government statistical publications;
(l)   other government publications – NEDO;
(m)   specialist and trade publications.

The Registrar of Companies

The Registration Department of the Department of Trade and Industry has offices at Companies House, 55 City Road, London EC1Y 1BB, and at Crown Way, Maindy, Cardiff CF4 3UZ; and, for Scotland, at Exchequer Chambers, 102 George Street, Edinburgh.

Rules for filing accounts
Section 242 of the Companies Act 1985 requires a company to lay accounts before its members in general meeting and to deliver them to the Registrar of Companies within certain time limits fixed by reference to its accounting year end. The limit for a UK public company is seven months, which can be extended by three months if the company has interests outside the United Kingdom.

The Stock Exchange requires listed companies to issue an annual report and accounts within six months of the end of the financial year being reported on (The Yellow Book, Section 5, Chapter 1, para. 20), but this may be extended for companies with significant overseas interests.

Other information to be filed
Companies are also required to file with the Registrar:

(a)   copies of their Memorandum and Articles of Association, and details of any subsequent changes;
(b)   address of the registered office, and the place at which the company's registers are kept, if not at the registered office;
(c)   details of the company's share capital and debentures;
(d)   details of each mortgage and charge on the assets of the company;
(e)   a list of the directors and secretary and any changes.

In addition, Section 363 of the Companies Act 1985 requires a company to file an *annual return*, which contains a summary of (b) to (e) above and a list of past and present members. Every third year the list must be a complete list of persons holding shares or stock in the company; in the intervening years only changes need be given, but in each year the return must show anyone whose name has appeared on the register as holding shares or stock in the company at any time since the last return. It is therefore possible to find out from Companies House if anyone has been a registered shareholder at any time, however short the period of ownership, although nominee names may hide the beneficial owner.

Inspecting a company's files
Companies' files are now maintained at Cardiff, and can be inspected either at Cardiff or at City Road, on payment of a fee of £1 per company. For this fee the searcher is provided with a microfiche of the company's file, which can be examined on their viewing equipment; hard copy can also be obtained at an additional 10p per page. The microfiche belongs to and may be taken away by the searcher, so anyone with suitable microfiche equipment can consult the file at leisure in his own office.

No postal search facilities are currently available through the Registrar, but there are a number of search agents who will provide the service on payment of a suitable fee, for example Jordan & Sons Ltd, Jordan House, 47 Brunswick Place, London N1 6EE.

The microfiche facilities available at City Road,

London and at Cardiff are virtually identical, and there is no significant time difference in the recording of information at the two offices. For instance, information on charges registered in London is available on the microfiche file in Cardiff within the hour.

Analysing a group

Most group accounts contain a general breakdown of their activities, but much more detail can often be obtained by examining the accounts which each subsidiary and associated company has to file at Companies House.

Extel Cards

Extel (Extel Statistical Services PLC, 37–45 Paul Street, London EC2A 4PB) is the leading UK provider of financial information services, both on data tape and in printed form. The best known printed services are Extel Cards, which provide information on industrial companies in the United Kingdom and overseas. Extel's card services in the United Kingdom include the following:

1. The *UK Listed Companies* service, covering every company listed on the British and Irish Stock Exchanges. Two individual cards are issued for each company:
    (*a*) An Annual Card, which summarises the company's activities and lists its subsidiaries and associated companies, its board members, its share and its loan capital (with history). Tables of profit and loss items for the last ten years and dividend payments for the last five years are given, together with the latest balance sheet, a summary of the chairman's most recent statement and a whole host of other information ranging from the company's registered number to its net asset value.
    (*b*) A Cumulative News Card, issued as and when dividends are announced and when other major items of news justify.
2. The *Analyst's* service, which complements the *UK Listed Companies* service and covers over 1,300 leading listed companies, giving a ten-year record (analysed and adjusted) of capital changes, balance sheets, profit and loss accounts, share prices, dividends, etc.
3. The *Unlisted Securities Market (USM)* service, which includes cards for all companies whose shares are traded on The Stock Exchange's Unlisted Securities Market.
4. The *Unquoted Companies* service, which is an extension of the *UK Listed Companies* and *USM* services. It contains similar information on more than 2,000 unquoted companies, on the same system of continuous updating year after year.

The *UK Listed Companies* service, which is an essential part of any stockbroker's or professional investor's office, costs over £1,500 per annum, takes up about eight cubic feet of filing cabinets and needs two or three hours' clerical effort per week to cope with the steady stream of new cards; but copies of individual cards can be purchased from Extel's extra card department for a few pounds.

A less expensive and more condensed form of information on listed companies is provided by Extel's *Handbook of Market Leaders*, which is published twice a year. It covers the 750 companies in the *FT* Actuaries All-share Index, and gives a share price graph as well as other information covering a five-year period. Extel also publishes an *Unlisted Securities Market Handbook*.

ICC Datacards

This recently started service can provide a single-page computer printout on any limited company trading in the United Kingdom, providing its accounts have been filed at Companies House. The page contains basic information on the company, the balance sheets and profit and loss accounts for four years, and a large number of ratios calculated for those years. ICC Datacard Services Ltd, 28/42 Banner Street, London EC1Y 8QE.

The Hambro Company Guide

This is an alternative to Extel's *Handbook of Market Leaders*, which used to be published bi-annually, giving about the same amount of information on each company and covering over 2,500 companies. In addition, it carried further information on some of the companies, provided and paid for by each company (e.g. the summary of the chairman's statement and annual results as advertised in the financial press); this enabled it to be sold at less than half the price of the Extel handbook. It has been in abeyance since 1982, but the new publishers, Hemmington Scott, 90/93 Cowcross Street, London EC1M 6BH, plan to restart publication quarterly in November 1985, covering 3,000 listed, USM and OTC companies.

Macmillan's

Macmillan's Unquoted Companies, a book compiled by the ICC Information Group, contains financial information on the top 10,000 unquoted companies in Britain (those with a turnover of around £3 million or more). It was first published in May 1985 at £87.50.

McCarthy Information Services

The Press provides a major source of news and information on companies, but keeping track of what appears on any particular company is a time-consuming and somewhat hit-and-miss affair. Fortunately McCarthy's (McCarthy Information Ltd, The Manor House, Ash Walk, Warminster, Wiltshire BA12 8PY) provides an excellent *Quoted Company* service, the reading list for which includes:

Birmingham Post	*Lloyds List*
Daily Express	*Mail on Sunday*
Daily Mail	*Marketing Week*
The Daily Telegraph	*The Observer*
The Economist	*Private Eye*
Euromoney	*The Scotsman*
Financial Times	*The Standard*
Financial Weekly	*Sunday Express*
Glasgow Herald	*Sunday Standard*
The Guardian	*Sunday Telegraph*
Investors Chronicle	*Sunday Times*
Irish Independent	*The Times*
The Irish Times	*Yorkshire Post*

All relevant news, comment and articles on a company are cut out and reproduced on information sheets and a new sheet is circulated to subscribers, on a daily basis. In addition, McCarthy's provides a range of other services, including services on Australian, North American and European companies, on USM and UK unquoted companies, and on industries, banking and property. McCarthy's also runs a service called *Mirac*, which provides the reports and accounts of all listed and USM companies and of all nationalised industries on microfiche.

Finsbury Data Services

Finsbury Data Services, 68/74 Carter Lane, London EC4V 5EA, provides three electronic business information systems over the public telephone network: a press abstracts service called *Textline*, a news headlines service called *Newsline* and a company financial data service called *Dataline*, which includes a forecasting model facility. The annual subscription to the services, including a remote terminal and printer, is around £10,000.

Datastream

Datastream is a brilliantly conceived computer-based system which provides detailed information both on individual companies and on companies within a specified sector of the market. Analysis of individual company accounts can be obtained on a five-year basis, covering profit and loss account, balance sheet and financing table, together with key accounting ratios, while the same information for a single year can be displayed on up to five companies at a time.

The system is accessed from remote visual display units (VDUs) situated in subscribers' offices and, once the initial programme has been selected, a series of questions is displayed on the VDU to enable the user to specify exactly what he requires. The information is then displayed on the VDU and can be printed out on a Datastream printer if hard copy is required.

Datastream also provides a chart plotting facility, macro-economic data, price monitoring and performance measurement, a portfolio performance program and a news channel.

The Datastream system, pioneered by stockbrokers Hoare & Co. Govett, is now run by Datastream International Ltd, 58–64 City Road, London EC1Y 2AL, which obtained a listing on The Stock Exchange in March 1983, but was then taken over by the Dun & Bradstreet Corporation in May 1984.

Over 500 remote terminals serve financial and investment institutions both in the United Kingdom and in Europe; the annual subscription for a single terminal (VDU and keyboard) is more than £10,000 or, alternatively, for a small monthly subscription, access to the Datastream system can be obtained on a metered dial-up basis.

Key Notes

Each Key Note provides a concise introduction to a sector of British industry. The series covers more than 150 sectors, and each note includes:

(*a*) a summary and interpretation of the latest production and trade statistics from government, industry and market sources;

(*b*) an appraisal of the market background, highlighting recent developments and future prospects;

(*c*) financial data on the sector and ratio analysis of the major companies in the sector; *and*

(*d*) sources of information: an index of recent press articles and a list of trade associations, trade publications and statistical studies.

Key Notes cost £75 each, or £4,500 p.a. to subscribe to the entire service; they are available from Key Note Publications Ltd, 28/42 Banner Street, EC1Y 8QE. The company is a subsidiary of Inter Company Comparisons Ltd (see page 167).

The Economist Intelligence Unit (EIU)

The EIU produces a wide range of business as well as economic publications, including special reports (e.g. *The UK Passenger Car Market: Developments, Issues and Prospects to 1990*, published in 1984 at £75), and periodical reviews (e.g. *Paper and Packaging Bulletin* quarterly), which cost £150 or so per annum. The EIU's London headquarters are at 27 St James's Place, London SW1A 1NT.

Government statistical publications

Although the Department of Trade and Industry does produce a weekly magazine, *British Business*, containing the latest information on a variety of statistics, the best overall presentation of the huge range of statistics prepared by government departments is given in the *Monthly Digest of Statistics*, published by the Central Statistical Office of the Government Statistical Service.

Other statistical publications include:

Financial Statistics (monthly) – gives the key financial and monetary statistics of the United Kingdom.

Economic Trends (monthly) – commentary and a selection of tables and charts providing a broad background to trends in the UK economy.

Annual Abstract of Statistics – contains many more series than the monthly digest and provides a longer run of years.

United Kingdom National Accounts – known as the 'Blue Book', which is published annually and gives detailed estimates of the national accounts including consumers' expenditure over the previous ten years.

Business Monitor – monthly and quarterly publications giving statistical information from various government departments on a wide range of subjects, e.g. Motor vehicle registrations, monthly from the Department of the Environment; Acquisitions and mergers of commercial and industrial companies, quarterly from the Department of Trade and Industry.

A useful booklet *Government Statistics – a brief guide to sources* is available free from the Central Statistical Office, CO:CSO Section, Great George Street, London SW1P 3AQ.

Other government publications – NEDO

Government departments produce a wide range of publications on individual industries, in particular National Economic Development Committee reports from the National Economic Development Office, NEDO. All NEDO publications are listed in a free booklet *Nedo in Print*, obtainable from NEDO Books, Millbank Tower, Millbank, London SW1P 4QX.

Specialist and trade publications

Trade magazines published by trade associations may contain useful statistical information compiled from the association's own members, as well as general news about the industry, while independent specialist magazines provide useful background information in their particular sphere. Some independent periodicals are published on a private subscription-only basis, for example the market intelligence reports on consumer goods, retailing, leisure and personal finance in the United Kingdom, published by Mintel Publications, 7 Arundel Street, London WC2R 3DR.

Finally, on a broader note, an independent view and forecasts on the UK and world economy are contained in the *National Institute Economic Review*, published by the National Institute of Economic and Social Research, NIESR. The NIESR, 2 Dean Trench Street, Smith Square, London SW1P 3HE, is an independent non-profit-making body, which conducts research by its own staff and in co-operation with the universities and other academic bodies.

Chapter 22

INFLATION ACCOUNTING

(References: SSAP 16 *Current Cost Accounting*; ED 35 *Accounting for the effect of changing prices*.)

Introduction

This·chapter deals with the subject of inflation accounting in five parts. The first two (Why inflation accounting is needed, and The development of inflation accounting systems) are designed for anyone completely new to the subject.

The reader who is already familiar with the background to inflation accounting can go straight to the third and fourth parts (SSAP 16 explained, and SSAP 16 discussed), or to the fifth and final part (Where do we go from here?).

WHY INFLATION ACCOUNTING IS NEEDED

In attempting to present a true and fair view of a company's affairs, accounting systems have two principal enemies: inflation and subjective judgement.

Historical cost (HC) accounting

In a time of stable prices, the historical cost system works well. What an asset cost is seldom in dispute, and although the directors have to assess the expected useful lives of fixed assets, and their likely disposal values, there is limited scope for subjective judgement. Furthermore, the quality of historical cost accounts has steadily improved over the years, largely thanks to the efforts of the Accounting Standards Committee. SSAPs have considerably reduced the number of options available to company directors and, though problems do still remain, not many people other than accounting theorists would seriously suggest that historical cost be abandoned as the basis of accounting in a period of stable prices.

HC accounting with inflation

In a period of substantial price rises (i.e. inflation), historical cost accounting has five main weaknesses:

1. *Depreciation inadequate for the replacement of fixed assets.* Historical cost accounting seeks to write off the cost of fixed assets over their effective lives. It does not set out to provide a fund from which the fixed assets can be replaced at the end of their lives. Nevertheless, in a period of stable prices, sufficient cash could be set aside over the life of an asset to replace it at its original cost. In times of inflation, insufficient is provided in this way to enable the business to replace its assets. For example, where an asset is written off on a straight line basis over ten years, the total provisions for depreciation as a percentage of cost are:

Inflation rate	Depreciation as % of cost (Constant pounds)
5%	79.1%
10%	64.4%
15%	53.8%

2. *Cost of sales understated.* In historical cost accounts, stock consumed and sold is charged against sales at its original cost, rather than at the cost of replacing it. But, in

148

order to retain the same stock level, the company has to finance the difference (and has to do so entirely out of profits after tax since the abolition of stock relief). This is perhaps most easily understood if we add a few figures. Assume that the company has in stock one item which cost £25. It sells it for £40, and replaces the stock for £35. Corporation Tax is payable at, say, 40%. Historical cost accounts say that the company made a profit of £15; but if it is to maintain its original stock level, it has to use £10 of the 'profit' of £15 simply in order to stand still and, with no stock relief, the tax man would want a further £6, leaving a 'net profit' of −£1.

3. *Need for increase in other working capital not recognised.* In most companies, debtors are greater than creditors, so, on an unchanged volume of business, 'debtors minus creditors' increases with inflation, requiring extra money to be provided for working capital. Historical cost accounts fail to recognise that this extra working capital is necessary to maintain the operating capacity of a business and that it has to be provided for the business to remain a going concern.

4. *Borrowing benefits not shown.* Borrowings are shown in monetary terms, and if nothing is repaid, and nothing further is borrowed, borrowings appear stable. This is a distortion of the picture, because a gain has been made at the expense of the lender (since in real terms the value of the loan has declined): some people feel that this gain ought to be reflected in the accounts.

5. *Year-on-year figures not comparable.* In addition to being overstated due to:

    (*a*) inadequate provision for depreciation,

    (*b*) understated cost of sales, and

    (*c*) no provision for increase in other working capital,

profits are stated in terms of money which has itself declined in value. Similarly, sales and dividends are not comparable with those of other years, because they are expressed in pounds of different purchasing power. For example, compare MARKS & SPENCER's pre-tax profits for the years 1979 to 1984 with the same figures adjusted by the Retail Price Index to produce pre-tax profits in constant pounds, as shown in the table below: the unadjusted figures suggest steady progress when in real terms pre-tax profits advanced only 5% in five years. When reported pre-tax profits appear fairly static, as in DISTILLERS' figures below, they are, in reality, in serious decline.

The reporting of profits in inflated pounds gives a far too rosy impression of growth in profitability. This tends to lull both managers and shareholders into thinking that their company is doing very much better than it really is, it encourages unions and employees to expect wage increases that are unmatched by real (as opposed to reported) profit growth, and it also can and does encourage government measures that are very harmful to the long-term prosperity of a company, e.g. the imposition of price controls or excess profits tax made on a completely false impression of profitability.

Before going on to discuss how inflation accounting has developed over the last few years, it is worth looking at the impact that even quite modest rates of inflation can have on the value of money if they persist for several years.

MARKS & SPENCER *Pre-tax profits as reported, and after adjustment by the Retail Price Index*

Year ending 31 March	1979	1980	1981	1982	1983	1984
Reported pre-tax profits (£m)	161.6	173.7	181.2	222.1	239.3	279.3
Average RPI for the period	202.6	233.2	272.4	302.8	323.8	338.8
RPI rebased: 1979 = 100	100.0	115.1	134.5	149.5	159.8	167.2
Pre-tax profits (constant £m)	161.6	150.9	134.7	148.6	149.7	167.0

DISTILLERS *Pre-tax profits as reported, and after adjustment by the Retail Price Index*

Year ending 31 March	1979	1980	1981	1982	1983	1984
Reported pre-tax profits (£m)	180.1	193.9	181.0	178.5	200.8	191.6
Average RPI for the period	202.6	233.2	272.4	302.8	323.8	338.8
RPI rebased: 1979 = 100	100.0	115.1	134.5	149.5	159.8	167.2
Pre-tax profits (constant £m)	180.1	168.5	134.6	119.4	125.7	114.6

The staggering impact of inflation

As Example 22.1 shows, the effect of inflation on the value of money over a number of years is staggering.

Example 22.1 Effect of inflation on the value of £1

Annual rate of inflation	After 5 years	After 10 years	After 20 years
2½%	88.3p	78.1p	61.0p
5%	78.3p	61.3p	37.6p
7½%	69.6p	48.5p	23.5p
10%	62.0p	38.5p	14.8p
12½%	55.4p	30.7p	9.4p
15%	49.7p	24.7p	6.1p
17½%	44.6p	19.9p	3.9p
20%	40.1p	16.1p	2.6p
25%	32.7p	10.7p	1.1p

Another way of putting this is to say that with inflation running at 7½% per annum, a modest level by recent standards, a company must double its profits every ten years to maintain their real value, and if inflation is up to 15% per annum, profits must be doubled every five years. In fact, we would go further than that: because of the inadequacy of historical cost accounting, the majority of companies should treble rather than double their historical cost profits in those periods in order to hold their own in real terms. Of course, any company that *does* succeed in maintaining real profits in times of high inflation is doing remarkably well. See Appendix 3 for table showing the effect of inflation in the United Kingdom on the Retail Price Index.

THE DEVELOPMENT OF INFLATION ACCOUNTING SYSTEMS

Additional depreciation

Some companies realised a number of years ago that, even with the modest rates of inflation the United Kingdom experienced in the 1960s, the provision for depreciation was insufficient to cover the cost of replacements, and they therefore made additional provisions for this purpose. Doing so gave a more realistic picture of profitability, but it did not reduce the liability for taxation: the extra depreciation had to be provided for out of profits after tax.

Details of the methods of providing for this extra depreciation varied, but the basic principle was to revalue fixed assets periodically and re-calculate depreciation on the new values. Both PILKINGTON and ASSOCIATED PORTLAND CEMENT (now the BLUE CIRCLE GROUP) were pioneers in the field, and Pilkington still does provide for additional depreciation in its HC accounts.

Current purchasing power accounting (CPP)

An Exposure Draft, ED 8 – *Accounting for changes in the purchasing power of money* – was issued in 1973 recommending that companies adopt what came to be known as current purchasing power accounting (CPP). The main features of ED 8 were that:

(a) companies would continue to keep their records and present their basic annual accounts in historical terms, i.e. in terms of the value of the pound at the time of each transaction or revaluation;

(b) in addition, all listed companies would present to their shareholders a *supplementary statement* in terms of the value of the pound at the end of the period to which the accounts related;

(c) the conversion of the figures in the basic accounts into the figures in the supplementary statement should be by means of a general index of purchasing power of the pound (the Retail Price Index);

(d) directors should provide in a note to the supplementary statement an explanation of the basis on which it has been prepared, and should comment on the significance of the figures.

CPP accounting was concerned solely with removing the distorting effects of changes in the general purchasing power of money on accounts prepared in accordance with established practice (i.e. on a historical cost basis). It did not deal with changes in the *relative* values of non-monetary items (which can and do occur in the absence of inflation).

CPP accounts were criticised on a number of grounds. Among these were the following:

1. Shareholders were faced with a choice between two sets of figures which frequently gave very different results. Both could not be correct.

2. CPP accounting enhanced the profits of companies which were heavily borrowed, particularly those showing low profits on a historical cost basis. This was because assets on which perhaps little or no profit was being made were shown by CPP to be increasing in

value in line with inflation (i.e. maintaining their real value), while money borrowed to acquire them was treated as declining in real value. The more heavily borrowed the company, the more the profits became boosted by CPP, as for example in GRAND METROPOLITAN's 1974 accounts, illustrated here.

GRAND METROPOLITAN *Extracts from 1974 accounts*

	£000
Ordinary shareholders' funds	429,436
less Goodwill	295,361
OSF net of goodwill	134,075
10% CULS 1991/96	121,114
Other loan capital	281,219
Bank overdrafts and short-term borrowings	130,396
Total debt	532,729
Earnings per share (historical)	7.3p
Earnings per share (CPP basis)	35.2p

---

3. The Retail Price Index is not a true index of general purchasing power and it may quite badly represent the effects of inflation upon a particular individual or company.

In the event, in spite of being adopted by quite a large number of public companies, CPP accounting was overtaken by the appointment of the Sandilands Committee, which was set up in 1974 under the chairmanship of Mr (now Sir) Francis Sandilands.

Current cost accounting (CCA)

The Sandilands Report

The Sandilands Committee reported to the Chancellor of the Exchequer and the Secretary for Trade in June 1975 and its report was published three months later: the Committee rejected the proposals contained in PSSAP 7 (a provisional SSAP on CPP, which had been issued as a follow-up to ED 8 pending the Sandilands findings), and recommended instead the development of a system to be known as current cost accounting (CCA), in which:

(*a*) no adjustment is made for inflation (i.e. for changes in the 'purchasing power' of money);

(*b*) assets and liabilities are shown in the bal-

ance sheet at their 'value to the business', which can be very much a matter of subjective judgement;

(*c*) 'operating profit' is struck after charging the value to the business of assets consumed during the period, thus excluding holding gains from profit and showing them separately.

The Sandilands report also recommended that current cost accounting should become the basic published accounts of companies as soon as practicable.

ED 18

In response to the Sandilands recommendations, the Inflation Accounting Steering Group (IASG, or the 'Morpeth Committee') was set up by the accountancy profession under the chairmanship of Mr (now Sir) Douglas Morpeth to co-ordinate the introduction of CCA, and its proposals for a system of CCA, endorsed by the Accounting Standards Committee, were published by the ASC as an Exposure Draft (ED 18) towards the end of November 1976.

The Hyde Report

ED 18, although technically impressive and supported by formidable explanatory handbooks, was widely regarded as too complicated, too subjective; some even felt that it was unauditable. This led to members of the Institute of Chartered Accountants in England and Wales voting at an extraordinary meeting that current cost accounting should not be made compulsory.

As a result of this extraordinary meeting, the Accounting Standards Committee set up the Hyde Committee, with the task of providing guidance, as an interim measure, on how information on the effects of inflation should be provided in the published accounts of listed companies.

The report of the Hyde Committee was published in December 1977. It recommended that supplementary information should be provided in the form of three separate adjustments to the profits computed on a historical cost basis. Two of these, depreciation and cost of sales, are a simplified form of CCA and the third, gearing, was designed to take account of the effect of net monetary items. It was from the Hyde recommendations that the standard accounting practice on CCA, SSAP 16, was developed and expanded to include a fourth adjustment, the *monetary working capital adjustment*.

SSAP 16 EXPLAINED

Introduction

SSAP 16, which is currently in abeyance, is an adaptation of the historical cost (HC) system, to recognise two basic concepts:

1. that the profitability of a company should be assessed after deducting the amount of money it needs in order to stand still in real terms, *and*
2. that the assets of a company should be shown at their value to the business.

The SSAP 16 system of CCA calculates the profit of a business by making adjustments to the HC profit and loss account. These adjustments allow for the impact of price changes on the funds needed to continue the existing business and maintain its operating capacity. An adjustment is also made to allow for the way in which the business is financed.

The CCA adjustments

Three *operating adjustments* are normally made to the HC trading profit to allow for the impact of price changes:

1. the *depreciation adjustment,*
2. the *cost of sales adjustment,*
3. the *monetary working capital adjustment.*

These adjustments to the HC trading profit produce the *current cost operating profit*, which takes no account of the way in which the company is financed.

The *current cost pre-tax profit* is then obtained by deducting interest paid, and by making a fourth adjustment:

4. the *gearing adjustment,*

which adds back part of the operating adjustments to allow for the proportion of assets financed by borrowings.

Price indices

Price indices are used in calculating the operating adjustments, to reflect relevant price changes. The most appropriate index or indices should be selected in each case, and may be:

(a) a price index prepared by government agencies, *or*
(b) a generally recognised privately produced index, *or*
(c) an index compiled by a business on the basis of its own experience.

Indices should be consistently applied in succeeding periods. The Government Statistical Service publishes each year a book *Price Index Numbers for Current Cost Accounting (PINCCA)* which contains, in addition to wholesale and retail price indices, a myriad of industry-specific and asset-specific indices, together with price indices for road motor vehicles, buildings and works. It is updated each month by a *PINCCA* monthly supplement, published in the *Business Monitor* series.

Depreciation adjustment

The depreciation adjustment allows for the impact of price changes on the cost of replacing fixed assets. It is the difference between depreciation based on the CCA value of fixed assets (their 'value to the business') and HC depreciation.

The *value to the business* is either:

(a) the net current replacement cost (gross current replacement cost *less* depreciation)

or, if less,

(b) the *recoverable amount*, which is the greater of:
    (i) the net realisable value of an asset (the realisable value net of expenses of disposal), and
    (ii) the amount recoverable from its future use (i.e. the discounted stream of estimated future earnings).

This is probably easier to understand diagrammatically, as shown in Example 22.2 opposite.

The *total* amount of CCA depreciation is not shown in the CCA profit and loss account, but it can be calculated from the accounts. For example, the 1984 accounts of BLUNDELL-PERMOGLAZE HOLDINGS, the paint and building products group, showed:

	£000
HC accounts	
HC tangible fixed assets	7,728
HC depreciation	779
CCA accounts	
CCA tangible fixed assets	9,517
CCA additional depreciation	290
Total CCA depreciation (not shown)	1,069

Cost of sales adjustment

The cost of sales adjustment (COSA), which allows for the impact of price changes on stock, is the difference between the value to the business of the stock consumed at the date it was consumed (i.e. the cost of replacing it) and the original cost of the stock.

Several methods of calculating the COSA are described in appendices to the *Guidance Notes on*

Example 22.2   Calculation of 'value to the business'

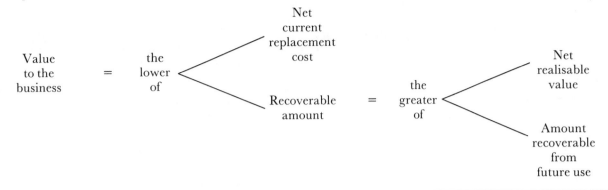

SSAP 16, including the *averaging method* illustrated below. This is a straightforward method suitable for use when stock levels have not fluctuated violently.

Calculation of cost of sales adjustment using the averaging method

	£000
Opening stock	6,591
Closing stock	6,644
	+53

Index numbers for cost of stock
Opening stock	98.4
Closing stock	102.4
Average index for period	100.0

Adjust opening and closing stock to average current cost for the year:

		£000
Opening stock	$= 6{,}591 \times \dfrac{100.0}{98.4} =$	6,698
Closing stock	$= 6{,}644 \times \dfrac{100.0}{102.4} =$	6,488
Volume change in stock	$=$	-210

Cost of sales adjustment (£000) $= +53 - (-210) = 263$

£263,000 was, in fact, the cost of sales adjustment for Blundell-Permoglaze in 1984, but the arithmetic was somewhat more complicated: £263,000 was the sum of the cost of sales adjustments calculated separately in each of the three divisions, each division using several different series of indices appropriate to various types of stock – raw materials, containers, rollers, finished goods, etc.

The cost of sales adjustment may be shown separately, or it may be combined with the next adjustment, the monetary working capital adjustment. If combined, they are called the 'working capital adjustment'.

Monetary working capital adjustment

The monetary working capital adjustment (MWCA) allows for the additional (or reduced) finance needed for monetary working capital as a result of changes in input prices of goods and services used and financed by the business.

Monetary working capital (MWC) is the aggregate of:

(a)   trade debtors, prepayments and trade bills receivable;

plus

(b)   stocks not subject to a cost of sales adjustment. These may include:
  (i)   stock relating to long-term contracts, net of progress payments;
  (ii)   seasonal agricultural produce;
  (iii) stock held for dealing purposes; *and*
  (iv)   land held for development;

less

(c)   trade creditors, accruals and trade bills payable.

If bank balances or overdrafts fluctuate materially with the volume of stock or with items in MWC, 'That part of bank balances or overdrafts arising from such fluctuations should be included in monetary working capital, together with any cash floats required to support day-to-day operations of the business.'

The MWCA is calculated by applying the appropriate indices; for example, Blundell-Permoglaze used the indices for finished goods to calculate their MWCA in 1984.

BLUNDELL-PERMOGLAZE HOLDINGS *Calculation of monetary working capital adjustment by the averaging method*

	1984 £000	1983 £000
Debtors	8,080	7,186
Creditors	5,190	4,236
Monetary working capital	2,890	2,950

Overall decrease in MWC (£000) = 2,950 − 2,890 = 60.

Indices of finished goods
Opening 100
Average 102.7
Closing 105.2

Adjust opening and closing MWC to average current cost for the year:

£000

Opening MWC $= 2,950 \times \dfrac{102.7}{100} = 3,029$

Closing MWC $= 2,890 \times \dfrac{102.7}{105.2} = 2,821$

'Volume' decrease in MWC 208

Monetary working capital adjustment (£000) = 208 − 60 = 148.

Gearing adjustment

We have seen that the operating adjustments represent the amount a company has to allow for additional depreciation, stock and monetary working capital because of price changes.

Current cost accounting then assumes that these operating adjustments will be financed partly by equity and partly by borrowings, in the same proportion as the company's operating assets have been financed over the previous period. The borrowing proportion is called the 'gearing proportion'.

As the gearing proportion of the operating adjustments will not need financing from current cost earnings, it is added back by means of the gearing adjustment.

Gearing adjustment =

Gearing proportion × Operating adjustments

where

Gearing proportion = $\dfrac{\text{Average net borrowing}}{\text{Average net operating assets}}$

and *net borrowing* is the excess of:

(*a*) all liabilities and provisions fixed in monetary terms (including convertibles and deferred tax, but excluding proposed dividends) other than items included in monetary working capital

over

(*b*) all current assets other than those subject to a cost of sales adjustment or included in monetary working capital,

and *net operating assets* are fixed assets (including trade investments), stock and monetary working capital, as shown in the current cost balance sheet.

The totals of net operating assets and of net borrowing and their main elements should be disclosed in notes to the current cost balance sheet.

Example 22.3 shows the effect of the gearing adjustment on an antique dealer, firstly if he is 100% equity financed and secondly if he is 100% financed by borrowing. In it, the actual prices of stock are used in calculating the COSA (rather than indices), a method suitable for companies dealing with large individual items of stock, e.g. a motor distributor.

Example 22.3 Gearing adjustment applied to an antique dealer

Let us suppose that a self-financed antique dealer buys a Georgian mahogany bureau for £550, sells it six months later for £700 and, on the same day, replaces it for £640. In CCA accounts he would be shown as making £150 on the first bureau, less £90 cost of sales adjustment = £60 profit; since he has no borrowings, there is no gearing adjustment. This, of course, reflects what would happen in practice: he would need all but £60 of the proceeds of the sale to replace his stock.

If, on the other hand, the antique dealer had no capital and had borrowed £550 from the bank to buy the first bureau, then *provided* the bank was happy to lend him £640 to buy the second bureau, his profit on the first bureau would be £700 less £550 repaid to the bank, less bank interest (£550 for six months at, say, 20% = £55).

CCA accounts would *assume* that the bank was happy for him to maintain his 100% gearing proportion, and would show:

		£
Trading profit		150
less Cost of sales adjustment		90
		60
*Gearing adjustment	(90)	
Interest paid	55	
		(35)
Current cost profit before taxation		95

*Gearing adjustment = gearing proportion (100%) × operating adjustments (in this case just a single cost of sales adjustment of £90) = £90.

Not many companies are financed entirely by equity, and only nationalised industries are financed entirely by debt (and are subject to special rules under SSAP 16), so the gearing adjustment normally adds back part of the operating adjustments. Blundell-Permoglaze, for example, in 1984 had average net borrowings of £4,137,750 and average net operating assets of £19,337,000, with operating adjustments of £701,000; thus:

$$\begin{array}{l}Gearing\\adjustment\end{array} = \frac{£4,137,750}{£19,337,000} \times £701,000 = £150,000.$$

Interest paid

Interest paid on net borrowing is normally shown with, and netted off against, the gearing adjustment, as shown in Blundell-Permoglaze's 1984 CCA accounts.

BLUNDELL-PERMOGLAZE HOLDINGS *Extract from CCA profit and loss account*

		£000
Historic profit before interest and taxation		1,446
Deduct: Current cost operating adjustments		
Cost of sales	(263)	
Monetary working capital	(148)	
Additional depreciation	(290)	
		(701)
Current cost operating profit		745
Add/(deduct):		
Gearing adjustment	150	
Interest payable	(205)	
		(55)
Current cost profit before taxation		690
Taxation		(395)
Minority interest		16
Current cost profit after taxation and minority interest		311
Dividends		(547)
Reduction in reserves		(236)

Taxation

SSAP 16 gives no special instructions on taxation. Normal practice is to show the same figure for taxation as the HC accounts.

Group accounts

Associated companies. The investing company's CC profit and loss account should include its share of the CC profits or losses of associated companies

or, where current cost figures are not produced, the directors' best estimate of them.

Minority interests. HC minority interests less the minorities' share of CCA adjustments, calculated on a company-by-company basis.

Current cost balance sheet

The basic principle of a current cost balance sheet is that it should reflect the value of assets to the business, and this is the reason why there are two main differences between an HC and a CC balance sheet:

1. Fixed assets are stated at their *value to the business*, as defined on page 152.
2. There is an additional reserve: the *current cost reserve*, which includes:
   (*a*) unrealised valuation surpluses on fixed assets, stock and investments, *and*
   (*b*) the cumulative net total of all CCA adjustments (i.e. all the past current cost operating adjustments less all the past gearing adjustments).

Presentation of current cost accounts

Under SSAP 16 current cost accounts must be presented by companies listed on The Stock Exchange, and also by unlisted companies (other than wholly owned subsidiaries) which satisfy at least two of the following criteria:

1. Annual turnover of £5 million or more.
2. Assets of £2.5 million or more in the *historical cost* accounts at the beginning of the period.
3. 250 or more employees in the UK or Ireland.

Insurance and property companies, investment and unit trusts, and non-profit-making organisations are exempted (SSAP 16, para. 46).

Current cost accounts may be presented *either* as supplementary accounts to HC accounts, *or* as the only accounts, provided they are accompanied by sufficient supplementary HC information to enable the user to ascertain the HC profit.

Comparability with previous years

SSAP 16 recognises that CCA figures in different years are not comparable unless they are adjusted to a common price basis. The Accounting Standards Committee intends to develop a standard on the subject; meanwhile, companies are encouraged to give adjusted comparative figures, and to adjust figures in any five- or ten-year statements. The extract from DISTILLERS' group current cost accounts overleaf illustrates one way of presenting adjusted comparative figures.

DISTILLERS *Extract from group current cost accounts*

	1984	1983 Amounts updated (note 2)	1983 Amounts as at March 1983
Profit and loss account	£m	£m	£m
Turnover	1,134.1	1,185.8	1,127.2
Trading profit per historical cost accounts	181.6	212.2	201.7
Depreciation adjustment	(31.7)	(34.8)	(33.1)
Cost of sales adjustment	(40.5)	(42.8)	(40.7)
Monetary working capital adjustment	(3.9)	(2.9)	(2.8)
Current cost operating profit	105.5	131.7	125.1
Share of loss of related company	(3.5)	(3.2)	(3.0)
Income from investments	7.2	7.0	6.7
Interest	1.9	0.7	0.7
Current cost profit before taxation	111.1	136.2	129.5
Taxation	(62.7)	(73.7)	(70.1)
Current cost profit after taxation	48.4	62.5	59.4
Gearing adjustment	3.0	2.9	2.8
Current cost profit attributable to shareholders	51.4	65.4	62.2
Extraordinary items	(12.3)	(13.0)	(12.4)
Dividends	(49.5)	(49.7)	(47.2)
Current cost surplus (deficit) for the year	(10.4)	2.7	2.6
Earnings per share	14.15p	18.01p	17.13p
Dividends per share	13.65p	13.68p	13.00p

Note 2 Corresponding Amounts
In order to show the effect of general inflation and provide a more realistic basis for comparison, the figures originally reported for the previous year have been updated by a factor which compensates for the estimated change in the value of the £. (The updating factor applied to the 1983 figures is 1.052 based on the general index of retail prices which was 345.1 for March 1984 compared with 327.9 for March 1983.)

SSAP 16 DISCUSSED

An improvement on historical cost accounts

In a period of inflation, current cost accounts produced under SSAP 16 are a *better guide* to the profitability of a company, and possibly to the value of its assets, than HC accounts, because they do make allowances for the amount a company needs to earn to continue the existing business (the operating adjustments) and for the benefits of borrowing (the gearing adjustment), but in our view the system has some major shortcomings:

1. It is very complicated: even the Accounting Standards Committee's step-by-step guide *CCA the Easy Way* covers 145 pages of A4 – this book's page size.
2. There is so much scope for discretion that

similar companies can (and do) produce wildly different figures for individual adjustments.

3. The figures produced each year are not comparable with figures for the previous year, unless they are adjusted to a common price basis.
4. The system does not provide any part of the basis on which a company is taxed: this is hardly surprising given so much scope for discretion.

The basic concept of allowing for the continuance of the existing business and for the maintenance of its operating capability, which is defined in SSAP 16 as 'the amount of goods and services which the business is able to supply with its existing resources . . . represented in accounting terms by the net operating assets (fixed assets, stock and monetary working capital)', may be fine in theory, but presents many difficulties in practice. We will consider each CCA adjustment in turn.

Depreciation adjustment

A problem here is that SSAP 16 normally requires the depreciation charge to be based on current replacement cost, but opinions differ on what should be done if the company does not intend to replace an asset at the end of its useful life with an identical asset. SSAP 16's guidance notes suggest making a realistic estimate of what it would now cost to acquire an asset which has the same service potential as that of the existing asset when acquired, i.e. the *modern equivalent asset.*

Take, for example, a company that buys two screw-making machines for £5,000 each; after five years, during which time the value of money has halved, it could buy a replacement machine that has double the output and costs £10,000. It could be argued that this would maintain the company's operating capability (in screws per hour) and that the straight line current cost depreciation for the fifth year should be £10,000 ÷ 5 = £2,000 for the two old machines, the same as the HC depreciation charge; i.e. no CCA depreciation adjustment.

On the other hand, the shareholders might justifiably think that they had had £10,000 of profit-earning assets five years ago, and so in today's pounds they should have £20,000 of profit-earning assets, not £10,000 worth, and in maintaining the real profit-earning capability of the company they would be right.

This approach leaves management free to select the best £20,000 of profit-earning assets it can find, rather than spending the money on, possibly by now, less profitable screw-making capacity. In fact, screw-making is likely to be less profitable now, as competitors can buy screw-making capacity at half the real cost five years ago.

From the taxation point of view, depreciation adjustments are totally irrelevant in the United Kingdom. Capital allowances are based on the historical cost of assets, although 100% first-year allowances (FYAs) did enable companies to gain relief on the cost of assets in their year of purchase, i.e. before their book cost was eroded by inflation. Unfortunately, FYAs are being phased out.

Cost of sales adjustment

This adjustment allows for the maintenance of a company's stock, but SSAP 16 gives so much discretion in the choice of indices and methods of calculation that the Inland Revenue does not consider it would be a satisfactory measure for the purposes of tax relief. For some years relief was given on the value of opening stocks multiplied by the movement in an 'all-stocks' index, regardless of the level of closing stocks. What the Inland Revenue was saying, eminently sensibly, was that it would allow sufficient tax relief for a company to maintain the *real* value of its stocks over the year, but would leave the choice of whether it did so entirely to the company. This was rough justice for a company whose stock prices had gone up much faster than the 'all-stocks' index, and overgenerous where stock prices were going up more slowly, but it was fundamentally fair, because it allowed companies to provide for the maintenance of the real value of their assets free of tax. Stock relief was discontinued in the 1984 Budget.

Monetary working capital adjustment

This adjustment also has a great deal of scope for discretion on the choice of indices and method and, in addition, the company has to decide what part of bank balances and overdrafts should be included in monetary working capital. It is therefore hardly surprising that taxation takes no account of a company's increased needs for monetary working capital; this produces gross inequalities between different types of business.

An efficient supermarket chain, which sells its goods for cash before it pays its suppliers, will have its stock entirely financed by its suppliers. For example, TESCO's 1984 accounts showed:

	£m
Stocks (goods for resale)	179.9
Debtors	9.9
Trade creditors	225.3
Cost of sales adjustment	7.0
MWC adjustment	(7.3)

But if the value of money halves in five years, and the value of stocks doubles, TESCO is most unlikely to need a penny to finance the increased monetary values of unchanged stock levels.

On the other hand, a financial institution which requires a free equity capital of, say, £2.5 million in order to take deposits of £100 million will get no tax relief in the same five-year period, even though this free equity capital (equity capital less fixed assets) is a bank's equivalent of stock which *cannot* be financed by borrowings; it will therefore need to retain £2.5 million out of after-tax profits in order to maintain the same real level of business. It is hardly surprising that financial institutions fight shy of current cost accounting without tax relief.

Gearing adjustment and current cost balance sheet

Although the idea behind the gearing adjustment is a perfectly reasonable one, since a proportion of the increase in capital needed to maintain a company's existing level of business is likely to be financed by borrowings, it does make the assumption that the company has, or can arrange, additional borrowing facilities.

In addition, the calculation of the gearing proportion relies on the asset values in the current cost balance sheet being realistic. This may not always be the case. Take, for example, a UK company which, in the early 1980s, owned a large and previously profitable chemical plant producing a 'commodity chemical' (i.e. one where the selling price is dictated by price levels in the international market, with little or no scope for passing on increased costs). At the end of the year the plant barely broke even, due to high wage settlements and strong sterling and, unless sterling weakened, there was little or no prospect of any improvement due to surplus world capacity. As the plant had hitherto been profitable, it was in the current cost balance sheet at net current replacement cost, £10 million.

Should the company have written the plant down to recoverable amount, which was zero as there was no prospect of being able to sell it and no immediate prospect of future earnings? Or should it have taken a longer view, relying on the cyclicality of the chemical industry and the prospects of sterling returning to a more realistic level to restore its profitability? The concept of prudence might suggest that it should have been written down, but doing so would have made a large difference to the company's gearing proportion, compared with a company that decided to take the other view, i.e. the gearing proportion and thus the gearing adjustment could have been considerably altered by the writing down (or upward revaluation) of assets. With hindsight, the longer view would have been correct, as sterling did subsequently weaken, but at the time nobody *knew* that it would do so.

Although it would be logical for a company's taxation to be calculated after adding back the gearing adjustment, the discretion allowed to a company in assessing the balance sheet values of its assets is far too great to provide a serious basis for taxation.

SSAP 16 in practice

Although most listed companies endeavoured to comply with SSAP 16 when it was first published in March 1980, the large majority have now abandoned producing current cost accounts, and some give their reasons for doing so, e.g.:

BEJAM – '. . . the Board is unconvinced of their value (in relation to the costs of production) in the light of the present debate as to the future of SSAP 16.'

CADBURY SCHWEPPES – '. . . the CCA approach produced fluctuations in the profit figures, which were a consequence of the method of accounting rather than of changes in the fortunes of the Company.'

EUROTHERM – 'The Directors consider it inappropriate to prepare current cost accounts given . . . the currently confused state of the accounting profession regarding a suitable method for the preparation of such accounts.'

ED 35

When SSAP 16 was introduced, the Accounting Standards Committee (ASC) undertook, so far as possible, to make no changes for three years so as 'to enable producers of accounts and users to gain experience in dealing with practical problems and interpreting the new information'.

In the light of reports from the CCA Monitoring Working Party, submissions from various accounting institutions, results of sponsored research studies and the reactions from business and industry in general during the first three years of operating SSAP 16, the ASC published a proposed compromise solution in July 1984: ED 35 *Accounting for the effects of changing prices*.

ED 35 reported widespread agreement that companies ought to reflect the effect of changing prices in their financial statements, but 'there was no consensus on how this ought to be done'. The inclusion of two separate sets of accounts did not command general support, so ED 35 proposed a single set of accounts with information on the effect of changing prices shown in a note where not given in the accounts themselves; current cost balance sheets, 'often taken to show the current value of the business, which they do not do', were to be discontinued, and only the current cost of fixed assets and stocks were to be shown. ED 35 did not find sufficient agreement within the ASC for it to replace SSAP 16, so SSAP 16 currently remains a Standard, though it is increasingly being ignored:

WATTS BLAKE BEARNE – 'Following the expiration of the three years' trial period for SSAP 16 and the subsequent publication and apparent rejection of ED 35 as a modified version of this Standard, it appears that there is now even less consensus over how the effects of inflation should be demonstrated in Financial Statements.

Your Directors have therefore decided to discontinue the annual publication of the Group's inflation-adjusted figures until a consensus is reached whereby their presentation will serve some practical and meaningful purpose.'

WHERE DO WE GO FROM HERE?

The nub of the matter is whether we are trying to achieve:

(*a*)   a system that allows for the general effect of inflation, *or*

(*b*)   what the Sandilands Committee was asked to produce, a system to 'allow for changes (including relative changes) in costs and prices'.

We believe that PSSAP 7, *Accounting for changes in the purchasing power of money*, was along the right lines, and that the root cause of the present disarray is the attempt to allow for relative changes, rather than for inflation.

Measuring inflation

The Sandilands Committee took the view that inflation was 'not a phenomenon capable of independent and objective measurement' and, in line with government thinking at the time, rejected the concept of using the Retail Price Index (RPI) to index accounts.

As the RPI has since been used satisfactorily by government to index personal tax allowances, for Index-linked gilt-edged securities and SAYE schemes and, most recently, for the indexation of acquisition cost in CGT calculations, there seems little doubt that the RPI is now a generally accepted measure of inflation in the United Kingdom.

What inflation accounts should achieve

The first point is that if the cost of a fixed asset is written off in pounds of falling value, the provision for depreciation is inadequate. In order that the total amount written off over the useful life of a fixed asset should be its cost (less residual value) expressed in *pounds at the date of purchase*, each annual depreciation charge needs to be adjusted by the movement in the RPI since the asset was acquired. Fixed assets should therefore appear in the balance sheet at cost less accumulated depreciation, adjusted for inflation into balance sheet date pounds.

The second point is that, in calculating the cost of goods sold, the opening stock should be ad-justed for the RPI movement during the year so as to eliminate stock profits due to general inflation.

Thirdly, the amount of additional working capital required by a company due to the effects of inflation should be deducted in calculating distributable profits.

Fourthly, the benefit of inflation in reducing the real value of borrowings and the adverse effect of inflation on holdings of cash should be taken direct to reserves, to reflect the fact that part of interest paid or received represents capital repayment.

Finally, figures for previous years should be adjusted to balance sheet date pounds, so that like can be compared with like, a point well recognised by the Central Statistical Office (imagine how misleading their financial statistics would be if they weren't expressed in constant pounds!), and already acknowledged by the ASC in recommending in SSAP 16 that companies should give 'comparative figures adjusted to a common price basis with the period's results and also adjust any 5/10 year statements similarly'.

Because inflation accounting would allow for the general effect of inflation but not for any relative change in price levels, inflation accounts would, in long periods of zero inflation, produce the same figures as historical cost accounts.

The future

Until the purpose of inflation accounting is agreed and a system of inflation accounting is introduced accordingly, we believe that the accountancy profession will continue in disarray and that HC accounts will continue to lull many managers and shareholders into thinking that their companies are doing considerably better than they really are, and will continue to encourage unions and employees to seek wage increases that are not justified by real (as opposed to reported) profits.

We also believe that unless the system so developed is acceptable to the Inland Revenue (with capital allowances based on cost adjusted for inflation) and can therefore become the *only* accounts a company produces, the continuation of two sets of accounts will always pose the problem of 'Which one is to be believed?'.

Chapter 23

TRENDS AND RATIOS

This chapter deals with the calculation of trends and ratios, describing each ratio in turn with an indication of the size of ratio one would expect, while the next and final chapter, Chapter 24, contains a suggested pro-forma for analysis, with a line-by-line explanation of each item.

How to tackle the analysis

Now that we have been right through the balance sheet and profit and loss account explaining each component in detail, we come to the heart of the matter: how to set about analysing a report and accounts. We suggest this is best tackled in stages:

1. Take a quick look at the balance sheet and profit and loss account to get a general idea of the size of the company, its capital structure and its profitability. Also look at the historical summary (if provided) to see if the company is growing, cyclical, stagnant or declining, and look at the breakdown of turnover by activity and geographically if one is given. It is also worth while reading any 'report to employees' that may be enclosed with the accounts, to help get a general picture of the company before getting down to any detail.

2. Read carefully through the chairman's statement and the directors' report, underlining any interesting points, and then go through the balance sheet and profit and loss account item by item, reading each accompanying 'Note' as you go; put a circle round anything unusual. In particular, check the 'statement of accounting policies' for anything abnormal and the auditors' report for any qualification or reservation.

3. The trends and ratios should now be calcu-

lated. In doing so the analyst should remain on the *qui vive* for interesting points and not allow himself to get mesmerised by number-crunching, because the figures produced at this stage are not an end in themselves. They are merely a means of helping the analyst assimilate what is happening in the company, providing him with pointers to the reasons behind good or poor performance, and they will often give warning of increasing risk or even of impending disaster.

4. The final stage is the interpretation of the trends and ratios, and the assessment of likely current profits and future prospects. Here the analyst should compare performance with that of similar companies and/or with the industry's averages (using ratios), and should consult other sources of information on the company and on the industry or industries in which the company operates.

The use of percentages and ratios

Any assessment of a company is likely to include a look at:

(*a*) the company's performance in previous years, *and*

(*b*) a comparison with other companies.

The use of percentages and of various ratios helps in the assessment of trends and in comparisons with other companies, and in particular may highlight aspects of a company that merit closer scrutiny.

Methods of relating items of information

There are four basic ways in which one item of financial information can be related to another:

1. A line-by-line comparison can be made of the current year's accounts with those of the previous year. This is sometimes called *horizontal analysis*.
2. The horizontal analysis can be extended over several years, usually by giving the figure for an item in the first year of the series a value of 100 and relating subsequent years' figures to base 100. This is sometimes termed *trend analysis*.
3. 'Common size' balance sheets or income statements can be prepared, each balance sheet item being expressed as a percentage of the balance sheet total and each profit and loss account item as a percentage of sales or earnings. This is sometimes called *vertical analysis*.
4. *Ratios* can be produced by comparing one item in a balance sheet or profit and loss account with another for the same period, or with the current price of the company's shares.

TRENDS

Horizontal analysis – comparison with the previous year

This is possibly the simplest method of comparing one year's figures with another and involves working out the percentage change from the previous year of each main component of the accounts, as in Example 23.1 (ROWNTREE MACKINTOSH's 1984 profit and loss account).

Percentage changes in themselves may reveal a certain amount about a company's performance, but they are of most value in prompting further enquiry. The horizontal analysis in Example 23.1 might, for instance, prompt the following questions (letters in brackets refer to lines marked in the example):

[A] 21.5% is a big increase in *turnover*: was it a uniform increase throughout the group? (Note 1 revealed a 76.4% increase in North America, where the full effect of two acquisitions had come through for the first time in 1984.)

[B] Note 1 also revealed that *trading profit*, excluding North America, increased by only 10.1%.

[C] Was the 58.2% increase in *interest paid* due to higher borrowings or to higher interest rates, or to lower *interest received*, or to a combination of all three?

[D] Why was the increase in *taxation* less than the increase in pre-tax profits? What is the position on ACT?

[E] Do the *extraordinary items* include reorganisation costs or the closure of loss-makers (which will help to improve profits in the future)?

These are the sort of questions that should be asked, and answered, by an alert analyst.

Example 23.1   Horizontal analysis of profit and loss account: ROWNTREE MACKINTOSH

	1983 £m	1984 £m	% change	
Turnover	951.9	1,156.5	+21.5	[A]
Cost of sales	617.1	739.0	+19.8	
Gross profit	334.8	417.5	+24.7	
Distribution costs	39.1	48.3	+23.5	
Marketing, selling and administrative expenses	226.5	280.0	+23.6	
Other operating income	(4.2)	(4.6)	+9.5	
Trading profit	73.4	93.8	+27.8	[B]
Interest paid less received	12.2	19.3	+58.2	[C]
Profit before taxation	61.2	74.5	+21.7	
Taxation	14.9	16.5	+10.7	[D]
Profit after taxation	46.3	58.0	+25.3	
Extraordinary items	13.5	11.5	−14.8	[E]
Profit attributable to Rowntree Mackintosh PLC	32.8	46.5	+41.8	
Dividends	15.7	18.4	+17.2	
Added to reserves	17.1	28.1	+64.3	

Horizontal analysis – half-yearly comparison

The fact that a company's annual figures for sales and profits show an increase on the previous year doesn't always mean that the company's performance is on a rising trend: it may have peaked out *during* the year.

This can be checked quite quickly by looking at the separately published interim results. If the increase over the previous year's first half is larger than the increase for the year as a whole, then there must have been a slowdown in the second half (Example 23.2).

Notice that in Example 23.2 we have compared each half-year in 1984 with the *corresponding* period in the previous year. This is because most businesses are to some extent seasonal, i.e. sales and profits are not evenly distributed between the first and second half. (For example, building materials suffer in the winter, and non-food retailers benefit heavily from Christmas.) Comparison of the second half of a year with the first half can therefore be misleading: in our example the improvement in the first half was clearly not maintained in the second half, although the results for the two half-years of 1984 were very similar.

Trend analysis – comparison over several years

Where comparison of a single company's figures is made over more than two years, the normal method is to take the earliest year's figure as a base of 100 and scale subsequent years accordingly, i.e. divide each year's figure by that for the first year, and multiply the result by 100 (Example 23.3).

The use of published historical summaries

Although the five- or ten-year summaries usually included in companies' reports and accounts need to be approached with caution, as we discussed in Chapter 19, most companies go to a good deal of trouble to present as fair a picture *as is possible on a historical cost basis*, and so the published summary can be very useful for a quick analysis of trends, even if slower and more detailed research is subsequently needed.

However, the main drawback to any analysis of trends over several years in times of high inflation is that the figures can be very misleading, with static or even declining performances in *real* terms appearing to have an upward trend in the reported figures.

A rough idea of the effects of inflation over the years can be gained by comparing the trend of turnover and trading profit with the trend in the Retail Price Index (RPI – see Appendix 3). Continuing with Rowntree Mackintosh in Example 23.4, we have adjusted the average RPI for 1980 to 100, with subsequent years scaled pro rata.

This admittedly is a very crude adjustment, but it certainly brings the figures much closer to the

---

Example 23.2   Horizontal analysis and comparison of interim figures

	1983 £000	1984 £000	Change
Year's sales	3,425	3,764	+9.9%
Year's pre-tax profits	595	651	+9.4%

but the *interim* figures showed:

1st-half sales	1,470	1,880	+21.2%
1st-half pre-tax profits	213	316	+48.3%

Few companies show their second-half figures, so they have to be obtained by subtracting the interim figures from the full year's figures. In this case:

2nd-half sales	1,955	1,884	−3.6%
2nd-half pre-tax profits	382	335	−12.3%

Example 23.3   Trend analysis: ROWNTREE MACKINTOSH

	1980	1981	1982	1983	1984
Turnover (£m)	629.8	688.0	770.5	951.9	1,156.5
Index (1980 base = 100)	100.0	109.2	122.3	151.1	183.6
Trading profit (£m)	44.8	48.0	55.9	72.6	93.8
Index (1980 base = 100)	100.0	107.1	124.7	162.0	209.4

Turnover and trading profit rose roughly in line until 1983 and 1984, when increases in turnover of around 23% brought 30% increases in trading profit. How did increases in earnings per share compare?

	1980	1981	1982	1983	1984
Earnings per share (pence)	20.9	21.4	24.5	31.0	36.0
Index (1980 base = 100)	100.0	102.4	117.2	148.3	172.2

Earnings per share have not increased as fast as trading profit, which could be caused by higher interest charges or higher taxation, but is most likely to be due to the issue of additional ordinary shares during the period.

real state of affairs than no adjustments at all: in real terms, both turnover and trading profit fell in 1981.

We will be discussing ratios later in this chapter, but it is perhaps worth pointing out here that where both the items in a ratio are expressed in terms of the currency at the time of reporting, dividing one by the other removes the direct effect of inflation. For example, the ratio of Rowntree Mackintosh's trading profit to turnover in Example 23.5 gives a true picture of how profit margins steadily improved each year between 1981 and 1984.

Trends in rates of growth

One last point before we leave horizontal analysis: the question of growth rates. If the rate of growth is fast, the figures reported year by year can give the impression that the company's growth is accelerating when it is, in fact, slowing down. Consider, for example, the figures of 'MIRACLE GROWTH PLC' in Example 23.6.

It is true that the increase in profits each year has been greater than the increase in the previous year in simple or absolute terms, but the compound or percentage growth rate has actually been slowing down each year.

Vertical analysis

So far we have discussed only working across the page, comparing each item with the previous year to get the percentage change, or looking at several years to see the trend of an item. If we work vertically, calling the total 100, we can construct 'common size' statements giving a percentage breakdown of the account items, as in Example 23.7.

The advantages of this method are, firstly, that the items are reduced to a common scale for inter-company comparisons and, secondly, that changes in the financial structure and profitability of a company can be seen in relation to the capital employed. For example, the change in Rowntree Mackintosh's short-term borrowings into short-term funds in 1984 represented a change of 7.4% in the capital employed, while deferred taxation went from zero to 1.1% of capital employed. Had these percentages been expressed in absolute terms – year-on-year change – short-term borrowings would have fallen by 127.4% and the percentage change in deferred taxation would have been infinite.

The use of vertical analysis over several years helps to show how the financial structure of a company is changing.

Example 23.4   Trend analysis adjusted for inflation by RPI: ROWNTREE MACKINTOSH

	1980	1981	1982	1983	1984
Turnover (1980 = 100)	100	109.2	122.3	151.1	183.6
Trading profit (1980 = 100)	100	107.1	124.7	162.0	209.4
Average RPI (adjusted)	100	111.9	121.9	127.1	133.4
$\dfrac{\text{Turnover}}{\text{Adjusted RPI}}$	100	97.6	100.3	118.9	137.6
$\dfrac{\text{Trading profit}}{\text{Adjusted RPI}}$	100	95.7	102.3	127.5	157.0

Example 23.5   Trading profit/Turnover ratio: ROWNTREE MACKINTOSH

	1980	1981	1982	1983	1984
Turnover (£m)	629.8	688.0	770.5	951.9	1,156.5
Trading profit (£m)	44.8	48.0	55.9	72.6	93.8
$\dfrac{\text{Trading profit}}{\text{Turnover}}$	7.1%	7.0%	7.3%	7.6%	8.1%

Example 23.6   Horizontal analysis of fast growth: 'MIRACLE GROWTH PLC'

	1980	1981	1982	1983	1984
Pre-tax profits (£000)	100	130	166	206	248
Year's increase (£000)		30	36	40	42
Percentage increase over previous year		30.0%	27.7%	24.1%	20.4%

Example 23.7   Vertical analysis of a balance sheet: ROWNTREE MACKINTOSH

	1983 £m	1984 £m	Common size statements 1983 %	1984 %
Fixed assets				
Land and Buildings	156.9	169.0	32.2	30.4
Plant and Machinery	202.8	239.5	41.6	43.2
	359.7	408.5	73.8	73.6
Current assets				
Stocks, debtors	305.0	344.0	62.5	62.0
Other creditors (due within 1 year)	(163.5)	(181.6)	(33.5)	(32.7)
Creditors (due over 1 year)	(13.5)	(16.0)	(2.8)	(2.9)
	487.7	554.9	100.0	100.0
Capital and reserves				
Share capital	82.0	83.0	16.8	14.9
Reserves	267.0	309.6	54.8	55.8
Shareholders' funds	349.0	392.6	71.6	70.7
Minority interests	0.1	0.1	—	—
Deferred taxation	—	6.0	—	1.1
Other provisions	9.5	15.6	1.9	2.8
Loan capital	99.9	148.6	20.5	26.8
Short-term borrowings (funds)	29.2	(8.0)	6.0	(1.4)
	487.7	554.9	100.0	100.0

Example 23.8   Five-year review of capital employed: ROWNTREE MACKINTOSH

		1980 £m	%	1981 £m	%	1982 £m	%	1983 £m	%	1984 £m	%
Ordinary share capital	[A]	54.1	17.9	67.8	20.1	70.0	20.0	79.3	16.3	80.3	14.5
Reserves	[B]	186.4	61.7	249.5	74.0	275.5	78.6	267.0	54.7	309.6	55.8
Ordinary shareholders' funds	[C]	240.5	79.6	317.3	94.1	345.5	98.6	346.3	71.0	389.9	70.3
Preference capital		2.7	0.9	2.7	0.8	2.7	0.8	2.7	0.6	2.7	0.5
Minorities		1.7	0.6	0.2	0.1	1.2	0.3	0.1	0.0	0.1	0.0
Deferred taxation	[D]	—	—	—	—	—	—	—	—	6.0	1.1
Other provisions	[E]	1.5	0.5	3.6	1.1	3.6	1.0	9.5	1.9	15.6	2.8
Loan capital	[F]	39.0	12.9	24.1	7.1	31.4	9.0	99.9	20.5	148.6	26.8
Short-term borrowings (funds)	[G]	16.7	5.5	(10.9)	(3.2)	(34.0)	(9.7)	29.2	6.0	(8.0)	(1.5)
Funds employed	[H]	302.1	100.0	337.0	100.0	350.4	100.0	487.7	100.0	554.9	100.0
Extraordinary items	[J]	−5.3		1.9		5.3		−13.5		−11.5	
Retained profits	[K]	9.5		29.1		27.3		17.3		28.1	
RPI for December		275.6		308.8		325.5		342.8		358.5	
Adjusted capital employed	[L]	302.1		300.8		296.7		392.1		426.6	

Taking Rowntree Mackintosh's capital structure over five years (Example 23.8), one can see that Ordinary shareholders' funds (OSF) [C] went up from less than 80% of Funds employed [H] in 1980 to almost 100% in 1982, and then fell to around 70% in 1983 and 1984. Let's look for the main reasons for these changes:

[A] In 1981 a sharp increase in Ordinary capital, coupled with an increase in Reserves [B] that was far more than could have been accounted for by Retained profits [K], a fall in Loan capital [F] and a dramatic turn-round in Short-term borrowings (funds) [G] suggest, correctly, a major injection of cash by way of a rights issue: 67.8 ÷ 54.1 = 1.25, a 1-for-4 issue.

[B] In 1983 a small fall in Reserves and a large increase both in Loan capital [F] and in Short-term borrowings [G] suggest major acquisitions. In fact £157.1m was spent on acquisitions in the United States during the year, £35.6m of which was funded by the issue of shares, and £52.9m of goodwill on these acquisitions was written off against reserves.

Looking for further points of interest:

[D] The £6m provision for Deferred tax in 1984 was due to changes in UK corporation tax made in the Finance Act 1984.

[E] The £6m increase in Other provisions in 1983 and in 1984 was in respect of provisions for rationalisation costs foreseen but not yet incurred. These, plus the extraordinary items [J] in the same years, which were mostly rationalisation costs, show that Rowntree Mackintosh is in the middle of an extensive rationalisation programme: more than £20m already charged, and provision for a further £15m.

[F] The increase in Loan capital in 1984 was mostly balanced by a reduction in Short-term borrowings [G].

One general point before leaving the five-year review: Funds employed [H] appear to have increased by more than 80% between 1980 and 1984, helped by a rights issue and an £85m increase in debt. However, a rather more modest picture emerges if a simple adjustment is made to allow for inflation by *dividing* the funds employed at the end of each year by the Retail Price Index for December each year (taken from Appendix 3) and by *multiplying* it by the Retail Price Index for December 1980. Although this is admittedly very crude, the adjusted figures [L] show that, in real terms, the company's capital employed has increased only by a little over 40%, and less than half of this was due to retained profits.

THE USE OF RATIOS

Choice of ratios

With both a balance sheet and a profit and loss account each containing a minimum of 10 to 20 items, the scope for comparing one item with another is enormous, so it is important to be selective, both to limit the calculations required and, more importantly, to make the presentation of the selected ratios simple and readily understandable. No decision-maker wants a jungle of figures, so the ratios chosen should be the key ones, logically grouped.

Logical grouping

Ratios can conveniently be divided into three main groups:

1. *Operating ratios*, which are concerned with how the company is trading, and take no account of how the company is financed.
2. *Financial ratios*, which measure the financial structure of the company and show how it relates to the trading activities.
3. *Investment ratios*, which relate the number of ordinary shares and their market price to the profits, dividends and assets of the company.

In describing these ratios we give what we regard as the most useful and practical definition of each component. Although there is an increasing trend towards standardisation, individual analysts do not always agree on definitions, while companies do not all define ratio components in the same way, and some even 'misname' items in their accounts: MARKS & SPENCER, for example, until 1977 labelled pre-tax profit 'operating profit', a term which is usually regarded as synonymous with trading profit.

Some companies include a table of key ratios in their report and accounts, e.g. MARLEY in its five-year review, shown here.

MARLEY *Extract from five-year review*

Ratios

	1984	1983	1982	1981	1980
Borrowed money as % of total capital	**37.3%**	35.6%	38.2%	36.7%	33.7%

Return on capital	**17.5%**	15.8%	10.5%	11.5%	13.3%
Earnings per share	8.9p	8.9p	2.0p	3.0p	4.5p

These can be useful for looking at trends within the company concerned, but it is preferable to work out one's own ratios by a standard method,

so that they form a fair basis for inter-company comparisons. Marley, for example, has never provided for deferred taxation, so the figures it gives for earnings per share may not be directly comparable with the e.p.s. of other companies.

Typical ratio values

Useful general guidance on the ratio values one might expect to find in various sectors of UK

Example 23.9 Extracts from Industrial Performance Analysis

BUILDING & CIVIL ENGINEERING (MAJOR)

BALANCE SHEET

	82/83	81/82	80/81
Period of accounts			
Number of weeks	52	52	52
	£m	£m	£m
Fixed assets	1,026	874	791
Intangible assets	4	4	6
Intermed assets	647	546	487
Stocks	1,392	1,399	1,271
Debtors	728	665	702
Other current assets	502	337	310
Total current assets	2,622	2,401	2,283
Creditors	1,804	1,583	1,463
Short term loans	270	263	327
Total current liabilities	2,074	1,846	1,790
Net assets	2,225	1,979	1,777
Shareholders funds	1,979	1,712	1,561
Long term loans	246	267	216
Capital employed	2,225	1,979	1,777

PROFIT & LOSS ACCOUNT

	82/83	81/82	80/81
Sales	7,663	7,315	6,099
Profits	303	255	254
Interest paid	71	74	54

KEY RATIOS

Profitability ratios			
Return on capital	13.6	12.9	14.3
Profitability	7.0	6.7	7.1
Profit margin	4.0	3.5	4.2
Return on shareholders funds	15.3	14.9	16.3
Asset utilisation			
Asset utilisation	178.3	191.2	171.0
Sales/fixed assets	7.5	8.4	7.7
Stock turnover	5.5	5.2	4.8
Credit period	35	33	42
Liquidity ratios			
Liquidity	1.3	1.3	1.3
Quick ratio	0.6	0.5	0.6
Gearing ratios			
Gearing ratio I	0.3	0.3	0.3
Gearing ratio II	0.5	0.4	0.4
Gearing ratio III	19.0	22.5	17.5

CONSTRUCTION EQUIPMENT DISTRIBUTORS

BALANCE SHEET

	82/83	81/82	80/81
Period of accounts			
Number of weeks	52	52	52
	£m	£m	£m
Fixed assets	35	38	35
Intangible assets	0	0	0
Intermed assets	7	5	6
Stocks	79	82	90
Debtors	57	56	70
Other current assets	28	21	15
Total current assets	164	159	175
Creditors	95	70	80
Short term loans	15	34	35
Total current liability	110	104	115
Net assets	96	98	101
Shareholders funds	36	48	75
Long term loans	60	50	26
Capital employed	96	98	101

PROFIT & LOSS ACCOUNT

	82/83	81/82	80/81
Sales	380	381	401
Profits	5−	4−	11
Interest paid	3	5	5

KEY RATIOS

Profitability ratios			
Return on capital	5.2−	4.1−	10.9
Profitability	2.4−	2.0−	5.1
Profit margin	1.3−	1.0−	2.7
Return on shareholders funds	13.9−	8.3−	14.7
Asset utilisation			
Asset utilisation	184.5	188.6	185.6
Sales/fixed assets	10.9	10.0	11.5
Stock turnover	4.8	4.6	4.5
Credit period	55	54	64
Liquidity ratios			
Liquidity	1.5	1.5	1.5
Quick ratio	0.8	0.7	0.7
Gearing ratios			
Gearing ratio I	2.1	1.8	0.8
Gearing ratio II	0.2	0.2	0.3
Gearing ratio III	150.0−	500.0	31.3

industry is contained in a book called *Industrial Performance Analysis* published annually by Inter Company Comparisons Ltd. Example 23.9 shows extracts from the aggregated balance sheet and profit and loss account data it gives, together with key ratios calculated from the data. Analysts using this book should be careful to note the definitions of each ratio component, and in particular that 'total assets' includes goodwill and that 'capital employed' does not include overdraft.

Ratios and inflation

As we mentioned earlier, when discussing published historical summaries, where *both* items in a ratio are *monetary* and are expressed in terms of pounds of approximately the same date, dividing one term by the other removes the direct effect of inflation.

For example, Wages/Turnover can fairly be compared from year to year, but Trading profit/ Capital employed is distorted to some extent unless fixed assets are revalued or adjusted annually.

OPERATING RATIOS

Most well-run companies of any size make extensive use of ratios internally, to monitor and ensure the efficient running of each division or activity.

However, companies are obliged to publish only a limited range of profit and loss account information, and a geographical analysis of turnover and trading results of operations (see Chapter 12).

It is thus often impossible to make any detailed analysis of operations, although some companies include further information on turnover, net assets and profitability by principal activities or market segments; in addition, resort can be made to Companies House for accounts filed by subsidiaries, although these can be misleading if goods and services have been transferred within the group at unrealistic prices or if major adjustments have been made on consolidation. In any case, the accounts of subsidiaries are often not filed at Companies House until some considerable time after the group accounts have been published.

Main operating ratios

1. $$\frac{\textbf{Trading profit}}{\textbf{Sales (Turnover)}}$$

expressed as a percentage.

where   *Trading profit* = profit before interest charges and tax; investment income and the company's share of the profits of associated companies are not included

and   *Sales (Turnover)* = sales (excluding transactions within the group).

This ratio gives what analysts term the profit margin on sales; a normal figure for a manufacturing industry would be between 8% and 10%, while high volume/low margin activities like food retailing can run very satisfactorily at around 3%. This profit margin is not the same thing as the gross profit margin (the difference between selling price and the cost of sales, expressed as a percentage of selling price), which can be obtained only if the company reports cost of sales.

Unusually low margins can be set deliberately by management to increase market share or can be caused by expansion costs, e.g. new product launching, but in general depressed margins suggest poor performance.

Somewhat better than average margins are normally a sign of good management, but unusually high margins may mean that the company is 'making a packet' and will attract more competition unless there are barriers to entry (e.g. huge initial capital costs, high technology, patents or other special advantages enjoyed by the company). A good example of high margins attracting competition occurred in fitted kitchen furniture in the early 1970s: WRIGHTON, which had been long-established specialists in the business, with a well-earned reputation for excellent quality at reasonable prices, reaped the initial benefit as business boomed, and reported rising margins:

Year to 31 March	1971	1972	1973
Sales (£000)	3,347	4,096	5,684
Trading profit (£000)	234	364	731
Trading profit ÷ Sales	7.0%	8.9%	12.9%

Fitted kitchen furniture became a conspicuously good growth area, leading to intensified marketing effort by HYGENA and DAINTYMAID, both backed by large parent companies, and by the entry of SCHREIBER, the largest UK furniture manufacturer, and MAGNET JOINERY, door and window manufacturers with about 100 of its own depot outlets in the United Kingdom (before the merger with SOUTHERNS EVANS).

Wrighton's subsequent margins tell the tale of fierce competition and a downturn in housebuilding:

Year to 31 March	1971	1972	1973	1974	1975
Sales (£000)	3,347	4,096	5,684	7,007	6,876
Trading profit (£000)	234	364	731	705	338
$\dfrac{\text{Trading profit}}{\text{Sales}}$	7.0%	8.9%	12.9%	10.1%	4.9%

Trading profit margins are also important in that both management and investment analysts usually base their forecasts of future profitability on projected turnover figures multiplied by estimated future margins.

An alternative definition of trading profit, used by some analysts, is *before* deducting depreciation, the argument being that different depreciation policies distort inter-company comparisons. If this approach is used, then trading profit should also be *before* deducting hire charges, to bring a company that leases rather than owns plant and machinery on to a comparable basis. Our view is that depreciation is a cost and should be deducted in any calculation of profit; we therefore prefer to deal with cases where a company's depreciation charge seems unduly low (or high) by making an adjustment, rather than by adding back every company's depreciation charge.

2. $\dfrac{\text{Trading profit}}{\text{Capital employed}}$

= **Return on Capital Employed** (ROCE), expressed as a percentage.

This is a most important measure of profitability, for several reasons:

(a) A low return on capital employed can easily be wiped out in a downturn.

(b) If the figure is lower than the cost of borrowing, increased borrowings will reduce earnings per share (e.p.s.) unless the extra money can be used in areas where the ROCE is higher than the company's average.

(c) It serves as a guide to the company in assessing possible acquisitions and in starting up new activities – if their potential ROCE isn't attractive, they should be avoided.

(d) Similarly, a persistently low ROCE for any part of the business suggests it could be a candidate for disposal if it isn't an integral part of the business.

ROCE can be calculated either for the company overall or for its trading activities:

Capital employed (in trading) = Share capital + reserves − intangibles + all borrowings including bank overdraft + minority interests + deferred liabilities − associates and investments. Government grants are not included.

Capital employed (overall) Associates and investments are not deducted, while the *overall profit*

figure includes income from investments and the company's share of the profits of associated companies, in addition to trading profit.

The figure for capital employed should, strictly speaking, be the average capital employed during the year, but for simplicity's sake it is normally satisfactory to use the capital employed at the end of the year unless there have been major changes. Some companies label the total at the bottom of their balance sheet as 'capital employed', but using this figure can be deceptive, in that bank overdrafts and loans repayable within 12 months are netted out against current assets, giving a company that has perhaps an embarrassingly large short-term debt a better ROCE than a company whose debt is more prudently funded long-term.

Another variation used by some analysts is to deduct any cash from the overdraft or, where a company has a net cash position, to deduct net cash in calculating capital employed. Netting out cash against overdraft can be justified where cash and overdraft are both with the same bank and the bank is known to calculate interest on the net figure (overdraft − cash), but in general our view is that if a company feels it prudent to operate with a large cash margin it should be measured accordingly, and that if the company's cash is locked up somewhere (for example, if it has arisen from retaining profits overseas to avoid UK taxation) the situation should be reflected in the ratio.

For example, RUGBY PORTLAND CEMENT showed the following details in its consolidated balance sheet in 1984:

	£000
Cash at bank and in hand	43,386
Creditors falling due within 1 year:	
Bank loans and overdraft	35,189

but did not disclose the whereabouts of the amounts involved; we would therefore think it wrong to net out the bank loans and overdraft in this case.

Any upward revaluation of property is likely to reduce ROCE in two ways:

(a) it will increase capital employed (the surplus on revaluation being credited to capital reserve), *and*

(b) it will probably increase the depreciation charge, and thus reduce profits.

Similarly, a company that shows government grants as a liability and uses them to offset against the depreciation charges over the life of the assets concerned will show a poorer return on capital employed than a company which shows assets net of any government grants. We recommend that government grants should *not* be included in capital employed, on the grounds that the original investment decision to purchase any asset was (or should have been) made on a net-of-grants basis.

3.
$$\frac{\textbf{Sales (Turnover)}}{\textbf{Capital employed (in trading)}}$$

expressed as a multiple.

A rising ratio usually indicates an improvement in performance, i.e. the amount of business being done is increasing in relation to the capital base, but beware of an improvement in the ratio achieved when a company fails to keep its plant and machinery up to date; depreciation will steadily reduce the capital base and improve the ratio without any improvement in sales. Beware, too, of any rapid increase in the ratio, which may well be a warning signal of overtrading, i.e. trying to do too much business with too little capital.

In inter-company comparisons care should be taken to compare like with like: the ratio can be misleading unless the operations of the companies concerned are similar in their activities as well as in their products. For example, a television manufacturing group which is vertically integrated (makes the tubes, electronic circuits and the cabinets and then puts them together) will have much more capital employed than a company which merely assembles bought-out components.

A better measure of performance is that of value added compared with capital employed, but value added is not always included in published information. Because of the difference in operations that can occur in apparently similar companies we would place more importance on our previous ratio (Trading profit/Capital employed) than on the ratio of Sales/Capital employed.

Our first three ratios are, of course, interrelated:

$$\frac{\text{Trading profit}}{\text{Sales (Turnover)}} \times \frac{\text{Sales (Turnover)}}{\text{Capital employed}}$$

$$= \frac{\text{Trading profit}}{\text{Capital employed}}$$

and the equation helps to illustrate the four ways in which management can increase trading profit in relation to capital employed:

by increasing the first factor by

(*a*) reducing costs
(*b*) raising prices } by higher profit margins

by increasing the second factor by

(*c*) increasing sales volume
(*d*) reducing capital employed } by higher output per £1 of capital

The healthy way of reducing capital employed is to dispose of low profitability/high capital parts of the business when this can be done without adversely affecting the remainder. There was until recently another way of producing the same optical effect other than by running down capital investment: by leasing rather than buying plant and machinery (or by selling and leasing back fixed assets already owned), but this loophole has largely been closed by SSAP 21, which requires companies to capitalise *financial leases* and include them in the balance sheet (see Chapter 11).

Two other ways in which companies may reduce capital employed are by the factoring of debtors, and by the off-balance-sheet financing of stock, providing the cash realised is used to reduce borrowings.

Further operating ratios

The choice of further operating ratios depends on what aspect is being examined and the information available. We have chosen four which deal with the size of working capital items (Stocks, Debtors, Creditors and Working capital itself) in relation to Sales, and finally one measuring trading profit as a percentage of wages and salaries.

4.
$$\frac{\textbf{Stocks}}{\textbf{Sales (Turnover)}}$$

expressed as a percentage.

Stocks comprise stocks of raw materials and consumables, purchased components, work in progress (net of progress payments), finished goods, goods for resale, and payments on account (shown under stocks).

Except when stocks are built up in anticipation of sharp price rises, well-run companies usually try to carry the minimum stock needed for the satisfactory running of their business: they do so to minimise interest charges on the money tied up in stocks, to save the costs of extensive storage and to reduce the risk of being left with goods that can't be sold due to deterioration, becoming obsolete or going out of fashion. Although some distortion can occur with accelerating growth, because stock is a year-end figure while sales occur throughout the year (on average several months earlier), a rising stock ratio without any special reason is regarded as bad news, reflecting lack of demand for goods and/or poor stock control. A high ratio in comparison to similar companies is undesirable, although Stocks/Turnover ratios vary enormously with the nature of a business. At one end of the scale, and apart from advertising agencies and other service industries, ready-mixed concrete companies probably have one of the lowest Stocks/Turnover figures of any industry: aggregates are extracted from the ground when required and the product is delivered the same day, so all that is needed in stock is a supply of fresh cement and fuel, giving a typical Stocks/Turnover figure of 5%. At the other end of the scale a company which maintains depots of finished goods and replacement parts worldwide, like a power transmission and mechanical handling systems manufacturer, can reasonably be expected to have a ratio as high as 50% in order to maintain a first-class service to its customers all over the world.

For an average manufacturing company a Stocks/Turnover ratio of around 25–30% would be reasonable, increasing the larger and more complex the goods made; for instance, a helicopter manufacturer might have stocks and **WIP** representing 60–70% of turnover and this level could be subject to sharp fluctuations, depending on whether completed helicopters had been delivered to clients just before or just after the end of the year; in contrast, a company making a limited range of nuts and bolts could probably run on a few weeks' stock, though if supplies were subject to interruption and/or shortages it might be prudent to carry more raw materials, and if orders tended to be erratic a higher stock of finished goods would be needed.

Where the *Cost of sales* is available, it can be used instead of the sales figure and, taking the stock of *finished goods* (for a manufacturer) or *goods for resale* (for a distribution or retail business), the ratio Stocks/Cost of sales can be expressed as so many days or months of stock, or as stock turned over so many times a year. Many analysts take the average of the opening and closing stocks, as in Example 23.10, which has a smoothing effect, but doing so does dampen the effect of a major change in stocks over the period.

Example 23.10   Calculation of Stocks/Cost of sales

	1982 £000	1983 £000	1984 £000
Year-end stock	1,758	2,272	3,008
Average stock		2,015	2,640
Sales		10,830	12,490
Cost of goods sold		6,270	7,130
Stocks/Sales		18.6%	21.1%
Stocks/Cost of sales		32.1%	37.0%
Days of stock		117 days	135 days
Stock turned over p.a.		3.12×	2.70×

---

5. $\dfrac{\text{Trade debtors}}{\text{Sales (Turnover)}}$

expressed either as a percentage or, multiplied by 365, as the collection period in days.

For example, given Trade debtors of £820,000 and Sales (Turnover) of £5 million:

$$\frac{\text{Trade debtors}}{\text{Sales (Turnover)}} = \frac{£820,000}{£5,000,000} = 16.4\% \; or$$

$$\text{Collection period} = \frac{£820,000}{£5,000,000} \times 365 \text{ days}$$

$$= 60 \text{ days}.$$

Apart from 'strictly cash' businesses like supermarkets, with virtually zero debtors (e.g. TESCO's debtors average about 0.5% of sales), normal terms are payment at the end of the month following delivery, so with 100% prompt payment the average credit given would be between 6 and 7 weeks, making debtors about 12% of turnover. In practice, a figure of 20–25% is quite normal although some companies may, as a matter of policy, give more generous credit in order to give themselves a competitive edge, while others may factor their debts and thus show abnormally low debtors.

A falling collection period is generally a good sign – an indication of effective financial control – but it could show a desperate need for cash, involving extra discounts for cash and undue pressure on customers.

Where extended credit is given by hire-purchase facilities provided by the company itself, rather than through a finance company, the HP amount outstanding is usually shown separately, but unless the turnover figure is also broken down it isn't possible to calculate the ratios of HP debtors/HP turnover and Other debtors/Non-HP turnover separately.

6. $\dfrac{\text{Trade creditors}}{\text{Sales}}$

expressed as a percentage.

This gives some indication of the amount of credit a company is allowed by its suppliers, and quite a good indication, provided stock levels and profit margins are reasonably steady and the business is not highly seasonal.

A better measure would be Trade creditors/Cost of goods purchased, but the cost of goods purchased during the year is seldom disclosed, so the analyst has to content himself with Trade creditors/Sales. This ratio will still show up any change in credit allowed, so it is the trend which needs to be watched.

A company that is short of cash will be forced to

try to get as much credit as it can, despite losing discounts for prompt payment. (*En passant*, any indications of change of suppliers or refusal of credit by suppliers can be an excellent early warning of trouble, because suppliers are usually in very much closer personal day-to-day contact with a company than an analyst or the company's shareholders. Similar warning can be given by the refusal of major factoring companies to offer further credit: because they act for so many individual creditors, factors often have a much clearer picture of a company's overall position.)

An alternative ratio to use here is Trade creditors/Stocks, to see what proportion of the stocks is financed by the company's suppliers. This is of particular interest in retailing businesses, where 120% is a normal figure for an efficient food retailer like BEJAM.

In addition, bankers often study movements in the ratio Debtors/Trade creditors. When things are normal this tends to be stable. Violent change in either direction is a warning signal.

7. Working capital / Sales

expressed as a percentage
where *Working capital* = Stocks + Trade debtors − Trade creditors.

This shows how much capital is required to finance operations in addition to capital invested in fixed assets. It can vary from a tiny 1%, or even negative, for a food retailer to 50% or more for a heavy engineering company, and gives some indication of the likely additional cash needed with increased turnover. A falling ratio indicates the possibility of overtrading.

It is also interesting to compare this ratio with our first ratio, Trading profit to Sales, to see whether increased sales will generate sufficient extra profit to provide the extra working capital required. Allowing for Corporation Tax on the extra profit, Trading profit to Sales must be higher than Working capital to Sales for a company to be 'self-financing' in working capital terms.

8. Trading profit / Wages

expressed as a percentage.

Trading profit/Wages gives a direct indication of the effect of wage increases on profits. For example, a company whose trading profit is only 15% of wages is likely to be much more adversely affected by a wage increase of 10% than a company with a ratio of 50%.

Finally, Sales per Employee and Trading profit per Employee are also useful ratios: their trend gives some indication of changing productivity.

FINANCIAL RATIOS

Financial ratios fall into two broad groups, gearing ratios and liquidity ratios. Gearing is concerned with the proportion of capital employed that is borrowed, the proportion provided by shareholders' funds and the relationship between the two, while liquidity ratios are concerned with the company's cash position.

Gearing

Financial gearing can be defined in a multiplicity of ways, the two most common being:

(a) the Debt/Equity ratio, shown as Borrowings/Shareholders' funds in the *Investors Chronicle*, and called 'leverage' in the United States and elsewhere, *and*

(b) the percentage of capital employed represented by borrowings.

Whatever method is used to compute gearing, a company with 'low gearing' is one financed predominantly by equity, whereas a 'highly geared' company is one which relies on borrowings for a significant proportion of its capital.

To illustrate (Example 23.11 overleaf), let us take the bottom half of three different companies' balance sheets, making two adjustments:

(a) deducting any intangible assets in calculating ordinary shareholders' funds;

(b) including the bank overdraft and any other borrowings falling due within one year (these are normally netted out against current assets in a company's balance sheet, but are just as much a part of capital employed as long-term borrowings are).

As you can see, the Debt/Equity ratio is a more sensitive measurement of gearing than Debt/Capital employed, and it also gives a better indication of the effect of gearing on equity income, known across the Atlantic as the 'leverage effect', but it can be distorted by the treatment of deferred tax varying from company to company, or varying within a company from year to year.

Leverage effect

The effect of leverage can be expressed as a ratio: percentage change in earnings available to ordin-

Example 23.11   Calculation of gearing and Debt/Equity ratios

		Company A £000	Company B £000	Company C £000
Ordinary share capital		600	500	250
Reserves		850	800	300
Intangibles		—	− 250	—
Ordinary shareholders' funds	[A]	1,450	1,050	550
Redeemable preference capital (3.5%)	[B]	—	100	—
Minorities	[C]	150	150	150
Deferred tax		400	400	400
Loan capital (10%)	[D]	—	150	400
Overdraft (12%)	[E]	—	150	500
Capital employed	[F]	2,000	2,000	2,000
Debt/Equity (Leverage) $\left(\dfrac{B + D + E}{A + C}\right)$		0%	33%	128%
Debt/Capital employed $\left(\dfrac{B + D + E}{F}\right)$		0%	20%	45%
Gearing		None	Low	High

Notes:

[B]   The treatment of preference shares is a problem: although they are not debt they do carry a *fixed* rate of dividend that is payable ahead of ordinary dividends. On balance we favour treating them as debt if redeemable but otherwise as equity when looking at capital (because it would be misleading to ascribe the same Debt/Equity ratio to a company with, say, 60 debt/40 equity as one with 60 pref/40 equity).

[C]   Minorities have been included as equity in the calculation of Debt/Equity ratios, on the assumption that minority interests in subsidiaries are all pure (non-redeemable) equity.

---

ary shareholders brought about by a 1% change in earnings before interest and tax (EBIT).

Suppose each of the three companies in Example 23.11 has a return on capital employed (ROCE) of 10%, and that the rate of Corporation Tax is 35%; then earnings before interest and tax (EBIT) will be as shown in Example 23.12.

Example 23.12   Calculation of leverage effect

	Company A £000	Company B £000	Company C £000
EBIT	200	200	200
less			
Loan interest	—	−15	−40
Interest on overdraft	—	−18	−60
Pre-tax profits	200	167	100
Tax at 35%	70	58.5	35
Profits after tax	130	108.5	65
Preference dividends	—	3.5	—
Available for minorities and ordinary shareholders [G]	130	105	65
1% change in EBIT	2	2	2
Tax	0.7	0.7	0.7
Available for minorities and ordinary shareholders [H]	+1.3	+1.3	+1.3
Leverage ratio $\dfrac{H}{G} \times 100$	1.0	1.24	2.0

Leverage, of course, works both ways; if EBIT fell by 50% then earnings available to ordinary shareholders would fall to £65,000 (Company A); £40,000 (Company B); and Company C would be on the verge of making a loss.

Operational gearing

In assessing what level of financial gearing might be reasonable for a company, we must first look at the volatility of profits. This depends to a large extent on the sensitivity of profits to turnover, which we will call operational gearing (although the term operational gearing is sometimes used in the sense of overall gearing to include the effects of financial gearing as well).

The operational gearing of a company can be described as the ratio of the percentage change of trading profit which results from 1% change in turnover, and depends on the relationship between fixed costs, variable costs and net profit, where fixed costs are costs that are incurred regardless of turnover, and variable costs are directly proportional to turnover:

Operational gearing
   (Turnover − Variable costs): Trading profit
or (Trading profit + Fixed costs): Trading profit

Example 23.13 demonstrates this.

Example 23.13 Effects of operational gearing

	Turn-over	Fixed costs	Vari-able costs	Trad-ing profit	Operational gearing
	£m	£m	£m	£m	
Company D	100	20	70	10	3:1 (100 − 70:10)
Company E	100	70	20	10	8:1 (100 − 20:10)

If turnover increases by 10%:

	£m	£m	£m	£m	Change in profits
Company D	110	20	77	13	+30%
Company E	110	70	22	18	+80%

This is fine for both D and E, especially for E, which is much more highly geared operationally than D. But, as with high financial gearing, high operational gearing works against a company when turnover falls. Assume a 10% fall in turnover:

Company D	90	20	63	7	−30%
Company E	90	70	18	2	−80%

The effect of gearing can also be illustrated graphically on a 'profit/volume chart', as shown in Example 23.14.

Example 23.14 Profit/Volume chart

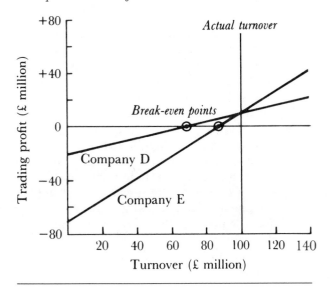

A profit/volume chart is constructed by plotting two points:

(a) trading profit against actual turnover
(b) fixed costs against zero turnover

and joining the two points together. The point where this line crosses the horizontal 'zero profit' line represents the level of turnover at which the company 'breaks even', i.e. makes neither a profit nor a loss. The steeper the gradient of the line the higher the operational gearing of the company. The break-even point can also be calculated:

Break-even turnover

$$= \frac{\text{Fixed costs} \times \text{Actual turnover}}{\text{Actual turnover} - \text{Actual variable costs}}$$

e.g. Company D $= \dfrac{20 \times 100}{100 - 70} = £66.67\text{m}$

Company E $= \dfrac{70 \times 100}{100 - 80} = £87.5\text{m}$

It is fairly obvious that a company with high operational gearing aggravates the problem by gearing up financially. Suppose, for instance, that Company E had borrowings that incurred interest charges of £3 million p.a.; Example 23.15 shows the effect on profits.

Example 23.15 Effect of high financial gearing coupled with high operational gearing

Turnover	Net trading profit	Interest charges	Pre-tax profits
£m	£m	£m	£m
100	10	3	7
110	18	3	15
90	2	3	−1

A company that illustrates the danger of high financial gearing on top of high operational gearing is BLACKWOOD HODGE, which is in the notoriously volatile subsector of Construction Equipment Distributors (see details of subsector ratios on page 166):

BLACKWOOD HODGE *Five-year profit record*

(£000)	1980	1981	1982	1983	1984
Profit before interest	18,814	20,187	14,147	3,003	12,836
Interest paid	13,819	18,070	17,835	14,497	9,796
Profit (loss)	4,995	2,117	(3,688)	(11,494)	3,040
Exceptional items	—	(1,100)	—	(9,123)	—
Pre-tax profit	4,995	1,017	(3,688)	(20,617)	3,040

It was probably only the drastic action taken in 1983, which incurred extraordinary items of £13,778,000 in addition to the exceptional items shown above, which enabled the company to survive.

Conversely, the directors of a property company with mainly completed developments let to substantial clients know that they have an assured rental income coming in each quarter, and they would not be considered imprudent to borrow heavily (i.e. gear up) provided the level of interest payments plus running expenses could not exceed the stream of rental income. We say 'could not exceed', because one of the ways property companies get into trouble is by borrowing short-term with a variable interest rate (e.g. on bank overdraft), rather than at a fixed rate; they then get caught out when interest rates go up faster than rental income.

Liquidity

The two ratios most commonly used in assessing a company's liquidity are concerned with current assets (stocks and WIP, debtors and cash) and current liabilities (creditors, bank overdraft and any debts due to be settled within the next 12 months):

1. **Current ratio**

    $$= \frac{\text{Current assets}}{\text{Current liabilities}}$$

2. **Quick ratio** (*or* 'Acid test')

    $$= \frac{\text{Current assets} - \text{Stock}}{\text{Current liabilities}}$$

Note that the Companies Act 1985 requires all amounts owing by the company to be included under creditors, with amounts due within one year and after one year being shown separately. We regard creditors falling due within one year as being synonymous with current liabilities, but the Companies Act 1985 does not require provisions for amounts expected to fall due within one year to be shown separately: they are included under the general heading of provisions. In our view provisions for amounts due within one year are current liabilities.

Current ratio

The Current ratio is a broad indicator of a company's short-term financial position: a ratio of more than 1 indicates a surplus of current assets over current liabilities. A current ratio of 2 or more used to be regarded as prudent in order to maintain creditworthiness, but in recent years a figure of about 1.5 has become quite normal, and a higher figure isn't necessarily a good sign: it may be due to excessive stocks or debtors, or it may

mean that the directors are sitting on an unduly large amount of cash which could be more profitably invested.

When looking at an individual company's current ratio, there is no simple rule of thumb on what the company's ratio 'ought' to be, because it so much depends on a number of different factors, including the following:

1. *The nature of the company's business.* If large stocks and the giving of generous credit terms are normal to the business, the current ratio needs to be higher than the general average, whereas a retail business with only cash sales, no work in progress and with stocks financed mainly by suppliers (i.e. creditors a large item) may be expected to have a lower than average current ratio.

2. *The quality of the current assets.* Stocks, for example, may be readily saleable, e.g. gold, or virtually unsaleable, e.g. half-completed houses in a property slump.

3. *The imminence of current liabilities.* A large loan due for repayment very soon could be embarrassing. It would be acutely embarrassing if gearing was already very high, there was no scope for an equity issue and neither cash nor further overdraft facilities were available. Even that is not perhaps as embarrassing as being unable to pay the wages next week, and next week's wages do not, of course, appear in the balance sheet.

    The key factor is whether a company has scope for further borrowings or is right up against its limits, but facilities available (as opposed to facilities being used) are rarely revealed in annual reports.

4. *The volatility of working capital requirements.* A company with a highly seasonal business pattern, for instance a Christmas card manufacturer or a UK holiday camp operator, may well make use of a much higher average level of borrowings during the year than the balance sheet shows, particularly as companies usually arrange their year end to coincide with low stocks and/or a low level of activity.

Because of these individual factors, the most informative feature of a current ratio is its normal level and any trend from year to year. A drop below normal levels is worth investigating, and a continuing decline is a warning signal that should not be ignored.

For example, MARKS & SPENCER's current ratio (opposite) stayed within fairly narrow limits throughout the years shown, except for a dip in 1980. This was due mainly to spending all its £50 million retained profits that year on additional

MARKS & SPENCER *Current ratios*

Year end 31 March	1978	1979	1980	1981	1982	1983	1984
Current assets (£m)	173.8	207.6	187.4	268.9	312.0	407.6	377.8
Current liabilities (£m)	182.2	241.0	230.5	300.0	369.2	442.5	450.8
Current ratio	0.95	0.86	0.81	0.90	0.85	0.92	0.84

METAL BOX *Current ratios*

Year end 31 March	1978	1979	1980	1981	1982	1983	1984
Current assets (£m)	315.0	384.3	385.7	449.5	492.9	519.7	403.0
Current liabilities (£m)	190.3	216.4	249.7	319.7	376.9	393.8	329.1
Current ratio	1.65	1.77	1.54	1.41	1.31	1.32	1.22

property, and to financing increased working capital by reducing short-term assets; but this still left a comfortable £33 million cash in the balance sheet. Apart from this one year, retained profits covered all expansion costs and provided additional working capital as and when needed, so there was no need to raise additional capital either from shareholders or through long-term loans.

The figures for METAL BOX show a much more volatile current ratio. A £36 million rights issue in the year ending 1979 helped to improve the ratio to 1.77 but it then dropped sharply in 1980, when capital expenditure was running at twice the level of depreciation and retained earnings put together, and short-term borrowings increased by £30 million.

The deterioration continued during 1981 and 1982, when more than £50 million was spent on reorganisation, and would have continued downwards in 1983 but for the sale and leaseback of the company's head office at Reading, which realised £23 million. In 1984 the ratio was distorted by the reduction of the South African subsidiary to related company status, which took £72 million off working capital and produced disposal proceeds of £39 million. Fortunately, profits in the same year picked up sharply, but unless this improvement is sustained a further downward trend in the current ratio will almost certainly signal a capital raising operation, probably another rights issue.

Quick ratio or acid test

As we have said, not all current assets are readily convertible into cash to meet debts; in particular stocks and work in progress may be able to be run down a certain amount, but not eliminated if the business is to continue. The quick ratio recognises this by excluding stocks from current assets and applies the 'acid test' of what would happen if the company had to settle up with all its creditors and debtors straight away: if the quick ratio is less than 1 it would be unable to do so.

Some companies whose normal terms of trade allow them to sell goods for cash before paying for them habitually operate with a quick ratio of well under 1 (0.4 is typical for a supermarket); so it is a poorer than average figure compared with other companies in the same industry, coupled with a declining trend, that signals possible trouble ahead. A feature that a low and declining ratio often highlights is a rising overdraft: the question then is, 'Are their bankers happy?' Fears in this direction may be allayed by a statement in the annual report about operating well within the facilities available, or by a statement at the time that new money is raised confirming that working capital will be adequate.

A large difference between the current ratio and the quick ratio is an indication of large stocks:

$$\text{Current ratio} - \text{Quick ratio} = \frac{\text{Stocks}}{\text{Current liabilities}}$$

Cash flow

If there is any doubt about the company's liquidity, the cash flow should be examined in as much detail as possible (see Chapter 18). There are two common definitions of cash flow:

Gross cash flow = depreciation plus profit after tax plus increase in deferred tax.

Net cash flow = gross cash flow minus dividends.

The question we need to ask is whether net cash flow in the current year will cover the company's cash requirements.

Cash requirements
There are three main areas to look at in identifying cash requirements:

1. *Repayment of existing loans* due in the next year or two, including convertible loans whose conversion rights are unlikely to be exercised. Loans repayable within 12 months should be shown under current liabilities.
2. *Increase in working capital.* Working capital tends, in an inflationary period and/or when a business expands, to rise roughly in line with turnover. It is useful therefore to use the Working capital/Sales ratio described earlier in this chapter to establish the relationship between working capital and sales (Example 23.16).
3. *Capital expenditure requirements.* Companies are required to report the amount of capital expenditure that has been contracted for and the amount that has been approved by the directors but not yet put out to contract.

Example 23.16   Calculation of the Working capital/Sales ratio

Sales £26m; Stocks £6m; Trade debtors £4m; Creditors £3½m. Calculate the Working capital/Sales ratio:

$$\frac{\text{Stocks} + \text{Debtors} - \text{Creditors}}{\text{Sales}} = \frac{£6\frac{1}{2}m}{£26m} = 25\%$$

Thus if the turnover of this company was expected to increase by 20% in the current year, it would be reasonable to assume that unless stocks were unusually high at the last year end or unless the increase in turnover is not going to follow the company's normal trading pattern, the company is likely to need an increase in working capital of £1.3 million (£26m × 20% × 25%).

The flexibility of the company's capital expenditure programme is important; there is much more risk in building one large process plant than in adding 50 outlets to a retail chain at about the same total cost over, say, 2½ years, because the former, once embarked upon, is a complete liability unless and until it comes on stream while the retail chain's expansion could be curtailed if, say, the economic trends turned downwards and capital expenditure had to be cut a year later, leaving 20 new outlets trading profitably. In general, 'great leaps forward' are more risky than step-by-step progress, especially in areas of high technology.

The size of a single project in relation to the overall size of the company is another important factor to watch: a new £25 million process plant that fails to come on stream as planned and loses £5–6 million a year for several years might break a smaller company but would cause no more than mild embarrassment to BP, and would be regarded as normal in government-financed nuclear power projects.

Cash shortfall

If the net cash flow looks like falling short of the cash requirements we have identified, then the company may have to take one or more of the following steps:

(*a*)   increase its overdraft (but is it at the limit of its facilities? – we probably don't know);

(*b*)   borrow longer term (can it do so within its borrowing limits?);

(*c*)   make a rights issue (is its share price at least 20% above par, is it at least a year and preferably two years since its last rights issue, and are market conditions suitable?);

(*d*)   acquire a more liquid and/or less highly geared company for paper (i.e. bid for another company using shares);

(*e*)   sell some assets (has it any listed investments which could be sold, or has it any activities which could be sold off without seriously affecting the business?);

(*f*)   sell and lease back some of the properties used in the business (has it any unmortgaged properties?);

(*g*)   cut back on capital expenditure that has not already been put out to contract;

(*h*)   tighten credit and stock control;

(*i*)   reduce or omit the ordinary dividend, and possibly even the preference dividend too.

If the company takes none of these steps it will run into an overtrading situation, which is likely to precipitate a cash crisis unless, as a last resort, it:

(*j*)   reduces its level of trading.

Contingent liabilities: net tangible assets

Contingent liabilities which are large in relation to the net tangible assets of a company or group can, with a run of bad luck (or bad judgement), be a serious threat to the financial stability of a business, and although the great majority of contingent liabilities never materialise, it is prudent to monitor what is going on. In group accounts, contingent liabilities of the parent company in respect of guarantees of borrowings by subsidiaries can, of course, be ignored, because the borrowings concerned are incorporated in the consolidated accounts, but all guarantees for associates and third parties should be included. Leasing commitments, if material, should also be monitored, and the particular points to watch for are guarantees and commitments outside the normal course of business and sharp increases in the amounts involved, as reflected by the ratio Contingent liabilities/n.t.a. BURMAH OIL COMPANY's 1972 accounts, illustrated in the next column, are an example of this.

The previous year's accounts had shown commitments of £204 million in respect of tanker in-charters, with out-charters of certain vessels covering £127 million, so the absence of any actual figure for out-charters in the 1972 accounts is, in itself, a little suspicious. A reasonable estimate of 'substantial' might be, say, 50%, leaving a £245 million unmatched commitment, equal to about 37% of net tangible assets, compared with 1971's unmatched figure of £77 million, only 12.7% of the net tangible assets that year. When the tanker charter market collapsed in 1973–74, BURMAH's unmatched in-charter commitments ran up huge losses for the company and it had to be rescued by the Bank of England.

BURMAH OIL COMPANY *1972 accounts: Note on commitments and contingent liabilities*

(*d*) Three subsidiaries have contractual commitments in respect of tanker in-charters and leased facilities involving hire charges (exclusive of certain operating costs) as follows:

Estimated as payable during:

1973	£ 20 million
1974 to 1977	115 million
1978 to 1982	140 million
1983 and thereafter	215 million

A substantial part of these commitments is already matched by tanker out-charters and other long-term arrangements.

INVESTMENT RATIOS

These are the ratios used by investors when deciding whether a share should be bought, sold or held. Most of them relate to the current price of the share, and therefore vary from day to day. The two most important ones are the Price Earnings Ratio (PER) and the dividend yield.

Price earnings ratio (PER)

$$PER = \frac{\text{Share price}}{\text{Earnings per share (e.p.s.)}}$$

where *share price* = the middle market price, which is the average of the prices at which shares can be sold or bought on an investor's behalf (the jobber's bid and offer prices respectively),

and *e.p.s.* = Profit attributable to ordinary shareholders ÷ Average number of ordinary shares in issue during year.

The calculation of earnings per share is described in detail in Chapter 14. The analyst will normally calculate two price earnings ratios: the 'historical PER', using last year's e.p.s., and the 'prospective PER', using his estimate of e.p.s. for the current year; he may also project his earnings estimates ahead to produce a PER based on possible earnings for the following year.

What the PER represents

One way of looking at the PER is to regard it as the number of years' earnings per share represented by the share price, i.e. *x* years' purchase of e.p.s., but this assumes static e.p.s., while in practice the PER reflects the market's view of the company's growth potential, the business risks involved and

the dividend policy. For example, a company recovering from a break-even situation, with zero e.p.s. last year, will have a historical PER of infinity but may have a prospective PER of 12 based on expectations of modest profits for the current year, falling to 6 next year if a full recovery is achieved.

The PER of a company also depends not only on the company itself, but on the industry in which it operates and, of course, on the level of the stock market, which tends to rise faster than reported profits when the business cycle swings up and to fall faster than profits in a downturn. The level of the PER of the *Financial Times* 500 Index shows this very clearly:

	500 Index	500 PER
Top of the bull market, 19 May 1972	227.30	19.88
Bottom of the bear market, 13 December 1974	63.49	3.71

The Actuaries Share Indices table published in the *Financial Times* every day except Mondays also gives the PER for each industry group and subsection, so any historical PER calculated for a company can be compared with its sector and with the market as a whole, although differences in the treatment of tax by individual companies do cause some distortion here; thus most analysts use e.p.s. calculated on a full tax charge to produce comparable PERs.

In general a high historic PER compared with the industry group suggests either that the company is a leader in its sector or that the share is overvalued, while a low PER suggests a poor company or an undervalued share. In each case check to see if the prospective PER is moving back into line with the sector, as a historic PER that is out of line may be due to expectations of an above-average rise in profits for the current year (in which case the historic PER will be higher than average), or to poor results being expected (which would be consistent with a low PER). In addition, if Datastream is available (see Chapter 21), it is worth checking the company's PER history to see where it lies in relation to its historical range and to the sector PER: all Datastream's PERs are calculated using fully taxed e.p.s.

Another useful rule of thumb is to be wary when a PER goes much above 20. The company may well be a glamour stock due for a tumble or, if it is the PER of a very sound high-quality company, the market itself may be in for a fall. One exception here is the property sector, where PERs are normally very high because property companies are, in the main, highly geared and use most of their rental income to service their debt, leaving tiny e.p.s.; investors normally buy property company shares more for their prospects of capital appreciation than for their current earnings.

Dividend policy and the PER

As the price of a share is influenced both by the e.p.s. and the dividend, a company's dividend policy affects the PER.

Some companies pay tiny dividends and plough back most of their profits to finance further growth. Shares in these companies are very popular, particularly with private investors seeking capital gain rather than income, and they will enjoy a glamour rating despite their low dividend; but the rating is vulnerable to any serious setback in profits, as there is little yield to support the price.

Dividends are more important to income-conscious institutional investors, whose yardstick is (or should be) total return: the sum of dividend yield and growth per annum. Thus, a company which reinvests its profits badly and fails to achieve growth will stand on a poorer rating than a company which distributes a higher proportion of its profits. However, in times of high inflation, a company distributing a large proportion of its reported profits (calculated on a historical cost basis) will tend to lose credibility if dividends are believed to exceed real earnings.

Dividend yield

As described in Chapter 13, dividends under the imputation system are actually paid net of tax at the basic personal rate, and carry an associated tax credit. Dividend yields are based on *gross* dividends per share, that is, on the dividends actually paid plus the associated tax credit; if the gross equivalent of a net dividend paid is not given in the report and accounts, it can be obtained by grossing up, i.e. by dividing the net dividend by (1 − basic tax rate expressed as a decimal):

Gross
dividend =
yield (%)

$$\frac{\text{Net dividend in pence per share} \times 100}{(1 - \text{basic tax rate}) \times \text{Ordinary share price in pence}}$$

The associated tax credit depends on the basic rate of tax at the time the dividend was paid (not the rate in the year it was earned), and the rates on the interim and final dividend may be different; for example, when the basic rate of tax was reduced from 33% in 1978/79 to 30% in 1979/80, the yield on the shares of a company which paid its interim dividend before the change and its final dividend after the change would have been calculated as follows:

December 1978   Interim dividend = 2p net,

grossed up $= \dfrac{2}{0.67} = 2.985\text{p gross}$

July 1979   Final dividend = 3p net,

grossed up $= \dfrac{3}{0.70} = 4.286\text{p gross}$

Total dividend = 5p net = 7.271p gross

Dividend yield (with a share price of 92p) =

$\dfrac{7.271}{92} \times 100 = 7.9\%$

Dividend cover

Provided the company is in a normal tax position with reasonably steady and mainly UK earnings, so that all the profits after tax can be distributed net with full tax credit, then, as Example 23.17 shows:

$$\text{Dividend cover} = \frac{\text{Earnings per share}}{\text{Net dividend per share}}$$

Example 23.17 is very straightforward, but when foreign tax on overseas earnings becomes significant, the maximum net dividend a company can distribute out of a year's profits is no longer the e.p.s. but something less, and the cover has to be worked out at a gross level.

Full distribution

Example 23.18 illustrates the dividend cover calculated on a 'full distribution' basis.

As explained more fully in Chapter 13, the maximum distributable gross dividends ('full distribution earnings') are the lesser of:

Example 23.17   Calculation of dividend cover

With a basic rate of personal tax of 30% and a Corporation Tax rate of 35%:

	Modest dividend £000	Maximum dividend £000
Pre-tax profits	2,000	2,000
Corporation Tax	700	700
Profits after tax	1,300	1,300
Ordinary dividends	520	1,300
Retained earnings	780	Nil

Tax payable

ACT: 30/70ths of net dividends	223	557
Mainstream tax	477	143
Total tax	700	700

Issued equity = 10m shares

Earnings per share = $\frac{£1.3m}{10m}$	13p	13p
Net dividend	5.2p	13p
Dividend cover	2.5 ×	1.0 ×

Example 23.18   Calculation of dividend cover: full distribution

Taking our previous Example 23.17, but assuming that half the profits are earned overseas and bear foreign tax (including any withholding tax on remission) at 50%, then the maximum distributable gross is:

Pre-tax profits	£2,000,000
less UK minimum mainstream tax	50,000
Foreign tax	500,000
Full distribution	1,450,000

70/100ths of this full distribution figure will be distributed as net dividends (£1,015,000), together with 30/100ths as the associated tax credit (£435,000).

With 10 million shares the full distribution earnings per share = 14.5p, while the modest 5.2p net dividend's gross equivalent, with a 30% basic rate of personal tax = 5.2 × 100/70 = 7.428p and

$$\text{dividend cover} = \frac{14.5}{7.428} = 1.95 \text{ times}$$

The overall tax position would be:

	Modest dividend £000	Maximum dividend (i.e. full distribution) £000	
Net dividend	520	1,015	
Tax credit (equal to ACT payable to company)	222.8	435	
UK pre-tax profits	1,000	1,000	
CT liability	350	350	
less ACT (max. 30% of UK pre-tax)	222.8 [a]	300	[A]
Mainstream tax (minimum 35% − 30% = 5%)	127.2 [b]	50	[B]
Overseas pre-tax profits	1,000	1,000	
UK CT liability	350	350	
Max. credit for overseas tax	350	350	
Overseas tax	500 [c]	500	[C]
Unrelieved overseas tax	150	150	
Unrelieved ACT	—	135	[D]
Total tax	(a + b + c) 850	(A + B + C + D) 985	
Profits after tax	1,150	1,015	
Issued equity = 10m shares			
Gross dividends	742.8	1,450	
Gross dividends per share	7.428p	14.5p	
Dividend cover	1.95	1.0	

(*a*) 'nil distribution' after-tax profits, grossed up; *or*

(*b*) total pre-tax profits, *less*
   (i) Minimum mainstream tax on UK pre-tax profits, charged at (CT rate − basic tax rate) and
   (ii) Foreign tax payable if all overseas profits are remitted to the United Kingdom;

and dividend cover $= \dfrac{\text{Full distribution e.p.s.}}{\text{Actual gross dividend}}$

Payout ratio

Before the introduction of the imputation system this ratio could be defined as the dividends distributed (gross) expressed as a percentage of the profits after tax, or as the reciprocal of the dividend cover, which gave the same answer.

Under the imputation system the payout ratio is less straightforward. Provided the company would not incur any extra tax liability on full distribution, the payout ratio is still the reciprocal of the dividend cover, but if full distribution increases the tax charge a difference arises. Taking the 'modest dividend' situation in Example 23.18:

(*a*) Payout ratio $= \dfrac{\text{Net dividends}}{\text{Profits after tax}} = \dfrac{520}{1,150} = 45.2\%$

(*b*) Reciprocal of dividend cover $= \dfrac{1}{1.95} = 51.2\%$

As the payout ratio reflects, by implication, the amount retained by the company, (*a*) seems the better definition as the company does, in fact, retain 54.8% of attributable profits if it pays out 45.2% in dividends.

Net asset value (n.a.v.)

This shows the book value of assets attributable to each ordinary share:

$$\text{n.a.v.} = \frac{\text{Ordinary shareholders' funds (OSF)}}{\text{Number of ordinary shares issued}}$$

Although the n.a.v. figure is *very* dependent on the balance sheet values of assets being realistic, it does give some indication of how much the price of a share depends on the ability of the company to generate profits and how much is backed by assets.

The net asset value is one reference point used in deciding on terms for an acquisition, assuming the potential biddee's assets are fairly valued or are adjusted for the purpose of the calculation. Where property has been revalued but the new value is only shown in a note to the accounts, i.e. the surpluses have not been credited to reserves, analysts will often show two figures, e.g. 'n.a.v. = 73p (94p including property revaluation)'.

Market capitalisation

The market capitalisation of a company is the market price of a company's ordinary shares multiplied by the number of shares in issue. The 'market cap' is a useful measure of the relative size of companies. For example, in the food retailing sector at 31 December 1984:

SAINSBURY	£2,060m
BEJAM	£174m
NORMANS GROUP	£25m

Chapter 24

PRO-FORMA GUIDE TO ANALYSIS

Although historical information summaries and analyses of company accounts are readily available from Extel Cards and Datastream, for those fortunate enough to enjoy these excellent services, there really is no substitute for poking around the accounts to spot, for example, when a company decides to include profits on the sale and lease-back of property above the line (because pre-tax profits would otherwise be down on last year?), or where a company has guaranteed extensive liabilities outside its normal business activities.

This chapter provides a pro-forma to help you poke round systematically and to work out key ratios. The first three sheets are designed for the analysis of a single year's accounts, and the remaining five sheets present a summary of a company's record over five years, to show the long-term trends of key ratios and percentages.

Analysts' views on the treatment of some items do vary and, under the Companies Act 1985, companies are given a choice of two balance sheet formats and four profit and loss account formats (CA 1985, Sch. 4). This pro-forma is only one way of tackling the figures; it should be modified, adapted and extended to cater for the company's choice of reporting formats and to suit the analyst's individual tastes, provided users are consistent in their treatment of items so that figures produced are on a fair basis for inter-company comparisons.

The following line-by-line notes, which provide cross-references to the relevant sections in earlier chapters, should be read in conjunction with the pro-forma. (It should be noted that some of the pro-formas have lines which are numbered but left blank: these are to accommodate any special items which may occur in individual cases.)

ANALYSIS SHEET 1 – PROFIT AND LOSS ACCOUNT

The main purpose of this sheet is twofold: to see if reported profits are distorted in any way and to examine the effect of an abnormal tax charge. This is done by 'normalising' profits and applying a 'full' tax charge (by deducting the potential liability for deferred tax as well as the reported tax charge) to produce 'normalised' e.p.s. The difference between normalised and reported e.p.s. then serves as a crude indication of the effect of SSAP 15 and other factors on the tax charge and, possibly, that something is abnormal about the way in which the company reports its pre-tax profits.

Line 1. Turnover or Sales
This figure should be after the deduction of trade discounts, and should not include transactions within the group, VAT or other sales-based taxes (see page 69).

Calculation of normalised trading profit

The method of calculating trading profit will depend on the profit and loss account format chosen by the company (see page 66). The pro-forma is designed for Format 1, and also includes 'Adjustments' to remove the effect of variations in accounting practices.

Line 2. Cost of sales
    Distribution costs
    Administrative expenses

These are described on page 71. If the company has chosen Format 2 or 4, the total of all deductions up to and including *Other operating charges* can be inserted in Line 2, unless a detailed breakdown is required (as in Example 2 in Chapter 12).

Line 3. Other operating income
Income from normal operations, not shown under any other heading (e.g. royalties).

Line 4. Adjustments
Although SSAPs have done much towards standardising the treatment and presentation of accounts, a number of companies include variations from normal practice which can make a significant difference to reported profits. These may arise in a number of ways:

(*a*) The provision of *extra depreciation* to allow for the inflated cost of replacing assets; this is an eminently sensible practice, but the extra depreciation should be added back into profits for inter-company comparisons. Any depreciation on intangible assets should also be added back, to produce a fair comparison with the great majority of companies that write intangible assets off straight away against reserves.

(*b*) *Capitalising expenses* and amortising them over the years in which benefits are expected to accrue, rather than charging the expenses at the time they were incurred. It may look fair, for example, to capitalise the cost of relocating a factory and to spread the charge over several subsequent years when the relocation will be saving rent, transport costs, etc., but the move may not turn out to be a success financially. The risk of capitalising expenditure was demonstrated only too clearly when ROLLS ROYCE, in capitalising research and development expenditure, relied on future profits from a new aero-engine and these profits did not materialise.

The standard accounting practice on research and development, SSAP 13, requires expenditure on research and development to be written off in the year of expenditure, except for specific projects where commercial success is reasonably assured (see page 67). We would also favour writing off all expenditure on intangible assets (e.g. relocation, staff training, advertising campaigns, etc.) and any expenditure a company has capitalised in this way during the year should be deducted from pre-tax profits.

(*c*) *Capitalising interest*. When a company builds a new factory it is reasonable to capitalise interest on money borrowed for the project during construction as this would be included in the capital cost if the project was put out to contract or a newly completed factory was purchased, but if completion is delayed or the start of production is postponed because of lack of demand, then interest on the investment should be written off as an expense (see page 68).

Another variation of capitalising interest is on land banks and on sites awaiting development or redevelopment; the risk here is that the original cost plus subsequent interest may easily exceed the market value of the asset in its present condition, although some might argue that if the company has succeeded in 'rolling up' the interest on the associated debt (has been allowed to add the interest to the capital sum borrowed, rather than paying it when due), then it is reasonable to capitalise the interest on the other side of the balance sheet (i.e. add it to the book value of the asset concerned).

We feel that the capitalising of interest before construction has started or after planned completion should be treated with suspicion, and we recommend that any interest that has been capitalised in these circumstances should be deducted from pre-tax profits.

(*d*) *Extraordinary expenses and losses.* As we have already discussed (on page 87), the definition of extraordinary items as opposed to exceptional items (see page 88) leaves a certain amount of scope for differences of opinion. For example, the treatment of losses on foreign currency borrowings (see page 119), and the details of items the company has treated as extraordinary, need careful examination: any 'non-extraordinary' items should be deducted from reported profits.

(*e*) *Extraordinary profits.* The converse to (*d*) may apply when a company makes profits other than in the normal course of business and does *not* treat them as extraordinary. The profits on any extraordinary items, for example on the sale and leaseback of properties or on the redemption of debt, should be excluded from pre-tax profits.

All these variations, except extra depreciation, tend to boost the reported profits of the company and should be viewed with healthy scepticism. In many cases they are genuine differences in practice, consistently and openly applied, in which case the analyst should adjust the profits to avoid getting an unduly optimistic view of the company, but there is also an unfortunate tendency for companies to adopt 'expediency accounting' to paper over the cracks when profits are crumbling. If there is any suspicion of this, a fine-tooth comb is needed to check:

(*a*) the auditors' report for qualifications;
(*b*) the statement or note on accounting policies (usually Note 1 to the accounts) for any changes;
(*c*) extraordinary items;
(*d*) movements to and from reserves.

Calculation of normalised pre-tax profit

The next four lines contain items of income and expenditure which are added to and deducted from Line 5, Normalised trading profit, to produce Normalised pre-tax profit in Line 10.

Line 6. Associates
This is the group's share of the pre-tax profits of associated and related companies (page 110).

Line 7. Investment and other income
This includes the Companies Act 1985 format items Income from other fixed asset investments, and Other interest receivable, *less* Amounts written off investments. Dividends are shown gross, i.e. plus associated tax credits (page 79).

Line 8. Earnings before interest and tax (EBIT)
This figure is used in the calculation of return on capital employed (ROCE) in Line 103 at the bottom of this sheet.

Line 9. Interest paid
This is on all borrowings (page 72) including overdraft; shown in the CA 1985 formats as Interest payable and similar charges.

Line 10. 'Normalised' pre-tax profit
This is the reported pre-tax profit adjusted by Line 4 to correct for any variations in accounting practices.

Calculation of normalised earnings per share

As discussed in Chapter 13, there are many factors that can make a company's tax charge differ from pre-tax profits multiplied by the standard rate of Corporation Tax; for example, non-offsettable losses where the actual tax charge is higher, and franked income and the non-remission of overseas profits where the actual tax charge is lower. However, the main cause of any difference, resulting in a lower tax charge, is, under SSAP 15, the amount of deferred taxation *not* provided because the company does not expect it to be payable in the foreseeable future.

Because SSAP 15 gives companies so much discretion over the provision, or non-provision, of deferred tax, we recommend that e.p.s. should be

calculated on a fully taxed basis, i.e. after the deduction of the 'potential amount of deferred taxation' the company would also have provided for if it had provided for *all* timing differences regardless of whether payable in the near future.

SSAP 15 requires this 'potential amount' to be disclosed, but if the information is not available a rough-and-ready practical rule is to deduct Corporation Tax at the standard rate from 'normalised pre-tax profits'.

Many analysts calculate a company's e.p.s. and PER on both an *actual* and a *full* tax basis, and some very sensibly started using 35% as the full rate in advance of financial year 1986 (the first year in which the 35% rate applies) in order to make year-on-year comparisons on a uniform basis.

Line 11. Taxation reported
The amount of taxation on ordinary activities shown in the company's profit and loss account.

Line 12. Potential deferred tax
The additional amount of deferred tax had the company provided for *all* timing differences.

Line 13. Estimated tax
Where insufficient information is given on potential deferred tax, omit Lines 11 and 12, and insert in Line 13 *either* the estimated tax = 'normalised pre-tax profits' × standard rate of Corporation Tax *or*, if higher, the reported tax charge.

Line 15. Minorities
This is the share of profits of the minority shareholders in subsidiaries not wholly owned by the company. In theory the profits attributable to minorities should be adjusted here to reflect a 'full' tax charge in the subsidiaries concerned, but this usually involves extensive research at Companies House. A crude adjustment can be made by grossing up minorities at the reported rate of tax and then applying a tax charge at the standard rate.

Line 17. Preference dividends
Actual amount paid, i.e. net of tax credit (page 85).

Line 18. Normalised profits attributable to ordinary shareholders
This is the attributable profit, having adjusted pre-tax profits to conform to normal reporting practices and having applied a standard tax charge.

Line 19. Ordinary dividends
Ordinary dividends paid and proposed for the year.

Line 20. Extraordinary items, as reported
Extraordinary items are items not arising in the

ordinary course of business, and in a company's accounts are added or subtracted below the line, i.e. after the profit on which earnings per share are calculated. They include extraordinary income, charges and tax.

Line 22. Ordinary shares in issue
This is the average number of ordinary shares in issue during the year, i.e. the number of ordinary shares which a company should use in its e.p.s. calculations; it normally appears in the accounts in a note on e.p.s.

Line 23. Normalised earnings per share
Line 18 divided by Line 22. The difference between this figure and the reported e.p.s. is, as we have said, a measure of the difference between a 'full' tax charge and the actual tax charge and of any variations from normal practice in reporting pre-tax profits.

Line 25. Reported fully diluted earnings per share
Companies are not obliged to report fully diluted e.p.s. unless dilution is material, but they can easily be calculated if required, as we describe on page 95. A similar calculation can be made using normalised profits attributable to ordinary shareholders to obtain normalised fully diluted e.p.s., but in practice the effect will be very similar to the effect on reported e.p.s., unless normalised profits differ widely from reported profits.

Line 26. Extraordinary items per share
This is just a convenient way of expressing extraordinary items to see if they are significant in relation to earnings per share.

Line 27. Dividend per share
As reported (i.e. net of tax), expressed in pence.

Lines 27 and 28. Dividend cover and Normalised cover
In straightforward cases where Corporation Tax liability is not affected by the proportion of profits distributed (i.e. where ACT on full distribution can be entirely offset against Corporation Tax, without penalty, see page 83) the covers can be obtained by dividing the reported e.p.s. or normalised e.p.s. by the dividend. If full distribution increases the tax liability, usually owing to overseas earnings, the dividend cover becomes complicated and, if not shown in the accounts, can only be calculated approximately (page 178).

Profitability ratios

The ratios in Lines 101 and 102 are measures of trading performance, and thus are based on capital employed in trading (see page 168), while ROCE (return on capital employed) in Line 103 is for the overall performance of the company, and is therefore based on the overall capital employed.

ANALYSIS SHEET 2 – ASSETS EMPLOYED

This page contains two key ratios, the current ratio and the acid test, both of which can be seriously distorted if current assets are overstated and/or current liabilities are understated. Care should therefore be taken to adjust for any incorrect classification: for example, the inclusion of a housebuilder's land bank as a current asset if it comprises more than a year's supply of building land. Note that Intangible assets are dealt with on Sheet 3.

Line 29. Land and buildings
The accounts will give the net book value (cost or valuation less accumulated depreciation). Unfortunately the figure for capital employed and thus the return on capital employed can be very much distorted by the assets being shown at unrealistically low values, and this distortion is most likely to occur when a high proportion of land and buildings has not been revalued in the last few years; so the details of revaluations, contained in the notes to the accounts, should be checked to see if valuations are reasonably up to date.

Line 30. Surplus on revaluation
Companies sometimes report that they have had

revaluations of land and buildings carried out, but have not written up the assets accordingly in their books. In these cases the surplus arising on revaluation can be added separately in Line 30 to produce a more accurate figure for capital employed, with a balancing entry on Analysis Sheet 3. Alternatively, Line 30 may be renamed to show a more detailed breakdown of fixed assets, e.g. where a company shows an unusual category of assets peculiar to the nature of its business, for example 'kegs and keg cider installations' in the case of H. P. BULMER. If this is done, a balancing entry is not, of course, required on Analysis Sheet 3.

Line 31. Plant and equipment
This includes Plant and machinery, and Fixtures, fittings, tools and equipment. It is normally shown at cost less accumulated depreciation, but a few companies revalue these assets periodically and provide additional depreciation on them (page 150). Where this is found, a 'normal' figure based on historical cost less accumulated depreciation may not be readily available, in which case note should be made that capital employed

will be overstated in comparison with other companies.

Payments on account
Where payments on account and assets in course of construction are shown under tangible assets in CA 1985 formats, amounts in respect of land and buildings should be included in Line 29 and for plant and equipment in Line 31.

Line 32. Investment grants
If investment grants are shown separately (as opposed to being deducted from the cost of an asset when it is acquired, see page 37), they should be deducted from the book value of fixed assets. If they have been included in the figure for reserves, they should also be deducted on Analysis Sheet 3 in calculating n.t.a. attributable.

Line 34. Associated and related companies
This figure is the cost of any investment in associated or related companies, less any amounts written off, plus the investing group's share of the post-acquisition retained profits and reserves of the associated or related companies (see Chapter 16). Loans to associated companies shown in the accounts under Investments should be included, less any amounts owing to them falling due after more than one year. Any amounts owed by or owing to associated or related companies shown under debtors or under creditors due within one year should be dealt with under those headings, as they affect current ratios (but if these amounts are large they should, strictly speaking, be excluded from the calculation of Return on capital employed in trading).

Line 35. Other investments
These are long-term investments, and may include Loans made by the company and Own shares. In our view this figure should include all investments that cannot readily be converted into cash at a price guaranteed within narrow limits; see comments on Line 39, and Chapter 7.

Line 36. Stocks and WIP
See Chapter 8.

Line 37. Trade debtors
Where trade debts to the company have been settled by bills of exchange which the company is holding to maturity, and the amount involved is shown as 'bills receivable' (page 59), this may be included in the figure for Trade debtors.

Line 38. Other debtors
Include prepayments and accrued income, and any other item shown under debtors (other than trade debtors).

Line 39. Cash and other liquid assets
See comments on cash on Line 46. Other liquid assets are near-cash items such as government securities and local authority bonds due for redemption or repayment within 12 months. Longer-dated gilt-edged securities may be included on the grounds that they are easily saleable although prices may fluctuate, but holdings of ordinary shares should not be included in current assets as their value can easily fall and, even if quoted, the shares may not be marketable in any quantity.

Line 41. Trade creditors
This item is the amount owing to trade creditors falling due for payment within one year. Where amounts due to trade creditors have been settled by bills of exchange which have not yet fallen due, the amount outstanding may be shown in the accounts under 'bills of exchange payable' (page 59). Trade bills may be included on this line, but all other bills payable should be included on Line 47.

Line 42. Taxation
This is the taxation and social security payable within the next 12 months, and includes the ACT payable on proposed dividends.

Line 44. Other short-term creditors
This includes payments received on account, accruals and deferred income, and other creditors falling due within one year. It does not include debentures, loans, overdraft and bills of exchange (see Lines 46 and 47).

Line 45. Subtotal
This subtotal is struck before the inclusion of Loans and overdraft (Line 46) and Bills of exchange payable (Line 47) so as to avoid these two items being deducted from assets in the calculation of capital employed (see page 168). Both items are types of debt and are included in Analysis Sheet 3 as methods of financing.

Line 46. Loans (under one year) and overdraft
This includes debentures, bank and any other loans falling due within one year, plus overdraft. Some analysts net out any cash against the overdraft (that is, deduct cash from the overdraft), thus showing a lower figure for overdraft and reducing the figure for capital employed. Where it is known that a company's bank nets out cash balances in calculating interest charges on overdraft, netting out can be justified. On the other hand, if cash balances are retained in overseas subsidiaries, or if the management chooses to maintain cash balances that are independent of overdrafts elsewhere in the group, it is not realistic to net them out (page 168).

Line 47. Bills of exchange payable
Bills of exchange issued under an acceptance

credit facility are only another method of borrowing (page 59) and can be treated in the same way as an overdraft; that is, by adding them in the Financing table on Analysis Sheet 3, rather than netting them out against assets in calculating capital employed on Analysis Sheet 2. Bills clearly identified as Trade bills should be included on Line 41.

Line 49. Trading capital employed
This is the sum of all assets except Associated and related companies and Other investments (and Intangible assets, which are dealt with on Analysis Sheet 3), less all current liabilities except Loans and overdraft (Line 46) and Bills of exchange payable (Line 47).

Line 50. Overall capital employed
Associates on Line 34 and Other investments on Line 35 are added to Line 49.

Lines 105 to 110. Ratios
Each of these ratios is described in Chapter 23.

ANALYSIS SHEET 3 – FINANCING

Line 51. Ordinary capital
The total nominal value of both ordinary and deferred shares which are fully paid. Where shares are partly paid, the total paid up should be shown separately.

Line 52. Share premium account
The details of premiums paid on the issue of shares for more than their nominal value (see page 17) is usually the first item in the note on Reserves.

Line 54. Intangibles
The most common intangible item is Goodwill (the cost of obtaining control in an acquisition over and above the value of assets acquired, see page 101), but any other intangible item included in a company's accounts (e.g. patents) should also be deducted here.

Line 55. Net tangible assets attributable
These are the net tangible assets attributable to the ordinary shareholders.

Line 30. Surplus on revaluation
This is the balancing entry for any surplus on revaluation shown in Line 30 on Analysis Sheet 2.

Line 56. Redeemable preference shares
Redeemable preference shares need listing separately from *Other preference shares*, as we count them as debt in the capital structure of the company because they eventually have to be repaid.

Line 58. Minorities
This represents the interest of minority shareholders in partially owned subsidiary companies.

Line 59. Deferred taxation and other provisions
Deferred tax is mainly due to capital allowances being given to the company for tax purposes faster than the company applies depreciation in its accounts (page 77). Other provisions may include provisions made for pensions and product guarantees.

Line 60. Long-term creditors
Amounts falling due after more than one year, excluding loans, overdraft, bills of exchange and amounts owed to associated and related companies.

Lines 62 to 67. Debenture and other loans (over one year)
The best way of presenting information on loan capital and other loans depends very much on the debt structure of the company; it may be useful to show:

(a) the division between loans repayable in less than five years and more than five years, which Schedule 4, para. 48 of the Companies Act 1985 requires to be reported;
(b) debenture, unsecured loan stock, convertible loan stock, bank loans and other loans separately;
(c) the breakdown between sterling denominated and foreign currency loans.

Lines 46 and 47. Loans (under one year) and overdraft, and bills of exchange payable
As already discussed, these current liabilities are *not* netted out against assets in Sheet 2, but are included here in Sheet 3 as part of a company's financing.

Line 68. Total debt
This includes Redeemable preference shares (Line 56), Loans (over one year) (Lines 62 to 67), Loans (under one year) and bank overdraft (Line 46), and Bills of exchange payable (Line 47).

Line 69. Capital employed
This figure should be the same as Line 50, Overall capital employed, on Analysis Sheet 2. The cause of any discrepancy should be found and corrected.

Line 70. Net asset value
This is the book value of the assets attributable to each ordinary share:

$$\frac{\text{Line 55}}{\text{Line 51}} \times \text{nominal value of ordinary share}$$

Further calculations can be made to obtain a fully diluted net asset value (i.e. allowing for paying up partly paid shares, for converting convertibles and for exercising warrants), but in practice the difference this makes is seldom significant.

Line 71. Net asset value plus revaluation
Line 30 from Analysis Sheet 2, any surplus on revaluation that has not been written into the books, is added to Line 55 in calculating the net asset value.

Line 72. Contingent liabilities
This is an item all on its own, usually to be found tucked away near the end of the notes to the accounts; it is easily overlooked but can be very

important (see page 62). The figure that is required is the total of commitments and contingencies *outside* the group; that is, not including guarantees of borrowings by subsidiaries but including, for example, guarantees on behalf of associated companies.

Line 114. Contingent liabilities/n.t.a.
This ratio shows the extent of contingent liabilities outside the company or group in relation to the net tangible assets attributable to the ordinary shareholders. (A figure of more than 2–3% is unusual, and worth further investigation.)

Analysis Sheet 1 Profit and loss account

Line	Company:	Year to 19 . . . £ . . .	19 . . . £ . . .	% Change	Remarks
1	**Turnover or sales**				
2	− Cost of sales				
	− Distribution costs				
	− Administrative expenses				
3	+ Other operating income				
4	± Adjustments				
5	= **'Normalised' trading profit**				$1 - 2 + 3 \pm 4$
6	+ Associates				
7	± Investment and other income				
8	= Earnings before interest and tax				$5 - 6 = 7$
9	− Interest paid				
10	= **'Normalised' pre-tax profit**				$8 - 9$

Calculation of 'normalised' earnings per share

Line					
10	'Normalised' pre-tax profit				From 4 above
11	− Taxation reported				Lines 11 + 12, *or*
12	− Potential deferred tax				Line 13 on its
13	− Estimated tax				own
14	= **Normalised profits after tax**				$10 - 11 - 12 - 13$
15	− Minorities				
16	= Profits attrib. to company				$14 - 15$
17	− Preference dividends				
18	= **Norm. profits attrib. to ord.**				$16 - 17$
19	− Ordinary dividends				
20	± Extraordinary items				
21	= **Normalised retentions**				$18 - 19 \pm 20$
22	Ordinary shares in issue				Average for year
23	Normalised e.p.s.				$18 \div 22$
24	Reported e.p.s.				
25	Reported fully diluted e.p.s.				
26	Extraordinary items per share				$20 \div 22$
27	Dividend per share (Div. cover)				
28	Normalised cover				

Profitability ratios

Line					
100	Trading profit/Sales				$5 \div 1$ as %
101	Trading profit/Capital employed				$5 \div 49$ as %
102	Sales/Capital employed				$1 \div 49$ as %
103	ROCE				$8 \div 50$ as %
104					

Analysis Sheet 2 Assets employed

Line		19 . . .	19 . . .	% Change	Remarks
Company:		Year to			
		£ . . .	£ . . .		
Tangible fixed assets					
29	Land and buildings				
30	+ Surplus on revaluation				
31	+ Plant and equipment				
32	− Investment grants				
33	= Total tangible fixed assets				29 + 30 + 31 − 32
34	Associated and related companies				
35	Other investments				
Current assets					
36	Stocks and WIP				
37	+ Trade debtors				
38	+ Other debtors				
39	+ Cash and other liquid assets				
40	= Total current assets				Sum of 36 to 39
Current liabilities					
41	Trade creditors				
42	+ Taxation				
43	+ Dividends				
44	+ Other short-term creditors				
45	= Subtotal				Sum of 41 to 44
46	+ Loans (under 1 year) and overdraft				
47	+ Bills of exchange payable				
48	= Total current liabilities				45 + 46 + 47
49	Trading capital employed				33 + 40 − 45
50	**Overall capital employed**				34 + 35 + 49
Ratios					
105	Current ratio				40 ÷ 48
106	Acid test ratio				(40 − 36) ÷ 48
107	Stocks/Sales				36 ÷ 1 as %
108	Trade debtors/Sales				37 ÷ 1 as %
109	Trade creditors/Sales				41 ÷ 1 as %
110	Working capital/Sales				(36 + 37 − 41) ÷ 1 as %

Analysis Sheet 3 Financing

Line		19 . . .	19 . . .	% Change	Remarks
	Company:	Year to			
		£ . . .	£ . . .		
51	Ordinary capital (Nominal value each:				
52	+ Share premium a/c				
53	+ Other reserves				
32	− Investment grants				Only if in reserves
54	− Intangible assets				
55	= n.t.a. attributable				51 + 52 + 53 − 32 − 54
30	Surplus on revaluation				From Analysis Sheet 2 (if any)
56	Redeemable preference shares				
57	Other preference shares				
58	+ Minorities				
59	+ Deferred tax and other provisions				
60	+ Long-term creditors				
61	**= Subtotal**				Sum of 57 to 60

Debenture and other loans

Line		19 . . .	19 . . .	% Change	Remarks
62					
63	+				
64	+				
65	+				
66	+				
67	+				
46	+ Loans (under 1 year) and overdraft				From Analysis Sheet 2
47	+ Bills of exchange payable				
68	**= Total debt**				56 + (62 to 67) + 46 + 47
69	**Capital employed**				55 + 30 + 61 + 68
70	Net asset value (n.a.v.)				(55 ÷ 51) × Nominal value
71	n.a.v. plus revaluation				(55 + 30) ÷ 51 × Nominal value
72	Contingent liabilities				

Ratios

Line		19 . . .	19 . . .	% Change	Remarks
112	Debt/Equity				68 ÷ (55 + 58) as %
113	Debt/Capital employed				68 ÷ 69 as %
114	Contingent liabilities/n.t.a.				72 ÷ 55 as %

SUMMARY SHEET 1 – SUMMARY OF PROFIT AND LOSS ACCOUNTS

In practice it can be confusing to show normalised figures mixed in with figures actually reported, so the only special figures shown in the profit and loss summary sheet are:

(a) 'normalised' trading profit;
(b) adjustments – to indicate reporting variations;
(c) normalised e.p.s. – to show the effect of (b) and the application of a 'full' tax charge.

Where a company's reported profits do not require adjustment it may be found satisfactory to dispense with Analysis Sheet 1 and the calculation of normalised e.p.s.: the summary can then be compiled direct from the accounts, as the figure for percentage of pre-tax profits taken by taxation will show up any abnormal tax charge.

Summary Sheet 1 does not, however, allow each item's percentage change from the previous year to be shown unless the % column provided is used for that purpose instead of showing each item as a percentage of reported pre-tax profits.

SUMMARY SHEET 2 – SUMMARY OF ASSETS EMPLOYED

This summary sheet gives a slightly compressed version of the information in Analysis Sheet 2, and shows each item as a percentage of capital employed instead of the percentage change from the previous year. Here again the summary sheet can, with practice, be compiled straight from a company's accounts.

SUMMARY SHEET 3 – SUMMARY OF FINANCING

This is the counterpart to Summary Sheet 2 and similarly, with practice, can be completed straight from a company's balance sheet without using Analysis Sheet 3.

SUMMARY SHEETS 4 AND 5 – SUMMARY OF SOURCES AND APPLICATIONS

As discussed in Chapter 18, the contents and the presentation of source and application statements vary considerably from company to company, so it can be useful to put the information provided into a standard format. It may also be useful to look at the pattern over the years, in particular at the use of external financing (funds from other sources), the growth in working capital and the trends in liquidity. As with earlier sheets, these formats should be adjusted to taste and to cater for any special features of the company being examined.

In general our formats follow those in the Examples in SSAP 10, except that Applications of funds are shown as positive amounts on Summary Sheet 5, rather than negative amounts on the same sheet as Sources, and changes in Working capital and changes in Liquidity are shown separately.

Note, in particular, that Line S1 on the Sources page is Profit before tax *less* minorities. If minorities have not been deducted by the company then dividends paid to minorities should be inserted as an application (Line A3) and there will be no minority retentions on Line S6. As the treatment of minorities illustrates, the Sources and Applications pro-formas will often need modification to cater for the varied ways in which information is presented by individual companies.

Summary Sheet 1 Summary of profit and loss accounts

Company:

Line		19... £...	%	19... £...	%	19... £...	%	19... £...	%	19... £...	%	19... £...	%
1	**Turnover or sales**												
5	'Normalised' trading profit												
6	+ Associates												
7	+ Investment income												
9	− Interest paid												
4	± Adjustments (removed)												
	= Reported pre-tax profits	100		100		100		100		100		100	
11	− Taxation reported												
	= Reported profit after tax												
	− Reported minorities												
	= Profits attrib. to company												
17	− Preference dividends												
	= Profits attrib. to ord.												
19	− Ordinary dividends												
20	± Extraordinary items												
	= Retentions												
23	Normalised e.p.s.												
24	Reported e.p.s.												
25	Reported fully diluted e.p.s.												
	Profitability ratios												
100	Trading profit/Sales												
101	Trading profit/Capital employed												
102	Sales/Capital employed												
103	ROCE												
104													

Year ending

Summary Sheet 2 Summary of assets employed

Company:		Year ending											
Line		19...		19...		19...		19...		19...		19...	
		£...	%	£...	%	£...	%	£...	%	£...	%	£...	%
29	Land and buildings												
30	+ Surplus on revaluation												
31	+ Plant and equipment												
32	− Investment grants												
33	**= Total tangible fixed assets**												
34	Associated and related companies												
35	Other investments												
36	Stocks and WIP												
37	+ Trade debtors												
38	+ Other debtors												
39	+ Cash and other liquid assets												
40	**= Total current assets**												
41	Trade creditors												
42	+ Taxation												
43	+ Dividends												
44	+ Other short-term creditors												
45	**= Subtotal**												
46	+ Loans (under 1 year) and overdraft												
47	+ Bills of exchange payable												
48	**= Total current liabilities**												
49	Trading capital employed												
50	**Overall capital employed**		100		100		100		100		100		100

Ratios

105	Current ratio												
106	Acid test ratio												
107	Stocks/Sales												
108	Trade debtors/Sales												
109	Trade creditors/Sales												
110	Working capital/Sales												

Summary Sheet 3 Summary of financing

Company:										
Line		Year ending								
		19....		19....		19....		19....		19....
		£...	%	£...	%	£...	%	£...	%	£...	%
51	Ordinary capital										
52	+ Share premium a/c										
53	+ Other reserves										
32	− Investment grants										
54	− Intangibles										
55	= n.t.a. attributable										
30	Surplus on revaluation										
56	Redeemable preference shares										
57	Other preference shares										
58	+ Minorities										
59	+ Deferred tax and other provisions										
60	+ Long-term creditors										
61	= **Subtotal**										
62											
63	+										
64	+										
65	+										
66	+										
67	+										
46	+ Loans (under 1 year) and overdraft										
47	+ Bills of exchange										
68	= **Total debt**										
69	**Capital employed**		100		100		100		100		100
70	Net asset value (n.a.v.)										
71	n.a.v. + revaluation										
72	Contingent liabilities										

Ratios

113	Debt/Capital employed										
114	Contingent liabilities/n.t.a.										

Summary Sheet 4 Summary of sources of funds

Company:		19...	19...	19...	19...	19...
Line		£...	£...	£...	£...	£...
S1	Profits before tax (*less* minorities)					
S2	± Extraordinary items					
S3						
Non-monetary Adjustments						
S4	+ Depreciation					
S5	+ Other provisions					
S6	+ Minority retentions					
S7	− Retained in associates					
S8	± Exchange adjustments					
S9	− Profit on disposal of					
S10	+ Loss fixed assets					
S11						
S12						
S13						
S14	**= Generated from operations**					
Funds from other sources						
S15	+ Rights issue of shares					
S16	+ Other issues of shares					
S17	+ Increase in loans					
S18	− Decrease in loans					
S19	+ Sale of fixed assets					
S20	+ Sale of investments					
S21						
S22						
S23	**= Sources total**					

Summary Sheet 5 Summary of application of funds

Company:

Line		19.... £....	19.... £....	19.... £....	Year ending 19.... £....	19.... £....	19.... £....	19.... £....
A1	Tax paid							
A2	+ Dividends paid							
A3								
A4	+ Purchase of fixed assets							
A5	+ Purchase of subsidiaries							
A6	+ Investment in associates							
A7	+ Purchase of investments							
A8								
A9	+ Purchase of goodwill							
A10								
A11	+ Increase } in working − Decrease } capital							
A12	+ Increase } in net − Decrease } liquid funds							
A13	**= Application total**							

Working capital

A14	± Increase (decrease) in stocks							
A15	± Increase (decrease) in debtors							
A16	± (Increase) decrease in creditors							
A11	= Net increase (decrease)							

Liquidity

A17	± Increase (decrease) in cash							
A18	± (Increase) decrease in overdraft							
A12	= Increase (decrease) in liquidity							

APPENDICES

APPENDIX 1 – CURRENT SSAPs AND EDs

The following Statements of Standard Accounting Practice and Exposure Drafts were current in December 1985.

		Date of issue
SSAP	Explanatory foreword (Revised May 1975)	Jan 1971
SSAP 1	Accounting for the results of associated companies (Revised Apr 1982)	Jan 1971
SSAP 2	Disclosure of accounting policies	Nov 1971
SSAP 3	Earnings per share (Revised Aug 1974)	Feb 1972
SSAP 4	The accounting treatment of government grants	Apr 1974
SSAP 5	Accounting for value added tax	Apr 1974
SSAP 6	Extraordinary items and prior year adjustments (Revised Apr 1975)	Apr 1974
SSAP 8	The treatment of taxation under the imputation system in the accounts of companies (Revised Dec 1977)	Aug 1974
SSAP 9	Stocks and work in progress	May 1975
SSAP 10	Statements of source and application of funds	Jul 1975
SSAP 12	Accounting for depreciation	Dec 1977
SSAP 13	Accounting for research and development	Dec 1977
SSAP 14	Group accounts	Sept 1978
SSAP 15	Accounting for deferred taxation (Revised May 1985)	Oct 1978
SSAP 16	Current cost accounting	Mar 1980
SSAP 17	Accounting for post balance sheet events	Aug 1980

		Date of issue
SSAP 18	Accounting for contingencies	Aug 1980
SSAP 19	Accounting for investment properties	Nov 1981
SSAP 20	Foreign currency translation	Apr 1983
SSAP 21	Accounting for leases and hire purchase contracts	Aug 1984
SSAP 22	Accounting for goodwill	Dec 1984
SSAP 23	Accounting for acquisitions and mergers	Apr 1985
ED 32	Disclosure of pension information in company accounts	May 1983
ED 34	Pension scheme accounts	Apr 1984
ED 35	Accounting for the effects of changing prices	Jul 1984
ED 36	Extraordinary items and prior year adjustments	Jan 1985
ED 37	Accounting for depreciation	Mar 1985
ED 38	Accounting by charities	Nov 1985

In addition to SSAPs and EDs, the Accounting Standards Committee (ASC) in 1984 introduced a new form of consultative document, the *Statement of Intent (SOI)*, designed to give early indication of how the ASC proposes to deal with a particular accounting matter. The first SOI, *Accounting for Pension Costs*, was published in November 1984. It also introduced the *Statement of Recommended Practice (SORP)*, to give guidance on topics where an SSAP would not be justified. Companies will be encouraged to comply with SORPs, but they will not be mandatory.

APPENDIX 2 – PRESENT VALUE

£1 received in a year's time is worth less than £1 received today, because £1 available today could be invested to earn interest for the next 12 months. If £1 now could be invested at a rate of interest i (expressed as a decimal), it would be worth £$(1 + i)$ in a year's time. If the £$(1 + i)$ at the end of the year was left invested, it would be worth £$(1 + i) \times (1 + i) = £(1 + i)^2$ at the end of the second year, and £$(1 + i)^3$ at the end of the third year, and so on; in other words, it would earn compound interest at the rate of i per annum.

Present value is like compound interest in reverse: the value of £1 received in a year's time is worth £$1 \div (1 + i)$ now, and £1 in two years' time is worth £$1 \div (1 + i)^2$ now, and so on. For example, if i (known as the discount rate) is 10% p.a., then the present value of £1 received in a year's time is £$1 \div (1 + 0.10) = £0.9091$. Similarly the present value of receiving £1 in two years' time is £$1 \div (1.10)^2 = £0.8264$, and £1 in three years' time is £$1 \div (1.10)^3 = £0.7513$, and £1 in n years' time is £$1 \div (1.10)^n$.

Tables of *present values* are available for various rates of interest and periods of years. The table below is a very simplified and abbreviated version of one:

Present value of 1 in n years' time

n	1%	2%	3%	4%	5%	10%	15%

n	1%	2%	3%	4%	5%	10%	15%
1	.990	.980	.971	.962	.952	.909	.870
2	.980	.961	.943	.925	.907	.826	.756
3	.971	.942	.915	.889	.864	.751	.658
4	.961	.924	.889	.855	.822	.683	.572
5	.951	.906	.863	.822	.784	.621	.497
10	.905	.820	.744	.676	.614	.386	.247
20	.820	.673	.554	.456	.377	.149	.061

Rate of interest (the discount rate)

Present value tables refer to the value of 1, rather than the value of £1, because they can be used for any currency: the 1 may be $1, DM1, 1 peseta or 1 of any other currency you care to name.

The present value concept (which is also the basis of discounted cash flow, DCF) can be applied to any streams of future income and to repayments of capital. For example, £20 nominal of 5% loan stock redeemable in three years would be worth the interest payments of £1 at the end of each year plus the £20 in three years' time, all discounted at 10% per annum, to give a present value of:

$$\frac{£1}{(1.10)} + \frac{£1}{(1.10)^2} + \frac{£1}{(1.10)^3} + \frac{£20}{(1.10)^3}$$

$$= £0.909 + 0.826 + 0.751 + 15.026 = £17.512$$

The calculation of the present value of a steady stream of income can be assisted by the use of annuity tables, an annuity of 1 for n years simply being an annual payment of 1 for n years; such a table is set out below.

In our previous example, the present value of £1 per annum for three years, discounted at 10%, could have been obtained from the annuity table: three years at 10% = 2.487.

In practice, interest on fixed-interest securities is usually paid half-yearly in arrears (i.e. at the end of each half-year), and so the half-yearly discount rate, which is the square root $(1 + i)$, is used to discount each half-yearly interest payment. For example, £100 of 5% Loan Stock with three years to redemption, discounted at 10% per annum, would have a present value of:

$$\frac{£2.50}{(\sqrt{1.10})} + \frac{£2.50}{(\sqrt{1.10})^2} + \ldots + \frac{£2.50}{(\sqrt{1.10})^6} + \frac{£100}{(1.10)^3} =$$

$$2.3837 + 2.2728 + \ldots + 1.8784 + 75.1315 = £87.8734$$

Annuity table: present value of an annuity of 1 for n years

n	1%	2%	3%	4%	5%	10%	15%
1	.990	.980	.971	.962	.952	.909	.870
2	1.970	1.942	1.913	1.886	1.860	1.736	1.626
3	2.941	2.884	2.829	2.775	2.723	2.487	2.283
4	3.902	3.808	3.717	3.630	3.546	3.170	2.855
5	4.853	4.713	4.580	4.452	4.329	3.791	3.352
10	9.471	8.983	8.530	8.111	7.722	6.145	5.019
15	13.865	12.849	11.938	11.118	10.380	7.606	5.847

Rate of interest (the discount rate)

APPENDIX 3 – RETAIL PRICE INDICES SINCE 1950

From 1974 onwards the Retail Price Index (RPI), as published in the Government Statistical Service's *Monthly Digest of Statistics*, has been based on 100 at 15 January 1974. Before this, the series was based successively on 100 at 17 June 1947, 17 January 1956 and 16 January 1962; in the table below all these earlier figures have been adjusted to base 100 at 15 January 1974.

Space has been left for the reader to insert RPIs month by month in the future, as they are announced. Alternatively, *Accountancy* magazine (the journal of the Institute of Chartered Accountants in England and Wales) includes an updated table in an early edition (usually February) each year.

Year	Jan	Feb	Mar	Apr	May	Jun	Jul	Aug	Sept	Oct	Nov	Dec	Average for year
1950	35.3	35.3	35.3	35.6	35.6	35.6	35.6	35.3	35.6	35.9	36.2	36.2	35.6
1955	43.1	43.1	43.1	43.4	43.4	44.3	44.3	44.0	44.3	44.9	45.5	45.5	44.1
1960	49.3	49.3	49.3	49.3	49.3	49.8	49.8	49.3	49.3	49.8	50.2	50.2	49.6
1961	49.9	49.9	50.3	50.3	50.8	51.2	51.2	51.7	51.2	51.7	52.1	52.1	51.0
1962	52.1	52.2	52.4	53.1	53.3	53.6	53.4	53.0	52.9	52.9	53.1	53.3	53.0
1963	53.5	54.0	54.1	54.2	54.2	54.2	53.9	53.7	53.9	54.1	54.2	54.3	54.0
1964	54.6	54.6	54.8	55.3	55.8	56.0	56.0	56.2	56.2	56.3	56.7	56.9	55.8
1965	57.1	57.1	57.3	58.4	58.6	58.8	58.8	58.9	58.9	59.0	59.2	59.5	58.4
1966	59.6	59.6	59.7	60.5	60.9	61.1	60.8	61.2	61.1	61.2	61.6	61.7	60.7
1967	61.8	61.8	61.8	62.3	62.3	62.5	62.1	62.0	61.9	62.4	62.8	63.2	62.3
1968	63.4	63.7	63.9	65.1	65.1	65.4	65.4	65.5	65.6	65.9	66.1	66.9	65.2
1969	67.3	67.7	67.9	68.7	68.6	68.9	68.9	68.7	68.9	69.4	69.6	70.1	68.7
1970	70.6	71.0	71.4	72.5	72.7	72.9	73.5	73.4	73.8	74.6	75.1	75.6	73.1
1971	76.6	77.1	77.7	79.4	79.9	80.4	80.9	81.0	81.1	81.5	82.0	82.4	80.0
1972	82.9	83.3	83.6	84.4	84.8	85.3	85.6	86.3	86.8	88.0	88.3	88.7	85.7
1973	89.3	89.9	90.4	92.1	92.8	93.3	93.7	94.0	94.8	96.7	97.4	98.1	93.5
1974	100.0	101.7	102.6	106.1	107.6	108.7	109.7	109.8	111.0	113.2	115.2	116.9	108.5
1975	119.9	121.9	124.3	129.1	134.5	137.1	138.5	139.3	140.5	142.5	144.2	146.0	134.8
1976	147.9	149.8	150.6	153.5	155.2	156.0	156.3	158.5	160.6	163.5	165.8	168.0	157.1
1977	172.4	174.1	175.8	180.3	181.7	183.6	183.8	184.7	185.7	186.5	187.4	188.4	182.0
1978	189.5	190.6	191.8	194.6	195.7	197.2	198.1	199.4	200.2	201.1	202.5	204.2	197.1
1979	207.2	208.9	210.6	214.2	215.9	219.6	229.1	230.9	233.2	235.6	237.7	239.4	223.5
1980	245.3	248.8	252.2	260.8	263.2	265.7	267.9	268.5	270.2	271.9	274.1	275.6	263.7
1981	277.3	279.8	284.0	292.2	294.1	295.8	297.1	299.3	301.0	303.7	306.9	308.8	295.0
1982	310.6	310.7	313.4	319.7	322.0	322.9	323.0	323.1	322.9	324.5	326.1	325.5	320.4
1983	325.9	327.3	327.9	332.5	333.9	334.7	336.5	338.0	339.5	340.7	341.9	342.8	335.1
1984	342.6	344.0	345.1	349.7	351.0	351.9	351.5	354.8	355.5	357.7	358.8	358.5	351.8
1985	359.8	362.7	366.1	373.9	375.6	376.4	375.7	376.7	376.5	377.1			
1986													
1987													
1988													
1989													
1990													

INDEX